THE HOUSE OF
THE PAIN OF OTHERS

Also by Julián Herbert in English

Tomb Song

THE HOUSE OF
THE PAIN OF OTHERS

CHRONICLE OF A SMALL GENOCIDE

Julián Herbert

Translated from the Spanish by Christina MacSweeney

Graywolf Press

This publication is made possible, in part, by the voters of Minnesota through a Minnesota State Arts Board Operating Support grant, thanks to a legislative appropriation from the arts and cultural heritage fund. Significant support has also been provided by Target, the McKnight Foundation, the Lannan Foundation, the Amazon Literary Partnership, and other generous contributions from foundations, corporations, and individuals. To these organizations and individuals we offer our heartfelt thanks.

MINNESOTA STATE ARTS BOARD

CLEAN WATER LAND & LEGACY AMENDMENT

TARGET.

Published by Graywolf Press
250 Third Avenue North, Suite 600
Minneapolis, Minnesota 55401

All rights reserved.

www.graywolfpress.org

Published in the United States of America
Printed in Canada

ISBN 978-1-55597-837-2

2 4 6 8 9 7 5 3 1
First Graywolf Printing, 2019

Library of Congress Control Number: 2018947075

Cover design: Kyle G. Hunter

Cover images: iStock

Map by Jeffrey L. Ward

For Mónica, who taught me to listen to others, and for Carlos Manuel Valdés, who taught me to listen to the dead.

Forget it, Jake. It's Chinatown.

Chinatown (1974)

CONTENTS

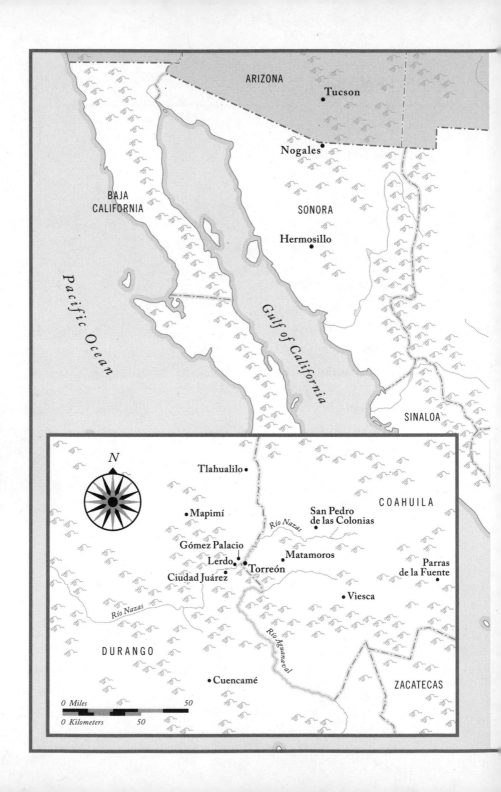

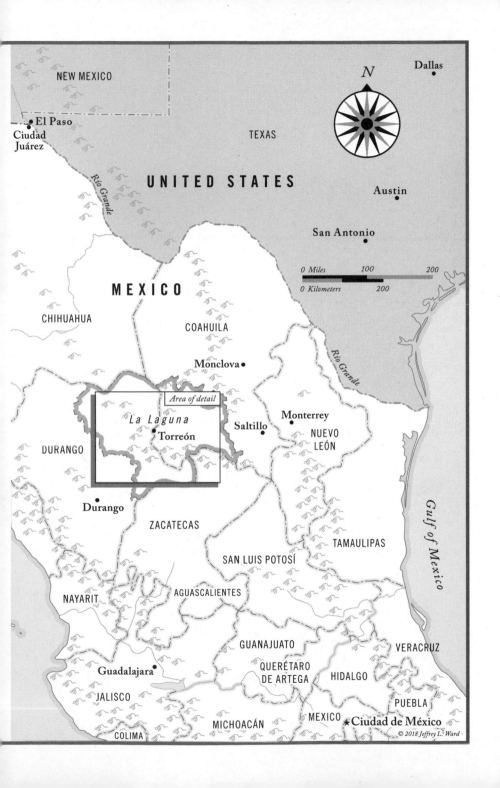

NEW MEXICO

El Paso
Ciudad
Juárez

TEXAS

N

Dallas

UNITED STATES

Austin

San Antonio

0 Miles   100   200

0 Kilometers   200

MEXICO

CHIHUAHUA

COAHUILA

Río Grande

Monclova

Area of detail

La Laguna
Torreón

Saltillo

Monterrey

NUEVO
LEÓN

DURANGO

Durango

ZACATECAS

SAN LUIS POTOSÍ

TAMAULIPAS

Gulf of Mexico

NAYARIT

AGUASCALIENTES

GUANAJUATO

VERACRUZ

Guadalajara

QUERÉTARO
DE ARTEGA

HIDALGO

JALISCO

PUEBLA

MICHOACÁN

MEXICO

★Ciudad de México

COLIMA

© 2018 Jeffrey L. Ward

THIS IS A WESTERN

LIM'S HOUSE

Walter J. Lim's former country house is a chalet-style building with green roof tiles and redbrick walls whose color is intensified by lines of white mortar. The roof is curved and seems to break like an emerald wave onto the garden, in which dwell, alongside younger orange and grapefruit trees, a pair of ancient mulberries. These trees—perhaps members of the same species growing in the Venustiano Carranza woods to the east, where the Chinese-owned market gardens that supplied the town with fresh fruit and vegetables once flourished—testify to an entrepreneurial dream: converting a locality famous for its cotton fields into a silk-producing region. There was no time for this dream to be realized. Six months after the outbreak of the Mexican Revolution, Francisco Madero's rebel troops entered the grounds and raped the woman who cared for the house. Later, a mob attempted to lynch Dr. Lim near Plaza 2 de Abril, despite the fact that he was wearing the Red Cross insignia on his left forearm. Walter J. somehow escaped to relate, some months afterward, his version of the small genocide perpetrated between May 13 and 15, 1911, in the northern Mexican city of Torreón, located in the region of La Laguna. Not all of his compatriots were so lucky: some three hundred Chinese immigrants were murdered, their corpses mutilated, their clothes removed, and their belongings looted. The bodies were dumped in a mass grave, dug on the order of an Englishman, by the outer walls of Ciudad de los Muertos: the city of the dead. Others ended up under the waterwheels on the road to the Venustiano Carranza woods, an area then known as El Pajonal.

"The doctor was never an imperial consul or chargé d'affaires," clarifies Silvia Castro, a thin woman with graying hair and an aquiline nose. "He was the leader of the local Chinese community, which is a very different thing. He'd already become a Mexican national before the massacre took place."

We are at the entrance to the Museo de la Revolución, of which the schoolmistress is director. That is to say, at the doors of the chalet that belonged to Lim in the early years of the twentieth century. The building—a ten-minute cab ride from Torreón's historic downtown—was subsumed within the city limits decades ago, and is now surrounded by a commercial zone and a middle-class residential area.

"This wasn't his home," adds Silvia. "He owned it, but didn't live here. His brother-in-law, Ten Yen Tea, took care of it. Lim's sister—the only Chinese woman mentioned in the archives—was here with her children when the rebels arrived. The doctor says they held the eldest girl at rifle point and forced her to say she'd marry them. Then they threw everyone out of the house and looted the property. The Ten family took refuge in the house of a man called Hampton."

We enter the vestibule, a very short, dark passage, where a ceramic oval set into the wall announces:

> This house was built by Dr. J. Wong Lim. It was later acquired by the Compañía Explotadora de Bienes Raices, S.A., and, according to a number of sources, functioned as a brothel. After this it belonged to Ignacio Berlanga García, and then Carlos Valdés Berlanga and his family. The house finally passed into the hands of Ramón Iriarte Maisterrena, who, during the Torreón Centenary celebrations, donated it as the seat of the Museo de la Revolución.

I'm amused by the parody of biblical genealogies the plaque devotes to private property. But it's curious that the text names the original owner as J. Wong Lim: all the documents I've come across, including a newspaper advertisement for his medical practice, introduce him as Walter J. Lim, Sam Lim, or JW: anglicized versions of his name. It's an unimportant detail, but also a temporal wink that suggests how deeply embedded in the oral tradition our knowledge of the massacre is.

I also find it ironic that Ramón Iriarte Maisterrena—former CEO of the Grupo Lala dairy company, a tutelary figure of Norteño conservatism, and perfect exemplar of the Spanish-American bourgeoisie: a prototype of unfettered capitalism—appears as the patron of the museum. I'd lay odds that, back in 1914, none of the heroes the premises extol would have considered its benefactor's prosperity desirable, or even legitimate. This is one of the paradoxes that give Torreón its sublime air: a city deeply devoted to the Porfirio Díaz regime that loves the revolution with teenage passion.

It's Monday. The exhibition rooms are closed to the public. In the shadows, I cross the freshly polished wooden floors, stand in windows resembling embrasures, squint to decipher cycloramas that, with concise paragraphs and blurred photographs, attempt to summarize a civil war that claimed a million lives (many of them victims of hunger and disease) in ten years. I ascend the pine staircase to the second floor. In one corner, I discover a mischievous image displayed in large format: the front page of *El Imparcial* glorifying the triumphs of Victoriano Huerta's army in 1914. But what actually catches my attention is a short note about the arrival of a new, relatively numerous Chinese diplomatic mission, composed of Chen Loh, Hu Chen Ping, T. Chen, and George H. Hu. I surmise that among their objectives was persuading Huerta to pay the 3,100,000 pesos in gold promised by President Madero after the unfortunate events in La Laguna. But Madero had been assassinated—on the orders of Huerta himself—one night in February 1913, without the permission of Western civilization, but with the approval of the Most Honorable Ambassador of the United States. I doubt it was part of the new revolutionary government's plans to repay the debts of a dead democrat.

"Would you like some tea?" Silvia asks.

I accept her offer.

We go to her office, a building in the courtyard behind the beautiful chalet. We talk. The schoolmistress gives me a summary of the book *Tulitas of Torreón*, shows me images from the revolutionary era taken by H. H. Miller, allows me to digitize the copy of the

English-language newspaper the *Torreon Enterprise* that stands framed on her desk, sets up an appointment with Ilhuicamina Rico, a local historian who has written about the prerevolutionary Magonista liberal movement in La Laguna . . .

"Here," she says, turning the screen of her computer toward me. "This is what the throng of needy souls looked like through the lens of Miller's camera on the day before the attack."

The photograph shows a collection of carts in supposedly military formation. No weapons are in sight. The vehicles are like the bodies of squatting, naked giants. The wood is rotten. The people—both men and women—appear to be in dire poverty.

"Those were the ones who attacked the Chinese," asserts Silvia. "They were a troupe of scoundrels who followed the revolutionary armies everywhere, with the clear intention of looting. The majority weren't even from around here. As Juan Puig notes at the end of *Between the Perla and the Nazas Rivers*,[1] the events of May 15 were an unplanned tragedy: a spontaneous reaction by the mass of common folk, taking out their frustrations on a particular group of immigrants because they thought they were *too different*. What happened had little or nothing to do with an act of xenophobia carried out by the people of La Laguna."

That is more or less the general consensus among Mexican historians, with only a few exceptions. It's a plausible thesis, and one that sits comfortably with Lagunero idiosyncrasy, the middle classes, and the annals of the nation. It is a thesis with which I disagree.

●●●●●

The slaughter of the Chinese community in Torreón is a revealing but buried episode of the Mexican Revolution, and it cannot be said that the zero historical (re)cognition of it is due to a lack of documentary evidence. Between 1911 and 1934, various oral and print versions of the events were in circulation. A number—I won't say a

---

1. *Entre el río Perla y el Nazas*

great number—of academics took an interest in the topic from 1979 to 2012. Read in Borgesian terms, one might say it is something that *wants to be told*: every few years, it refuses to die. This book is merely a version of that refusal.

In parallel, different interest groups—including, curiously, contemporary Chinese residents of Torreón—have done everything in their power to water down the story. And for this reason, it is difficult to access the nuances of its underlying causes.

I first heard about it as a child, from Julián Jiménez Macías, a boy from La Laguna whose precocious skirt chasing—one Halloween, while we were trick-or-treating along the dark streets of the Barrio del Alacrán—ended in my getting my head split open. As punishment, at his parents' instigation, that other Julián turned up at my bedside on two or three afternoons and attempted to make up for that whack to the head with reports on Llanos soccer games, tabloid scandals, and stories involving corpses. In the version he told me, the murderer of the Chinese immigrants had been a legendary phantom: Pancho Villa.

With the passage of time, I discovered other incarnations of the events, and more than once imagined dedicating an evening of prose to them. A pretext for this arose in 2012, when a new edition of *Between the Perla and the Nazas Rivers* was published. My intention was to write a review; a thousand words at most. I soon discovered I had too much information and, more importantly, too many different opinions. I was tempted by the idea of undertaking something longer, based on *Between the Perla* and other sources. "It'll be," I thought, "an essay of fifteen to twenty pages."

By the summer of 2014, I'd unearthed enough to consider embarking on a historical novel, but as soon as I began to invent, it became obvious I was betraying the material I'd gathered: the fiction had already been written by the National Spirit. What didn't exist was a *crónica*, in the hybrid Mexican sense of the term, with its blend of literature and journalism, objectivity and subjectivity. I decided to write an ambiguous story, a stylized cross section of history that would bring together the events of the past, and the dents they have left in the present (and in me). A "gonzo" reading applied to history. Not an epic or a tragedy, much less an academic thesis: an all-encompassing report.

In counterpoint to the above, as my research and its writing-up proceeded, I noted that the impulse toward the great Mexican novel had taken hold of me like a fever. In order to tell the story of the massacre, it seemed indispensable to include anecdotes about how I'd found my sources, and to note how strange it is that this small genocide continues to be a taboo subject for inhabitants of Torreón (especially among those in business). To explain how it was that Torreón had such a large Chinese community at the beginning of the twentieth century, it would be necessary to address the meteoric rise of the city, describe the semiaristocratic, semipicaresque condition of the region of La Laguna, attest to the coexistence of multiculturalism and racism within its traditions. To explain why the national Sinophobia reached its apotheosis in a freight rail terminal, I would have to go back to the origins of the Chinese diaspora, consider its consequences, and analyze the particular transnational character of that cultural and financial unity that extended, for one hundred years, through Canada, the United States, Mexico, and the Caribbean.

I would also have to make use of the satirical penny press of the Porfirio Díaz presidency and the earliest documents on illegal migration between Mexico and the United States, whose protagonists were not wetback *mojados*, but people of Cantonese origin.

And I couldn't fail to make use of the story of the first Confucian philosopher to tread the streets of a western town: Kang Youwei, the man who led the first revolution of the modern era in China, whose thinking would, moreover, have a degree of influence on Mao Zedong, and whose penchant for real estate speculation would be responsible for the founding, in the Mexican desert, of the Wah Yick banking and railroad company: the building housing this enterprise was the urban focus of the violence that resulted in the largest mass slaughter of Asians on the American continent.

At times I doubted if anyone born outside of La Laguna would be interested in the region's history. I mention it here because I feel the theatrical aspects of the massacre are important. But also because La Laguna is both old and exceptionally young; not dissimilar from, say, the humble Japanese fishing village that would, at the end of the nineteenth century, become the magnificent port of Yokohama. Both geographical and symbolic territories are the setting for an industrial and commercial liberal utopia, a secular religion that extracted from nothing worlds that, in certain eras, aged prematurely: almost at the same rate as a human being.

(I'm lying; I decided to keep my portrayal of Torreón due to a mere textual impulse: the desire to narrate the story of a city I love in the form of a parody—in the etymological sense Gérard Genette gives the word, namely, *a parallel ode*—of the twentieth-century Latin American novel.)

I like the idea that these pages contain not only a story, but also an essay: an oblique reflection on violence in Mexico. I spoke to historians to give my choice of criteria a solid foundation, I interviewed the cab drivers who crossed my path, I endeavored to see our national history reflected in the daily life of contemporary Torreón, I gathered as many juicy anecdotes as I could, without caring that this took me on mischievous digressions . . . The result is a medieval book: a denunciation dressed up as a military and economic chronicle, with a smattering of short biographical sketches, in (equally unsuccessful) imitation of both Stefan Zweig and Marcel Schwob. An anthology of others' texts, glossed and/or plagiarized in a language that eschews creative writing. A historical antinovel: overwriting: a stockpot with bony prefixes to season a greasy literary field that has run out of meat.

Why would anyone want to read such a book?

I asked myself that question in October 2014. I'd written 180 pages of *The House of the Pain of Others* when I was invited to speak about it at the Pontificia Universidad Católica in Chile. I was doubtful: If my regional *retablo* ran the risk of being of no interest to Mexicans, what was the point of talking about it to people living on the other side of the world?

I traveled to Santiago de Chile in the company of another writer,

Cristina Rivera Garza. The main topic of our conversation during that journey was one that to this day leaves me lost for words: the forced disappearance (declared a multiple homicide in February 2015 by the Mexican judicial system) of forty-three students from the rural teacher training college in Ayotzinapa, Guerrero State. At that moment—as we sleepily disembarked from our plane to meet our hosts, Professors Macarena and Fernando, and Cristina was detained for an hour by customs officers because she had forgotten to declare an innocent bag of almonds—we were unaware of what the case was about to become: a social and media phenomenon that would have a profound effect on the presidency of Enrique Peña Nieto. Although the forty-three are not the most serious example of mass disappearance to occur in Mexico, they do represent a fundamental fracture of society and the state. The Sweet Nation; paraplegic and diamante.

While I was speaking in the Centro Cultural Gabriela Mistral about whatever came into my mind, in dozens of Mexican cities there was an upsurge of indignation that would briefly become global. That night, reading the news in a hotel in Providencia, I decided that although the massacre in Torreón might not be of interest to anyone else, for me it functioned as a shield of Perseus: a circle, burnished by time, on the surface of which I could glimpse, without being turned to stone, the Medusa's head my country had become.

This is not the story you were expecting: it's the one I have.

•••••

The first mention was on May 16, 1911. One of the survivors managed to escape from Torreón, where the telegraph line had been cut, and made his way to Monterrey or Saltillo, from where he wired the businessman Wong Chan Kin in Ciudad Porfirio Díaz, informing him of the small genocide. Kin passed on the information to Shung Ai Süne, chargé d'affaires ad interim in Mexico City. He in turn finally alerted the moribund Porfirian regime. Both the national and foreign press ignored the news until May 22. This absurdity would be inexplicable were it not for the gunpowder beginning to clog the lungs of the Sweet Nation.

Toward the middle of May 1911, alongside other notable developments, plans were afoot to oust Porfirio Díaz, that extraordinary statesman who suffered from the delusion that modernity could be introduced to a country by offering fair-skinned people economic incentives to settle there, and ordering cavalry charges on the civilian population. On May 8, an army of nearly 2,500 men, led by Francisco "Pancho" Villa, Pascual Orozco, and Francisco I. Madero surrounded Ciudad Juárez. On the thirteenth, a force of irregulars from Durango and Coahuila—under the command of Emilio Madero and Jesús Agustín Castro, a young former streetcar conductor—laid siege to Torreón. That same day, Emiliano Zapata surrounded Cuautla, and checked the advance of the troops led by Victoriano Huerta, who avoided open battle for fear of leaving the nation's capital undefended. Ciudad Juárez fell on the tenth, Torreón on the fifteenth, Cuautla—after a week of fierce combat—on the nineteenth. Although it was more coincidence than a coordinated action by the insurgents, the simultaneous loss of these three battles cost Díaz's positivist Científicos the regime. By May 22, the old cabinet had been dissolved, and Díaz's resignation—which became effective three days later—was a foregone conclusion.

A news item was also published on that same May 22: in Torreón, Maderista troops had murdered—it was then calculated—224 Chinese and 7 Japanese residents. A number of articles appeared in the United States, Mexican, and Chinese press. Foreign coverage—much of it erroneous: the *New York Times* stated that Dr. Lim had been lynched—unanimously condemned the events. The Mexican press was divided: hysterical, obviously Porfirian indignation; a rigid defense of Maderismo, whose strategy consisted of putting the blame on the victims by accusing them of having taken up arms against the revolutionary army; and, finally, a cynical, racist form of whimsy that minimized the barbarity by arguing it wasn't as if the life of a Chinaman was actually worth as much as a Mexican's.

Four separate investigations were ordered.

Responsibility for the first, established at the end of May by Emilio Madero, fell to one Macrino J. Martínez, a Torreón revolutionary who, despite his lack of qualifications, was summarily appointed judge advocate. The second, headed by Jesús Flores Magón, was so slow and superficial it is hardly worth mentioning. The third, commissioned in August by the Ministry of Foreign Affairs, was led by Antonio Ramos Pedrueza, a respected jurist and member of the Twenty-Fifth Legislature (the last of Don Porfirio's regime). The fourth investigation, which also took place in August, was carried out in the name of the Chinese government, advised by officials from the United States. This committee was composed of Chang Yin Tang (who sent his private secretary, Owyang King, to Torreón in his place), and the lawyers Lewens Redman and Arthur W. Bassett. It also had the unofficial support of Judge Lebbeus R. Wilfley, who was involved in the redaction of a number of documents, and was a personal consultant to President Taft.

The investigation—if such it can be called—undertaken by Macrino J. Martínez was a hodgepodge of stultifying rhetoric, false statements, and malicious rumors whose only aims were to exonerate the Maderista soldiers and convince the public that the Chinese community had attacked the Republican Liberation Army first.

Flores Magón's conclusions were the last to be published: they were released in December 1911 and caused ten arrest warrants to be issued against the presumptive guilty parties.

The report by Ramos Pedrueza is not simply a significant historical text; it is also the main ideological basis for the theory Mexican historians hold concerning the massacre, a conscientious reading, in terms of jurisprudence, that confines itself to the events, ignores the context, and makes use of anthropological theory and the enigma of violence perpetrated by the nameless masses to offer an explanation that doesn't involve respectable people.

The indignation of the Chinese government was vented in a short report, published as a bilingual English/Spanish pamphlet, and printed on far better-quality paper than any of its Mexican counterparts. It is not as prolix as Ramos Pedrueza's (fifteen witness statements are only indirectly cited), but documents the most vivid and cruelest stories of the killings.

Over the years, the federal government put together a dossier of four files (thousands of pages), including articles from national and foreign newspapers; the dispatches and telegrams between various official bodies, some written in a hilarious coded language; the diplomatic correspondence between Mexico and the Chinese mission; reports by the investigative commissions; and the extremely troublesome formalities undertaken to establish the dates and amounts of indemnity to be paid to the Celestial Empire. The sheets of paper went on piling up until 1934, the year in which the personal Sinophobia of Plutarco Elías Calles, the Jefe Máximo, big chief of the revolution, acquired the status of official foreign policy and sank any hope of a resolution. The documents now reside in the Archivo Histórico Genaro Estrada of the Ministry of Foreign Affairs in Mexico City.

●●●●●

At the dawn of the World Cup held in Brazil in 2014, I met Laurent Portejoie in Mexico City. Our blind date had been arranged by the French embassy: the project, *(De)scribe the City*, was an exercise of the imagination in which a writer and an architect were supposed to travel around the Distrito Federal to generate a politico-aesthetic mechanism (a text, an image, a strategy) that would serve as a (re)formulation of the multiple urban (or orbital) fragments that make up the capital. I accepted the assignment out of opportunism: the French government would cover the travel expenses that would allow me to explore the Genaro Estrada archive in search of information on the massacre of the Chinese community in 1911. The meeting would have meant little to me had it not been for the fact that it was transformed, sooner rather than later, into a sentimental reality: Laurent and I became friends; the rhetorical imperative to compartmentalize ultimately became a mutual desire to share. First, our families: mine accompanied us on the trip, his was an obligatory element of every conversation. We also found common ground in an area of childhood that, despite being located in different countries and spoken in different languages, was relatively easy for us to access: the aesthetic impulse, the notion that anguish (in my case, the memory of a small genocide that occurred at the beginning of the twentieth century) can be mocked whenever there exists complicity between procrastinators.

Hélene Meunier and Martí Torrens, a married couple, were the catalyst for the meeting: Laurent doesn't speak Spanish or English, and my French consists of a couple of nursery rhymes. Thanks to these new friends, and their mastery of the environment and languages separating us, our perception of DF came close to those very expensive discoveries of the Lost Generation of Mexican writers, whose characters found the cosmopolitan experience inconceivable without the presence of eroticism, multiculturalism, political nostalgia, the forging of new friendships, consumption of intoxicants, absurd escapades . . .

A further addition to our improvised, fleetingly Chilango group of friends was Massimo, whom we rechristened Dottor Fetuso: an Italian photographer whose apartment, located in a luxury condo on the Paseo de la Reforma, became the headquarters of some of the indoor activities we undertook during the week. We were also accompanied by Arturo, the cab driver Laurent had met the previous year when he was on holiday in Mexico with his wife and daughters. Without Arturo, we would never have managed to get behind the scenes in Tepito, La Merced, or Santa Fe. He took us to their most unconventional corners: a recently raided Catholic church; the office of a small-time drug dealer with the face of a Disney princess and the vocabulary of a sixty-year-old hooker, whose power lay in having beguiled the hearts of half a dozen robust white-product salesmen; the Santa Fe gully bristling with steel barbs, trash, and tremendous danger for the on-site workers: a pool of poverty in the heart of an exclusive real estate development, a fissure of inhumanity that a multimillionaire construction magnate had ingeniously hidden with a billboard advertising *Forbes* magazine and Macallan single malt. On his cell phone, Arturo showed us aerial photographs that revealed a gigantic warren: Ciudad Satélite, the neighborhood designed by Luis Barragán as a sort of VIP Soviet dystopia.

Laurent is fifty-something and provincial; he was born in Bordeaux. I was then forty-three, and still had the chauvinist chip on the shoulder that unites the majority of Mexican Norteños. Many circumstances contributed to the success of our journey, but perhaps the main one was our inability to communicate. At first we could talk only through an interpreter, but very soon (bear in mind that we were spending the whole day together, with no other company, like the only small-town kids in a suburban college that was simultaneously one of the most populous cities in the world) we had to invent a private language—a kind of Frañol with the addition of mime, onomatopoeia, sketches, pop music, and plentiful beer—not only to talk about our experience of crossing on foot and by car several of the frontiers fracturing and cementing Mexico City, but also to explain any other human experience to each other. The friendship between two people who have to invent a common language to survive chaos is unshakable. That is why I can categorically state that, as we together traversed and (de)scribed the metropolitan area, we envisioned what we were doing not so much as an intellectual or political adventure but as a philosophical praxis: the foundation of a utopia based on complicity and the invention of a shared language. The exploration of the posthistoric possibilities of fraternity.

Laurent informed me that he'd bought a Polaroid camera just before leaving France. He wanted his visual record to have a specific component, something he hadn't used previously in his career as an architect and that, besides being vaguely outmoded, embodied our disadvantage in relation to the city: it was—viewed in relation to a digital camera—too physical, human, and clumsy. I was reminded of H. H. Miller, the American photographer who bequeathed us one of the few extant graphic reports of the massacre of the Chinese community.

Laurent is an eccentric artist who understands his work as something purely sensory. I only rarely saw him drawing during the days we spent together. But he made hundreds of audio recordings: the distribution of sound in space is one of the determining aspects of his architectural works. Often—for example, in La Merced or Tepito—his participation in the acoustic experience was anything but pleasant: he has trouble hearing on one side.

During our first conversation, we settled on the theme of the *frontier* insofar as it can be seen as an internal *constructio* of the city. Since we had been put up in a boutique hotel in the Colonia San Rafael, it occurred to us that the first frontier we should cross was San Cosme: the avenue separating our neighborhood from Santa María la Ribera. Very near the plaza with its Moorish pavilion, at the level of Díaz Mirón, we made a discovery that fitted in well with the spirit of our meanderings: the greater part of the architectural body of a leftover Porfirian facade had disappeared; what could be glimpsed behind it, through a crack in the front door, was a sixty-yard soccer pitch on the artificial turf of which children of nine or ten were running. The image was perfectly appropriate as, the afternoon before, the French team had thrashed the Swiss on the group stage. The city could be the quotient of dividing an old facade by what can be seen through a crack.

In front of a vacant lot, next to the Museo de Mineralogía, I attempted to explain to Laurent, in my stubby language, what the 1985 Mexico City earthquake meant for my generation: not just a traumatic experience but also an awakening to political life; the visceral sensation of belonging to society. I don't know whether it was from nostalgia or the paucity of my verbal resources, but I ended up in tears at the memory of the political failure that was, and continues to be, the outcome of our process: the election of Vicente Fox in 2000, and the consequent boom in the narco economy; the senselessness of Felipe Calderón's regime, which left over eighty thousand corpses on the streets and highways of Mexico; the return of the PRI to government, accompanied by new and more profound disasters: corruption, impunity, economic depression, the rise of armed paramilitary groups, thousands of forced disappearances . . . Laurent took his Polaroid from his manbag and shot the first image of our project: a scream-like portrait of me with a vacant lot in the background.

From then on, the shots continued in a precise but irrational way. It was never a matter of registering definitively visual moments, but rather ones that were emotively relevant. Aspects of the process reminded me of visual artists like Mario García Torres and Sol Lewitt. Something the latter wrote in his *Paragraphs on Conceptual Art* describes Laurent's process: "Conceptual artists are mystics rather than rationalists. They leap to conclusions that logic cannot reach." One of the successful products of this approach was a Polaroid my friend took from the fourteenth floor of the condo where Dottor Fetuso lives, on the afternoon when Mexico defeated Croatia. It shows a throng of fans walking toward the Angel of Independence. The euphoria of the crowd doesn't come across visually—the distance and quality of the shot make that impossible—but Laurent was trying for something else: to register what we later christened the "vertical frontier," the physico-socio-political boundaries between those who traverse the country at ground level and those who experience it from skyscrapers; a clearly mutual invisibility.

We visited many frontiers: the one separating La Condesa from San Miguel Chapultepec, with its interesting but failed project for residential space; the increasingly blurred borderline between Condesa and Roma; the division between Roma and Doctores, the clearest demarcation of which is that Roma has at least three times more functioning streetlamps; the one separating the Santa Fe of motorists from the pedestrian Santa Fe . . . We also traced out territorial analogies by making imprudent automobile journeys: driving, for example, from a public housing project to the Sonora market, where birds, reptiles, and mammals live piled up in tiny cages. We viewed Tlatelolco as both a historical site and a pragmatic space, and noted the impossibility of evading the emotional impact of the student massacre that occurred there in 1968, but also that is it equally impossible to find among its residential units a single frigging cantina where you can rinse the taste of that historical shit from your mouth: faithful disciple of priggish constructivism, Pani planned his residential utopia with urbanistic reticence toward such a pressing matter as the public consumption of alcohol. You have to cross Avenida Flores Magón into the tough Guerrero neighborhood to find a drink. And that's what we did: ending up swigging pulque and dancing salsa with the decrepit locals of the adjoining neighborhood, people who have never been to a technical college or university, who shoulder lamentable political baggage but who will be the only unadorned proletariat to survive when this nation of hypocritical outlaws goes down the drain.

The following day, Laurent returned to France, and I set about finding the Genaro Estrada archive. I was feeling so infatuated by the time I'd spent with my friend, crisscrossing the city with no fixed destination, that instead of checking out the address on the internet, I left the hotel, walked toward the monument to the Revolution, and asked random passersby where I might find the institution in question. My search led me to the central offices of the Ministry of Foreign Affairs, opposite the Alameda. After standing in a couple of lines, and discovering that none of the pencil pushers I consulted had the faintest idea where this historical archive belonging to the ministry they worked in might be located, I gave up and hailed a cab. The driver was an elderly man. I asked him to take me to my hotel and, for the heck of it, complained about the ignorance of public functionaries.

"So what are you looking for?" he asked.

"The Estrada archive."

"I'll take you there."

The vehicle transported me to the corner of Lázaro Cárdenas and Flores Magón, back in the residential unit designed by Mario Pani. It stopped at the cultural center (former headquarters of the MFA) that houses a memorial to '68.

"Here it is," said the driver, pointing to the building across the street.

Twenty-four hours earlier, I'd stood on that very corner, arm in arm with Laurent Portejoie; I'd been trying to explain another mass killing; not the small genocide of the Chinese in Torreón, but the massacre of the night of Tlatelolco. The difficulty of walking along a street with so many generations of skeletons jumping out at you!

•••••

In 1932 Eduardo Guerra devoted a terse little paragraph to the 1911 massacre of the Chinese community in his *History of Torreón*,[2] which endorses the malicious rumor that it was the Celestial subjects who opened fire on the revolutionary troops. This account marks the beginning of a third phase of the history of the event: its interpretation by historians.

Over the next forty years, the story came to an impasse: it was rarely spoken of or written about. It was, at most, according to some of the older residents of La Laguna—children in 1911—a story to be told at the dinner table: the vignette depicting one of Emilio Madera's soldiers, who, having run out of bullets, grabbed a twelve-year-old boy by the legs, swung him around in the air, and smashed his head against a post.

In 1979 Leo M. Dambourges Jacques published an eighteen-page article titled "The Chinese Massacre in Torreón (Coahuila) in 1911." In broad outline, it narrates not only the events of that May but also the peculiar way in which the Chinese community established itself and prospered. Almost all the cited sources are in English.

Then, in 1989, a local doctor, Manuel Terán Lira, self-published the pamphlet *The Massacre of the Chinese in Torreón*.[3] This amateur chronicler (several people he interviewed jokingly referred to him

---

2. *Historia de Torreón*
3. *La matanza de los chinos (Torreón, 1911)*

as "Lying Lira") is one of the least authoritative but most influential voices in the popular mythology of La Laguna. Neither the research nor its grammatical dressing is strong. However, his libel contains one paragraph I find exciting:

> This writer remembers that in 1946, around the Municipal Pantheon, there still existed some very extensive open areas where, on the Day of the Dead, a number of luxury automobiles used to park. Then Chinese families in deep mourning would leave a glass-framed photograph on the ground, light a small lamp or candle, add a plate of white rice, kneel, pray silently, and after a while, retrieve the portrait, leave the rest, and retire, all this before the curious eyes of those present.

In 1992 the now-canonical account appeared: *Between the Perla and the Nazas Rivers*, by Juan Puig. In contrast to that of Terán Lira, his prose is peerless. Moreover, no one has studied the files in the Estrada archive more scrupulously. That is the book's strength, but also its weakness. Puig is familiar with neither the temperament nor the cultural history of La Laguna. His methodology eschews interdisciplinary approaches; his interpretation is surgical, but lacks amplitude. Puig bases his understanding of the origins of Torreón on two authors: Eduardo Guerra and Pablo C. Moreno. His information is not always erroneous, but it *is* outdated and, more importantly, he is too willing to pander to the narcissism that is characteristic of the region. Puig declares that the small genocide was "the first—but most sinister—expression" of Mexican anti-Chinese feeling, which seems to me inaccurate because, by 1911, Celestial citizens at all social, legal, and territorial levels, including even those of the imagination, had long been the victims of racism; the stench of lynching was in the air. In spite of these and other points of disagreement, I find Puig's work extraordinary. It would have been impossible to write these pages without having it at hand, and sometimes plagiarizing it.

In the midnineties the historian Carlos Manuel Valdés was commissioned by the federal Ministry of Public Education to write the free third-grade textbook on local history for Coahuila State.

Carlos incorporated into his pedagogic discourse some of the historiographical landmarks we Cohuilenses find most uncomfortable: the genocide of nomadic groups in the nineteenth century; the masterstroke of social engineering that was Governor Santiago Vidaurri's decree ordering the poisoning of all sources of potable water in the desert not belonging to settled communities; the possession and trading of black slaves in Saltillo in the colonial era; the Hunger Caravan: a heartrending march to Mexico City, organized by the miners of Nueva Rosita and their families in 1951; and the massacre of the Chinese community in Torreón. The MPE demanded that these four stories be cut from the book. Valdés responded that if this were to occur, he would prefer to retract the book from circulation. In the end, the volume was printed uncensored. One in the eye.

In 2005 Marco Antonio Pérez Jiménez wrote his undergraduate thesis on the small genocide. His prose is insufferable, but his intellect isn't: he contextualizes the power dynamics at the heart of Maderismo and takes into account the possibility of xenophobic tendencies among a section of that movement. He analyzes the influence of Ricardo Flores Magón as a source of anti-Chinese sentiment, and not only among the poor: it seems that some wealthy Laguneros sympathized with the anarchist wing of the Mexican Liberal Party (PLM) with which Magón was associated starting in 1906. For instance, Manuel "El Chino" Banda, who, as Antonio de Pío Araujo wrote in a letter to Magón dated May 18, 1907, "has a capital base of 100,000 pesos and is the owner of many urban properties in Torreón." Pérez Jiménez demystifies the lumpen aura in which Puig cloaks those who participated in the events: he offers proof that there is no reliable information about their social origin or actual power and, when there is, on several occasions the people involved appear to be businessmen, stewards, political leaders, landowners and their heirs.

Other footnotes to the story are added by Sergio Corona Páez, the official chronicler of Torreón.

"Everyone loves his own one-sided history," he said to me when I visited his office in the Universidad Iberoamericana. "They don't realize an uncensored version is more interesting. There are a great many myths. For instance, the one about our city being founded by German, English, North American, and Lebanese immigrants. For goodness' sake, the 1910 census showed foreigners to be scarcely five percent of the total population. The majority of Torreón's founders were poor Mexicans from the center and southern part of the country."

Corona is one of the few activists truly interested in reconstructing the circumstances of the crime. In 2011, working through the city council, he was the driving force behind an official historical apology, which he publicly handed to a Chinese diplomatic mission that was invited to the city for that purpose. Additionally, a memorial plaque was mounted on the wall of the building known as the Banco Chino, and a bronze statue of a Cantonese market gardener was installed in the Venustiano Carranza woods.

In the fall of that same year, Sergio Corona received a serious challenge to his status as official chronicler from a small group of Torreón citizens. The commemorative plaque disappeared from the Banco Chino. Later, the municipal police found the statue of the market gardener toppled to the ground, surrounded by a swarm of flies that had been attracted to the urine and trash left there. Silvia Castro told me in confidence that the mayor at that time was courteous enough to present the sculpture to Manuel Lee Soriano, the president of the local branch of the Unión Fraternal. It's said—though I haven't been able to prove it—that Don Manuel keeps the piece in his home: far from the eyes of the open-minded, liberal, migrant society that to this day refuses to admit to itself what happened in the Chinese community between May 13 and 15, 1911.

•••••

I say good-bye to Silvia Castro and leave the Museo de la Revolución through the back entrance, an iron gate painted Mexican-flag green that leads onto a diagonal street running as far as Bulevar de

Independencia. Before closing the gate ("Give it a good tug," says the schoolmistress. "If not, people will get in without our knowing"), I take one last look at Dr. J. Wong Lim's house. Viewed from the rear, the building has a somber air. I don't know if this is because it stands beside the modest modern building housing the offices, or if perhaps it's due to the fact that the splendor I earlier perceived in the facade is achieved only in the presence of a civic brand of nature: a manicured lawn, colorful climbing plants, aged trees that have been carefully watered . . . That's how, I think, the back of any historical construction should be seen: as a zone of basic obscenity, the image of a structure that has been stripped of the adornments imposed by landscaping: that is to say, rhetoric. The idea of this stripping away reminds me of another story about the massacre.

It's said that, while they were killing the Chinese, some of Madero's men discovered their victims were in the habit of hiding their savings in their shoes. Word spread. And this is why the ad hoc gravediggers who threw the bodies into a pit noted that they were all barefoot.

I run across Independencia. There are no traffic signals or pedestrian bridges between the Soriana store and my hotel, so I weave through the midday traffic with characteristically Mexican valor, dodging cars under the scorching Mayrán desert sun. I imagine a spectral cohort: the ghosts of three hundred Chinese traversing— the asphalt burning their bare feet—the streets of a city that does not recognize them.

CAB (1)

I flag down a cab at the door of the hotel and ask to be taken to the Archivo Municipal Eduardo Guerra on Calle Manuel Acuña, a few blocks from the Plaza de Armas. Nearby is a commemorative-plaque business owned by Manuel Lee Soriano.

"And what do you know about the Chinese people who were killed here?" I blurt out to the driver.

"Well, I've heard of it, of course. A cannonball even hit the casino, where those idiots gathered to try to screw my General Villa. They owned everything in sight, you know. They were the richies. And my general wasn't one to do things by halves. He gave it to 'em good."

Anyone writing about the history of the killing of the Chinese will sooner or later (not without impatience) have to point out that Francisco "Pancho" Villa could not have participated in the events: he was already very busy capturing Ciudad Juárez, over six hundred miles away. But, no matter how often you repeat this fact, the vox populi drowns you out: everyone in the streets of Torreón will tell you it was Villa who ordered the massacre. There are at least two ways to interpret this. The first relates to the process of narrative economy that has incorporated the story into the oral tradition: Villa took Torreón two years after the killings, and that second battle was the debut of *his* Division of the North: possibly the most famous military body of the Revolution. This is what has stuck, mixed up with the social trauma of the genocide, in the collective memory. The second reading is riskier and more complex. A scapegoat from another region was needed because Laguneros have a hard time accepting the obvious: the Chinese community was murdered by a faction of the local population. La Laguna has an intoxicatingly virtuous glow, but it also has its defects, and one of those is *denial*. For some reason, the good people of Torreón have traditionally chosen to lay the blame for their misfortunes on *outsiders.* As a society, its critical ability outstrips that of the rest of the country: it is not only intelligent, but also ingenious, virulent, full of intrigue, and even poetic. An anarchist vein runs through its discourse. On the other hand, its capacity for self-criticism is virtually nonexistent.

The municipal archive is closed, but I am able to get as far as the lobby, where I meet the director of the institution, Dr. Rodolfo Esparza Cárdenas. He doesn't, however, have the keys to the reading rooms, and the archivists—whom they do in fact employ—have decided to take extended leave.

"They're unionized," the director explains.

He advises me that, in any case, there's precious little information about the period in question: the archive was torched by insurgent troops in 1911, 1914, and 1916. The scant documents available to the public dealing with early twentieth-century Torreón are in the Instituto Estatal de Documentación, in Saltillo, my hometown.

"We have a census of foreign residents, but it only goes back as far as 1922. And there's a copy of the business directory, made by Jacobo M. Aguirre in 1902, but who knows where it is. We were looking for it the other day, and it seems to have disappeared."

I ask for directions to Don Manuel Lee Soriano's office. He gives them to me with a warning: "The Chinese have never liked talking about the killings. You'd be better off asking him about something else."

Manuel Lee Soriano rarely comes into his office anymore. His secretary informs me he is elderly, sick (he had a cerebral hemorrhage just over a year ago). She says she'll try to make an appointment for me to see him at the club (I don't know what club she's referring to) because that's where he's been spending his mornings, chatting with friends to relieve his ailments. She adds that she can't be sure if it will work out, because Don Manuel doesn't like having fixed commitments, which is understandable, because he's a very old man and has worked his whole life: it's not that he doesn't want to, but the time for all that has passed. I beg her to ask if he might see me one day during the week. We leave it that she'll phone in the afternoon.

I go out into the street, stop a cab, and ask to be taken to the historical archive of the Universidad Iberoamericana, where I have an appointment with Dr. Sergio Corona Páez.

"And what do you know about the Chinese people who were killed?" I ask the driver.

"What's there to know? What he came to do to the poor little Chinamen here in our city makes Villa a bastard. He's not worth giving a shit about."

IN THE LAND OF LA LAGUNA

In 1848, Leonardo Zuloaga bought a hacienda from the Sánchez Navarro family. The property was called San Lorenzo de la Laguna, and Zuloaga constructed a dam on the reservoir contained within: El Carrizal, the reed bed. In addition, he ordered a small keep to be built in the middle of the reservoir. This tower [*torre* in Spanish] became so famous that by 1855 the property had become known as the Rancho del Torreón. When Zuloaga died a decade later, the land passed into the hands of Juan Fierro, who sold it back to Doña Luisa Ibarra, Zuloaga's widow, for 40,000 pesos. Doña Luisa may not have been the world's best administrator, and it is possible her status as a woman left her at a disadvantage given the customs of the business community of the era: for years she attempted without success to keep El Torreón afloat by means of leasing out land, selling off sections, and offering concessions. Under the allegation that the widow had sheltered the enemy during the Second Franco-Mexican War of 1861, the property was seized in 1867; Ibarra managed to recover it some months later. By 1868 El Torreón had become a *ranchería* of 225 inhabitants. The population must have decreased in the following years, since in 1878 the administrator, Ignacio Banda, declared "only the big house and some three or four shacks inhabited by poor people remained." In 1880 the industrialist Guillermo Purcell wrote in a letter, "Doña Luisa, and this is the general opinion, will be left in poverty." It was around this time that two things arrived on the scene—an ideology and an artifact, both of which would change the face of the region: Mexican positivism and the steam engine.

During the final third of the nineteenth century, a group of intellectuals—the self-proclaimed best minds of the nation, known as the Científicos—gathered around the dictator Porfirio Díaz and, inspired by the thinking of Auguste Comte, developed a project of modernization for Mexico. Despite the fact that their main concern was the design of practical strategies (an attitude favorable to the ingress of foreign capital, financial incentives, the nation-wide construction of mass transportation and communications infrastructures), they managed to slip into their discourse the most extraordinary atavism: the notion that the failure of the country's social structure was not due to the unfair distribution of wealth, authoritarianism, corruption, or ignorance, but to the preternatural inability of the indigenous peoples to become good citizens. They decided to "improve the species" (an immoral expression still in use here) by encouraging the immigration of Europeans. This phenomenon has been studied by many historians, so I won't linger on it, but will simply point out that the birth of Torreón as a town and its later elevation to the status of a city are ideologically inseparable from a eugenic utopia.

The project for the mass Europeanization of Mexico was a failure. While poor white immigrants disembarked by the thousands in the United States and Argentina, their longed-for arrival in Mexico was—to say the least—anticlimactic. In La Laguna, which can be considered the most resounding success of Porfirian social engineering, there were many more Mexican, Chinese, and both white and black American migrants than Europeans.

One member of the latter category was called Andrés Eppen Aschenborn.

Andrés Eppen came from an old Prussian family with roots in Rheinland-Pfalz. His parents, Friedrich and Charlotte, arrived in Mexico in 1831. They were both in their twenties, and their reasons for abandoning Germany are romantically hazy: a mixture of rejection of Rhenish political conditions and an idealized vision of the new republics of the Americas. Andrés was born in 1840 in Mexico City, but it is quite possible that he had no childhood memories of his time there: at the age of two, he was sent back to Europe with his mother and siblings. Perhaps disillusioned by the American reality, or maybe even having found marriage to be not all he had hoped for, Friedrich Eppen kept his wife and offspring at a distance for as long as he could. Andrés spent nineteen years in

Germany and France, where he studied artillery and graduated as a first lieutenant. He was a well-built, mustachioed twenty-year-old, over six feet tall, when he returned to the stranger that was his native land and unexpectedly found himself in the thick of the War of Intervention. Against all logic, he embraced the liberal Juárez cause. He enlisted as a private first class in the artillery corps of the Mexican army, and was steadily promoted until he regained his old rank of first lieutenant while fighting against his tutors in the French army. I wonder if, at the bottom of this decision, there is not some Freudian sediment: sublimating the figure of the unknown native land as a metonym for the absent father; a mixture of personal vengeance and a declaration of love to a ghost.

One day, when his detachment was passing through Mapimí, in Durango State, Andrés fell ill with typhoid. He collapsed in the street and was left behind in the town. It was a difficult moment for the national army: it had suffered enormous losses, there was neither food nor ammunition, and the harsh desert climate was more injurious than the invading army's bullets. If the feverish Andrés escaped ending up naked, abandoned to a certain death, it was perhaps because his clothes were too big to be of use to any other soldier. He crawled beneath the eaves of a roof to protect himself from the rain, and drank the water that seeped through the cracks. This was enough to allow him to survive until some local inhabitants discovered him, took him in, and cared for him during his convalescence.

This event marked him for life. When he was discharged from the army in Durango with the rank of captain, he decided to return to Mapimí and set himself up as a farmer, cheek by jowl with the people who had saved him. He bought land in the township and prospered for a number of years. Later, during a visit to San Fernando (a grim town—later to become the city of Lerdo—some two miles of low hills and gullies to the west of what we now call Torreón), he met Gualterio Hermann, agent of the German-owned Rapp, Sommer & Company, which had multiple links to the Porfirian government. Hermann invited him to work for the firm that Eppen would eventually hold a stake in. This put him in contact with Luisa Ibarra, Zuloaga's widow and one of the clients of the consortium.

There had been a long-standing project to establish a branch of the railroad system, Ferrocarril Central Mexicano (whose capital base was, despite its name, in the United States), that would connect Ciudad Juárez to Mexico City. Governor Francisco Gómez Palacio was praying for a stretch of track to pass through Durango, and he attempted to persuade his friend the president of the republic to support this aim. But the foreign investors believed that laying a line across the Durango Sierra was unlikely to offer them the profits they desired. Juan Puig cites the calculation that, when crossing the mountains, the maximum possible size for a convoy would be fifteen wagons, but on level ground, like that of the Rancho del Torreón, a single engine could pull fifty. This, together with the peak in cotton cultivation, sealed the fate of the Nazas River basin.

Andrés Eppen was tasked with convincing Luisa Ibarra to sell her vast estate, made up of eight adjoining haciendas, bequeathed to her by Zuloaga. The deal included both the uncultivated land, on which new settlements would be established, and the cultivable areas, which Rapp, Sommer & Company would in the following decades convert—with the addition of the Perímetro Lavín and Tlahualilo estates on the Durango side of the region—into the principal source of cotton in Mexico. The location chosen for the construction of the railroad terminal that would establish the town was the Rancho del Torreón. The cost of the transaction reached 220,000 pesos: approximately a thousand years of the local minimum wage. Who knows what Doña Luisa would have done with such an obscene sum? She died of pneumonia six years later, and as she never procreated, the surname of Zuloaga Ibarra died out with her in La Laguna.

The first train pulled into the estate on September 23, 1883. Five years later, another transportation company—with a reputation for being second-rate and unpunctual—the Ferrocarril Internacional, laid down its sleepers from Ciudad Porfirio Díaz, on the frontier with Eagle Pass, Texas, to the junction with the new station. From that moment, the expansion was unstoppable. The zones bordering the tracks were scrupulously divided into lots by Federico Wulff, a Texas engineer of German origin, contracted for the purpose by Eppen.

By 1888 the new western town was in a process of dizzying growth, as testified by the opening of the Gran Hotel Michou, soon to be renamed the Hotel de Francia. From then until the beginning of the Revolution in 1910, laws were passed exempting industrialists and estate owners from state and federal taxes for periods ranging from ten to twenty years. On September 16, 1889, Díaz informed Congress of a 380-mile-long telegraph line linking Torreón with the northern frontier. The 1890 census showed a total of a thousand inhabitants.

Drought and popular unrest due to scarcity of food characterized the year 1891. But by 1894, there were 2,736 permanent residents of Torreón, plus a floating population of 500. November 12 was the date when the train brought in the first gringo consul: Thomas R. Acres. Torreón was elevated to the status of a municipality, and its first mayor, Antonio Santos Coy, founded the Sociedad Casino: a group concerned with leisure activities that organized salons and card nights in the local railroad station.

The fiestas were not confined to holy days of obligation. A note published in the *Diario del Hogar* in the same year says:

We have games of chance at all hours, both during the day and at night, and particularly on Saturdays and Sundays, when people are paid for their work during the week. We hold public balls, with the presence of women, outdoors and even in the street. You won't believe this, because that's what any respectable person would do. High- and low-stakes games, brothels, and cantinas are all in abundant supply.

In one of his short stories, Daniel Sada reinvents an anecdote that serves as a metaphor for the junction of wealth, entertainment, and all things sinister that Torreón represented for Mexico. There's always something monstrous about miracles.

In 1894 a railroad wagon was reconfigured to act as a jailhouse, and was left on a siding. One day, to the shock of the alderman, Epitacio Morales, the Jimulco train accidentally coupled with this wagon-jail and very nearly carried it off, freeing the prisoners of the state prosecutor's office. The blunder was corrected and the cheers of the prisoners were stifled, but the story lived on.

Sada's version, "The PoMo Prison,"[4] is more poetic and stranger than the real event, and contains a tangible truth that surpasses the fetish of any supposed "historical truth." The Torreón that Sada imagines is a city made up not only of houses but also of machines and tracks on which everyday life is carried out. City hall and other public offices are all wagons, not buildings. The mayor opens a casino with the overt intention of making a killing off the rich, but immediately realizes his investment is endangered by their violent natures: the landowners have the unfortunate habit of settling the least disagreement with bullets, just like card sharps. To keep the clientele under control, the mayor places a jail-wagon next to the casino-wagon and threatens to incarcerate anyone who disturbs the peace. But the gunfights continue and, as the functionary would not dare force the wealthy to stand trial (it would be bad for business), he passes laws relating to the invasion of private land, laws no one understands, and which he uses as a pretext to lock up the poor of the town. The prisoners are exhibited as an example of the evil existent inside the Torreón jail: they are given, if anything, an orange or a half kilo of nuts a day, they have to shit where they sleep, the only fresh air they breathe passes into the interior of the wagon through a hail of bullets . . . The trick works: the rich men stop killing one another in the casino-wagon for fear of dying of starvation next to the have-nots in the adjoining prison. Time goes by. The convicts watch, through a crack, the population of the town growing, watch it becoming a city while they continue in perpetual confinement on the train, which

---

4. "La cárcel posma"

should signify movement but is in fact a dungeon. Until some anonymous hand finally decides to free them. This is not done by simply
coupling the wagon to an engine, as almost happened in the historical anecdote, but by stealing an entire stretch of the urban space. The
casino, the city hall, and all the other offices: half of Torreón is expelled down the tracks from Torreón, and only in this way can the
city and the convicts be mutually redeemed. In the end, the fugitives
run through the scrubland (less uncultivated than the city), and the
dream comes to an end with "If any of those prisoners, now sitting
comfortably in their houses, were to read these few lines, they should
know once and for all what I wish for them: I hope, since that time,
they've been getting what they deserve!"

What is implied in these lines is that the anonymous hand that
may have freed the prisoners, that may have stoked the engines,
and coupled the wagons, and taken the nomadic Torreón out of
Porfirian Torreón, is the hand of music, the hand of prose, the hand
of Daniel Sada pressing the keys of a typewriter. It's an outstanding short story.

In 1894 La Laguna was beset by drought and a smallpox epidemic. There was another upsurge of unrest among the have-nots.
Those twelve months were so bitter that for decades they were
known as the Year of Hunger. But the town held out. A bullring
was inaugurated; its terraces were badly constructed, and were the
site of a serious accident in 1897. Electricity was installed. The number of companies and stores increased.

Four years later, in 1898, a very unusual lawyer arrived in town
in the role of the commercial agent of a railroad company. His
name was Manuel José Othón, and he drank like an Irish priest
while drafting neoclassical poems. When not engaged in these activities, he negotiated concessions for his clients, completed the
necessary formalities for obtaining a notary's license, traversed on
foot, armed with a rifle, the great expanse of desert land around
the Hacienda de Noé, property of the landowner Santiago Lavín,
and lied by correspondence to Pepita Jiménez—his wife—about his
health and his possibly repeated acts of infidelity. And while he was

unsuccessfully attempting to stay sober and soberly falling for the ass of a younger woman (the divorced lady of a Spaniard, or the wife of a mechanic, or a single girl who owned a restaurant; from Saltillo or Durango or Lerdo; called Lupe Rodríguez or Gregoria Bustamante *La Machinena* or Guadalupe Jiménez, according to the respective testimonies of Artemio de Valle Arizpe, Armado Illarramendi, and Alfonso Toro), Othón found time to write a perfect, inscrutable piece of poetry: "Wild Idyll."[5]

Sonnet V

What a sickly, suffering panorama!
With the flatlands so relentless and doleful!
The dread that floats throughout so woeful
As if it were a field of fearful slaughter.
Shadow encroaching, encroaching, encroaching,
Appears to be, with its sheath of tragedy,
The vast soul, filled with the bitter reality,
Of those people who must depart despairing.
And there we exist, ground under oppression,
Beneath the heavy weight of all forgetting,
Tormented by the anguish of all passion.
In a leaden sky, the sun by now inert
And in the depths of our lacerated hearts
Is the desert, the desert . . . and the desert!

The printing press arrived in 1889, bringing with it Alberto Swain, who carved his own blocks of movable type from wood. He only ever made lowercase letters. From his type boxes came the early conservative journalism jointly produced by Delfino Ríos and Jacobo M. Aguirre, great-grandfathers of the intellectual caste of La Laguna.

In addition to the opulence forever embodied in the vast fields of cotton, in 1990 there were twelve important centers of industry,

---

5. "Idilio salvaje"

among which were a soapworks, a mill producing yarns and textiles, a smelter, a brewery, a brickworks, a factory making furniture, and another producing soda and candy. There was, furthermore, what was at that time the principal steelworks in the country, in which Don Evaristo, grandfather of the future revolutionary Francisco I. Madero, was a partner. A company refining the local *guayule* plant would soon be opened on the road to El Pajonal, and was for years the largest, most profitable in the region: the Continental Rubber Company.

The local population reached 13,845: in the course of a decade almost ten thousand people had come to live in the utopia called Torreón—it should be said that Torreón is, above all, an oxymoron: a Pragmatic Utopia. In 1901, thanks in part to the offices of the poet Othón—capable of combining with enviable skill business, drunkenness, and hendecasyllables—the electric streetcar was set in motion, connecting Torreón to nearby Ciudad Lerdo. To celebrate this pompous, grandiloquent event, Professor Pioquinto González, a Durango musician of thirty-one years of age, composed "De Lerdo a Torreón," a polka that would quickly become the rage throughout the entire north of the country and enter the popular memory. Significantly, the name of the piece has changed: nowadays it is known as "De Torreón a Lerdo."

Five urban streetcar routes were inaugurated. A new bullring was constructed, the Plaza 2 de Abril became the civic heart of the town, and new banking institutions were set up, one of which was owned by the Chinese community. In 1904 the first Chamber of Commerce was created, and the following year there was a surge in real estate speculation. In 1906 an indoor market was erected. In 1907 the town achieved the status of city. In 1909 the extraordinary artillery captain and Torreón's founder, Andrés Eppen, was buried with full honors. Only one year later, Torreón had forty thousand inhabitants, housed the third most important national freight rail terminal, was the principal city of Coahuila State and one of the best in the whole of Mexico.

If a single event could perfectly represent Porfirian political economy, it would be the founding of Torreón. But even if that historical period had depended exclusively on what was done in La Laguna, the Revolution that brought about the fall of Porfirio Díaz would still have broken out. The stories about the miracle occurring in the region omit the fact that the distribution of wealth was atrociously unjust. Yes, the development of the river basin was stunning, but the masses of its poor lived on the verge of financial ruin: wages oscillated between seventy-five centavos to one peso a day. From 1880 to 1936, La Laguna was a center of armed rebellion.

There is an anecdote that illustrates the outlook of the great local proprietors in relation to employment, profit and loss, and race. One day in 1895, the people of Torreón loudly demanded an audience with Mayor Francisco Villanueva. They informed him that on the outskirts of town, on the opposite side of the tracks, seven hundred black laborers had been abandoned to their fate by the administrators of the Tlahualilo hacienda. These workers came from Tuscaloosa, Alabama, and had been contracted to work in Mexico. When it was discovered that some of them were suffering from smallpox, fearing an epidemic, the cotton manufacturing company sacked them en masse with no advance notice or compensation and threw them off the property (although not far enough for them to be repatriated) with a brutality worthy of Southern slave owners.

The vast encampment remained on the outskirts for days, like a medieval print refuting the image of Porfirian positivism, until Poston, the consul, urged on by Villanueva, obtained the papers necessary for the repatriation of the seven hundred. They were herded onto a freight train with no attempt to isolate the infected, and transported like cattle back to the United States. This is one of the most serious racist deportations in the history of Mexico, and the fact that it came about in the same city where, sixteen years later, the worst slaughter of Chinese people on the American continent would occur seems to me sufficient to set a red light flashing in anyone's mind.

●●●●●

The second half of the sixteenth century, when explorers made their way deeper into the north of the country in search of agricultural areas capable of feeding the mining communities of the south, saw the beginnings of the *pays de la laguna*: a water supply system involving ten municipalities in Durango and five in Coahuila. The earliest maps identified two rivers—the Aguanaval and the Nazas—and many other bodies of water, with San Pedro on the northern border, and Santa María de las Parras to the south. Jesuit missions were soon scattered across the entire territory. The first plant to be cultivated in any volume was the vine, but, starting in the 1830s, the fields were turned over to cotton.

La Laguna prospered during the period of the Spanish viceroyalty. One factor that contributed to the particular makeup of the region, and that would, eventually, have a perverse ideological influence, was the monopolistic nature of private ownership: at the end of the eighteenth century, the marriage between the Conde de San Pedro de Álamo and the Marquesa de Aguayo merged almost the whole of the regional patrimony—from both the Durango and Coahuila sides—into one estate. This vast privatized district was very soon forced to come to terms with a number of irritating impositions: in 1787, under Carlos III's Bourbon reforms, it was legally divided into the colonial provinces of Coahuila and Durango. In addition to the loss of an intellectual pivot resulting from the expulsion of the Society of Jesus, this led to an intense cultural drama: a shocking event that, 227 years later, remains an open wound. However tacky it may seem, and although it might sound less like a problem of the shortcomings of Mexican federalism than a Near Eastern territorial conflict or frontier negotiations between former Soviet republics, there are still Laguneros who idealize their eighteenth-century status and advocate the reintegration of that transcendental Eden: legal separation from Durango and Coahuila.

At first glance, Lagunerismo has a strangely virtuous solidity. That impression changes on closer inspection. Carlos Castañón Cuadros recounts the multiple conflicts between the "upriver" landowners of Durango and their "downriver" counterparts in Coahuila: two groups of capitalists who had a history of often armed confrontation over water rights. This gives a less irrational slant to the administrative separation the colonial and Mexican governments imposed on the territory. Lagunero regionalism is, among many other things, a Far Western conflict: the struggle between the mediating state and unconstrained capitalism that rejected any external authority, preferring to solve its problems John Wayne style: with a Colt.

In the eighteenth century, a parish priest named Dionisio Gutiérrez denounced the "absolute and despotic" control of water by the administrators of the large haciendas that generated extreme poverty and depopulation in many areas. The situation hadn't changed much by the middle of the nineteenth century, and that is why Benito Juárez's liberal agrarian reforms caused indignation among local landowners, as can be inferred from the letters of complaint Zuloaga sent to Governor Vidaurri, or this paragraph by Carlos Castañón:

> On his arrival in Viesca, President Benito Juárez, who had already heard reports of the agrarian conflicts between Zuloaga and the inhabitants of Vega de Marrufo (now Matamoros), issued a decree increasing the land to be expropriated by the government to eighteen sites of *ganado mayor* [cattle, horses, and so forth], a total of 31,600 hectares. This decree replaced another, issued on February 28, 1863, which had been ignored by Santiago Vidaurri.

Why do I deem it relevant to set down these data in the chronicle of a small genocide? Because chauvinism is a cultural metonym par excellence in La Laguna, and no separatist regionalism is ideologically neutral; among its metaphors is xenophobia. You don't have to be a sociologist to be aware of two common aspects of this type of discourse: the rejection of the state's monopoly on violence, and the determination to defend local norms and customs (among them, the way in which private property and race are perceived), laws notwithstanding.

The Lagunero élan, the discriminatory systems involved in increasing its population, and its traditional economy are to some extent similar to those of the entities that lost the Civil War in the United States. Pretending that the slaughter of the Chinese is completely at odds with local chauvinism would be like saying it's impossible to get fries in a burger joint.

A contemporary anecdote demonstrates that these cultural metonyms transcend the popular imagination and middle-class indignation, and influence politics and finance.

In July 2014, Pedro Luis Martín Bringas (shareholder in the Soriana supermarket chain, and one of the thirty-five richest men in Mexico, according to *Forbes* magazine, 2013) started the ELLA (El Estado de La Laguna) movement, and put his own money into canvassing for the separatist cause by fielding candidates in Coahuila's municipal elections. As an organization, ELLA was not registered for the election, which meant its votes were not counted. Martín Bringas claimed to the press that 25 percent of the total vote went to his organization. He did not, however, offer any independent confirmation of this figure. He rounded off his tirade by denouncing the candidates from the conservative PAN (National Action Party), who had initially voiced their moral support for the movement, but differed in terms of political policy. Martín Bringas accused them of betraying the cause and confusing the electorate. This information is gathered from declarations Bringas made to the newspaper *El Siglo de Torreón*, a media organ that showed clear sympathy for ELLA during the campaign, and that, it can be said in passing, had once extolled the activities of the anti-Chinese clubs of the twenties and the pro-Nazi equivalents of the thirties.

•••••

In 1969, Texas Western Press published a unique volume in the genre of microhistory: *Tulitas of Torreón: Reminiscences of Life in*

Mexico. It is a first-person narrative, supplemented by photographs and letters, written by Evelyn Payne and based on many hours of taped conversations with her eighty-year-old mother, Gertrudis Jamieson, also known as Tulitas.

Tulitas Wulff was born in New York, where her family had moved from San Antonio. Her father, Fred, succeeded in finding employment as a draftsman in a construction company following a tough period in which he had to roll up the frayed cuffs of his pants and put cardboard insoles in his shoes. A few years after Tulitas's birth, Fred was invited to Mexico to draw up plans for a dam in the desert. He immediately accepted: his twelve-year-old daughter suffered from chronic bronchitis, and he imagined the dry climate would do her good. They arrived in 1881, decorated their first Christmas tree, and in time Fred and Linda produced four more children. They spoke English and ate sauerkraut (they were of German descent), but judged themselves to be Mexican.

Tulitas says:

I sometimes wonder about what would have happened if he had stayed in New York. We would have grown up to the tune of *Take Me Out to the Ball Game* instead of *La paloma*; we would have watched baseball instead of bullfights. Skyscrapers, Wall Street, Vanderbilts and Tammany in lieu of Porfirio Díaz, *enchiladas* and revolution.

Once Fred started to prosper, and Torreón began to emerge as an urban entity, Linda and the children moved temporarily to San Antonio, returning when the town had reached its apogee. Gertrudis remembers how difficult it was to keep a nursemaid, however lacking in charms she might be (apparently, Don Federico made strategic efforts to hire only plain nannies): there were so many men living in Torreón, and so few women, that no sooner would one show up than she had several suitors, sometimes younger, and occasionally handsome. Even the craggiest spinster found a husband within a few months.

Tulitas gives a humorous account of the self-imposed racism of Mexican society:

> Once when I was about 13, a most self-conscious age, we were invited to San Pedro to attend a very grand ball given by Francisco I. Madero (father of the Revolution) for the girl to whom he was engaged. As a special feature of the event all the young girls were supposed to march in two by two, and I, although I was younger than most of them, had been included. My partner was Rosita, aged about 16 and already very much a young lady. She was so thoroughly whitened that she looked like a clown, and I almost baulked at walking with her. Just as the procession was about to start Rosita's mother came rushing in, and I gave a sigh of relief, thinking that surely she would do away with the girl's make-up. But she only grabbed a powder puff, crying anxiously, "Rosita, ponte más polvito." (Put on more powder!)

Tulitas notes the Babelian aspects of the language spoken by the locals: she transcribes the scolding a mining captain gave to a worker incapacitated by a hangover.

"If you sauuy in the noche that you ain't goin to trabajar in the mañana, why the jel don't you dígame!"

One abiding feature of the landscape was the railroad, which marked, along with the nascent industries, the rhythm of the town:

> [The] train service was dilatory. The engineers considered themselves very important men—if one had a girl he wanted to visit, the train could wait till he did so. So the *mozo* [from the Wulffs' house] always made several trips to the station and when the premonitory rumblings and shiftings indicated that the schedule was about to go into operation again he rushed home to inform us, summon a *coche*, and load the bags into it. . . .
> The train tracks . . . ran right through the town and trains were often parked for hours, so you had to make a wide detour

around them. If you were afoot and daring enough, sometimes you took a chance and crawled over the couplings between the cars. Epimeño, another *mozo*, was sent to get a fifty-pound cake of ice. Returning, the ice firmly tied with a piece of rope, he found his way barred by a long freight train which had just pulled in and seemed likely to stay awhile. Epimeño decided to chance it, but just as he was crawling through, the train started off, and he was carried to Gómez Palacio, three miles away, before he could dismount. Having no money for the streetcar, he walked home in the blazing sun. The ice was long since melted when he got back, but he proudly showed us that the rope was still wet, evidence that he had really bought ice.

The hookers—euphemistically called "women of secondary affairs"—had chosen the siesta hours for their working shift. Any decent woman, and any man who deemed himself a gentleman, was banished from the street between lunch and sundown. The foreigners who insisted on staying outdoors during those hours—there was one in particular who made himself out to be a descendant of La Rochefoucauld: he used to sit naked to the waist at the door of his lodging, typing furiously—were considered by the Mexicans to be casting a slur on their families' names.

The trades undertaken by men were unexpected: although La Laguna was prospering, flexibility was still an advantage when it came to earning a living. In the early years, the good people of Torreón had only one barber, a man who charged a modest fee for the exercise of his craft. He therefore absented himself during the cotton-picking season, when he could earn more as a day laborer. For many years, gentlemen were hirsute until the end of the harvest.

Tulitas left Torreón at the age of thirteen, first for San Antonio and then San Francisco to complete high school. Until she reached seventeen—while she was attempting to grow her hair to her waist, and arrange it in the bouffant, pompadour style of a "Gibson Girl" (those sketches of young women made by the illustrator Charles

Dana Gibson, who, through such magazines as the *Social Ladder*, dictated the pinup fashion of the day)—her only source of news of La Laguna were the letters she received from her parents. Images filter through from that correspondence as if extracted from a dream:

> [Papa] was on horseback riding through waist-high brush when a sudden shower came up. Even with a raincoat on, he found himself thoroughly drenched. But the peons walking behind him emerged absolutely dry. It developed that when the rain began they had simply stripped, put their clothes in the peaked crowns of their sombreros, and moved along stark naked till the rain was over.

In San Francisco, Gertrudis attended class at the Hopkins Institute of Art, secretly read romantic novels set in Paris, put up with being excluded from university life (the majority of North American men of the era found the idea of studying with women repugnant), and once almost swooned on seeing a naked man in a life drawing class. At seventeen, she was informed that her mother, Linda, was to travel to California on paternal orders to bring all the children—except for Fidi, the eldest, who was then at university—back to Torreón.

It was January, and the train journey was not easy. Linda Wulff was ill, and Tulitas, as the eldest sister, was forced to take charge of the children. In Albuquerque there was a snowstorm, they had to change trains, and, to cap it all off, one of the sleepers they had reserved was already occupied. Gertrudis—who, exactly midway in the journey, was discovering the time had come for her entry into womanhood, to find a husband, and take on the adult world—walked tearfully through the corridors of the train until a gentleman who was traveling alone took pity on her and offered to spend the night in the men's restroom in order to give his cabin to the young woman and Alice, her adolescent sister. Gertrudis accepted the offer, but couldn't sleep a wink: her eyes were fixed on the sliding door of the compartment, and she refused to allow Alice to remove even her shoes. When her sister protested, Tulitas said, "You're lucky I let you take off your hat."

Federico was waiting for them on the platform in Torreón. During the time his children had been in United States, maintaining themselves not exactly in luxury on an allowance of four hundred dollars a month, the engineer had invested his energy and earnings in the construction of a small family mansion. The building was being erected on the southern side of the town, not too far from the railroad station, atop a small, steep hill with a view of the whole city. When she disembarked from the train, Tulitas was able to see her as yet unfinished future home in the distance. As the design was not unlike a miniature German castle, the people of Torreón called it a chalet. In time it would come to be known as La Casa del Cerro.

The moment she heard the first notes of the town band, Tulitas realized how much she'd been missing Mexico. She says:

> Even though it was only 7:00 a.m., very early for that very leisurely time and place, two good-looking young men were walking up and down the platform. Suddenly, Papa was bringing them over and introducing them. "Dr. Jamieson, and Mr. Fairbairn." If I had had any idea that I was looking at my future husband and his best-man-to-be, I might have felt differently. As it was, I was thoroughly irritated that Papa, with paternal blindness, had been stupid enough to introduce anybody when I was so wrinkled, dirty and generally awful-looking.

●●●●●

In La Laguna it's commonly said that Saltillo is just a bakery on the highway from Torreón to Monterrey. The reason behind this slur is that the traditional local delicacy is the famous Tlaxcalteca pulque bread. That worked well enough until a few decades ago, by which time Torreón was a metropolis whose excellent, enlightened public could be seen, according to the writer Paco Amparán, from the moon. Saltillo, for its part, was custodian of a provincial valley whose inhabitants referred to the revolutionary president Venustiano Carranza as "*el bulevar*" the only thing named after him. Then the expansion of Torreón began to decelerate, while in Saltillo it sped up. Nowadays, both cities have around a million inhabitants, and comparable industrial and commercial facilities.

The scorn expressed toward the provincial capital is a metonym of a greater, more deep-seated rejection: scorn for the center of the country (particularly DF) and its concept of nationhood.

Torreón celebrated its hundredth birthday in 2007. It is the youngest city in Mexico, and one of the youngest in all Latin America. Although it sells itself as an advanced society (and in many ways is), it also has a reactionary streak. Its reigning household gods (the railroad, the telegraph, and cotton) belong to high modernism, but are at the same time outdated: museum pieces. One feature that makes it unique is that, originally, there was no government building or Catholic church around the Plaza de Armas. It was all banks, hotels, offices, and a cinema: in 1910, Isauro Martínez opened the Pathé theater, where silent movies were shown.

One might think, and the people of Torreón would agree, that such a community guarantees a freer, more modern civic lifestyle than others, despite the remote punishments imposed on it by the Catholic-Juarista-Aztec order. That is only partly true. Torreón has an extremely strong local culture, and an almost tropical sexuality, both of which flowered in the desert, somewhere between a spaghetti Western and a *cumbia* party; but it is also a community that prefers to keep its skeletons in the closet.

Filemón Garza Cavazos, the city's mayor in the thirties, had, the decade before, belonged to the anti-Chinese club, a body whose members armed themselves with stout sticks and stood in front of the stores of their Asian competitors to scare off their customers. Every Lagunero historian knows that fact, but none will ever be inclined to mention it in an academic study or *crónica*: that businessman, politician, and founder of the city's most important newspaper is considered to have been one of the pillars of La Laguna society. Many other grandfathers, great-grandfathers, or granduncles who now head companies, foundations, and cultural projects were once active in the Club Svástica—sympathetic to the Nazi cause—or raised their champagne glasses at the doors of the casino when they heard that Victoriano Huerta had assassinated Madero. The names of these people are well known to the Torreón intelligentsia, and I have often heard them mentioned soto voce by that same intelligentsia. No one, however, dares to set down such stories in writing.

●●●●●

On the wall behind Dr. Sergio Corona Páez's desk is a panoramic photograph of the old city center. The image shows the railroad station, the Alianza market, and, dominating it all, the building that gave its name to the community.

"This is, in fact, the second tower," says Corona. "The first was destroyed in the summer of 1868 when the Nazas topped its banks. Ah, but neither of them was exactly an ornament: do you see the parapets and embrasures here? It was a small fortress for defense against the nomadic groups and outlaws that abounded in the region until the early twentieth century."

Even its name marks Torreón as a city founded on the language of violence, and no one can claim it to have been a stranger to violent metaphors. More recently, such metaphors have proliferated due to the influence of the narco cartels. If I mention this only in passing, it's because I believe it has already been sufficiently dealt with elsewhere. What interests me isn't the blunt discourse of brutality in La Laguna, but its most internalized, domestic expression.

In contrast to what happens elsewhere in northern Mexico, where the glaring sunlight imposes a Calvinist veto on the mention of certain parts of the body, the region enjoys an exultant sexuality, a quarrelsome, dusty version of the Caribbean aura that a friend summed up for me in this way: "I get to Torreón, I take off my dick, chuck it up into the air, and, for the rest of the week, no one lets me bring it down."

Prostitution has enjoyed good health since the times when the "women of secondary affairs" took to the streets during the siesta. Francisco L. Urquizo says that, during the revolution,

> Torreón's brothels were famous, and there were none better in the whole of the north of our country. . . . . The three high-class houses belonged to María Ortega, Paulina, and La Niña, and had between twenty and thirty women apiece. They were the ones that serviced the bosses and officers from the evening to the early hours. And then there were the lower-class whore-houses where the troops went.

To this day, the trade is plied in the downtown streets, where it's easy to pick up a girl, a boy, or a tranny for a modest sum. There are a great many cantinas where women charge "whatever you want to give me" to come in their mouths. And neither is there any short-age of escorts who advertise on the Web with charmingly modest obscenity: "Deep Throat, 15 *brazas*"; "Fellow travelers and loving couples welcome"; "Service door available twenty-four/seven."

Sometime ago, the poet and photographer Jesús Flores carried out an investigation: he became a self-employed homosexual pros-titute for a year, and succeeded in photographing himself and some of his clients before or after anal coitus in order to build up a graphic gonzo chronicle of male prostitution in La Laguna. As a by-product, he wrote a diary in verse under the pseudonym Sebastián Margot, to which he gave the all-encompassing title *Rough Top and Susceptible Bottom*.[6]

In the seventies, Torreón had the most famous tolerance zone in Mexico. Against all odds, what was also known as the Fourth Sector was not merely a grim, lowlife place; in reality it seems (in images of the time) cheerful, particularly in relation to its porno murals. Years after the brothel owners' conglomerate closed, and when the news came that the area was to be bulldozed, Héctor Moreno photo-graphed many of the pieces of pornographic art and published the

6. *Chacal y susceptible*

images in a small book: *Closed Down*.[7] It's one of the best documents I know of on popular sexuality: an intriguing, portable Pompeii.

It has to be said that in Torreón, sex goes way beyond whoring. There is an elemental elegance in the courtesy, frankness, and grace with which people here exchange muscles, fluids, and fats. It should also be said that this carnality has been threatened by violence, crime, and the deterioration of the social fabric. This is a shame: from my viewpoint, loss of sexual joy seriously damages the intangible patrimony of any nation.

Bearing this sensuality in mind, it's hardly surprising that the Colombian dance music *cumbia* became more popular here and in Monterrey than in any other Mexican city. In the eighties, Lucho Argaín's group La Sonora Dinamita wrote a song that went "Your Lagunero's going, black girl, / going and never coming back," to thank the inhabitants of Torreón for their love of this musical genre. Nor is it any surprise that, on generating its own *cumbiambera* identity with such groups as Tropicalísimo Apache and, a generation later, Chicos de Barrio, the added local flavor has taken a completely different direction from that of the sluggish, drug-induced dirges of the Colombian and Monterrey underground: not reducing the revolutions of the vinyl, but doubling the beat: applying the faster *chu-chu*, *chu-chu* of the güiro to the drum section, which is more or less the same as turning a rockabilly song into punk rola. Because Torreón is a lover on speed, a woman smoking crack, fucking doggy style until her knees bleed. And neither is it any surprise that the house style of dances (vertical expressions of a horizontal desire) is to close with a free-for-all: any event where the Chicos play that doesn't end in a pitched battle is a flop. How else to catalyze the sexual passion of a culture that yearns for violence than by cracking open the head of a guy from a different neighborhood before perhaps giving it to his woman?

There is another extreme theatrical scenario—inoffensive but with grandiloquent gestures—that the region considers its own: wrestling.

---

7. *Clausurado*

The sport is taken more seriously here than anywhere else in Mexico. The level is very high; it has specific rituals and a brand loyalty that is the envy of other franchises. The Durango side of La Laguna has produced veritable legends of pankration: Gran Markus, Mano Negra, Blue Panther, Último Guerrero, and Espanto Jr.

Chicos de Barrio wrote the theme song for a gringo cartoon series called *¡Mucha Lucha!*

But all those pastimes pale before soccer. No matter their gender, the people of Torreón are fanatical fans. And there is a reason for this: Santos, the local team, has had its glorious moments, including winning the occasional championship, and, although it lately seems to be on a downward slope, years ago the team achieved what is most difficult for a Mexican club: playing clean, the way world soccer's "man of letters," Eduardo Galeano, begged the sport to be played. Figures such as Jared Borghetti and Rodrigo "Pony" Ruiz, who both wore the green-and-white shirt in the franchise's most splendid years, and even slightly traitorous athletes like Oribe Peralta, are the objects of extreme levels of popular adoration.

And what name did the inhabitants of La Laguna, true junkies of violent analogies, give the eleven men of their tribe? The Guerreros.

The love for Santos is an incarnation of amour propre. For years, when the team played in the tiny Corona stadium (nothing separated the players from the crowd; from the stand you could practically spit in the face of a rival when he was taking a corner), there were no fans more imaginative or ferocious. At one time they had no enemies because all the other supporters were afraid to come to Torreón for fear of losing their self-respect or their teeth. This, added to the fact that Santos was the most solid team in Mexican soccer when playing at home, was the reason for the ground's arrogant nickname, which was retained even when the team moved to a larger, modern, and more luxurious facility; a motto inscribed on the wall, which, although we all love it, is still cruel, reads: The House of the Pain of Others.

In 1888 a young Chinese man alighted from the train in Torreón. Oral tradition has him carrying baskets of goods from his country: silk, herbal remedies, handicrafts, perfumes . . . He had sold all these products in train carriages and the markets of the towns he passed through during his journey across the desert. His name was Wong Foon Check. The Mexicans would come to know him as Foon-chuck. He had a long life. But that isn't what interests me at this stage.

Foon-chuck founded a school where Cantonese was taught, managed a hotel in which opium was smoked, and was the business partner of a man who was condemned to death by the form of torture known as *leng t'che*. But neither is that what interests me at this stage.

What I am interested in belongs to that instant: the image of a solitary young man, a stranger to everyone, with only a smattering of Spanish and a shy manner, who leaves the train in a newly founded city of the West. Look at him: he's twenty-four. He's carrying two baskets of merchandise. He doesn't know it, but, come what may, he has just destroyed the eugenic utopia of those who consider themselves the wisest men in Mexico.

CAB (2)

"And what they did, grandpa, is stick their bayonets into the children when the moms came out of their houses carrying them in their arms, and then they turned round like the guys in *300*, and fuck me if they didn't finish off the Chinitas as well."

I'm running late: the hours had flown by discussing Benjamín Argumedo with his biographer, the magistrate Jesús Sotomayor; I was due to meet Manuel Terán Lira in the restaurant of the Sanborns department store a quarter of an hour ago.

"Can't we take the Reforma diagonal?"

"Roadwork, grandpa," says the cab driver, a gold tooth glinting in his smile (it's been a while since I've seen someone younger than I with a gold tooth), as he looks at me through the rearview mirror. He continues his master class: "But you can get better information from that radio station . . . what's its name? . . . I can't remember what they call it, grandpa, but it's right there downtown, on Hidalgo. They can give you more information, because one of my old lady's sisters works there, and she says there are always Chinitos turning up."

I make my way through the store to the restaurant and ask the waitress for Dr. Terán Lira. She directs me to a table set slightly apart. There he is, accompanied by his wife: somewhere in his seventies, not very tall, not much meat on him, a straight back, an unkempt mustache, and a delightful face. He gets to his feet as soon as he spots me, walks over like he's welcoming me into his home, and introduces his wife, who shakes my hand, murmurs "Hola," smiles, and then fixes her eyes on her plate and neither looks at us nor speaks again.

Terán Lira offers me a seat and sits down opposite me while I order tea. He looks more like a retired rock star than a historian: he's wearing an old Texan hat with the brim curled upward, has slightly purple-tinted spectacles, almost-new black jeans, and a sleeveless T-shirt that makes him resemble a teenage skateboarder with prematurely wrinkled arms. If he had tattoos, he'd be able to get backstage without a pass at a Rolling Stones gig.

"This is about the Chinese," he says, handing me a booklet of no more than thirty pages. "But my thing, my thing really is Pancho Villa."

Enveloped in his charisma, I understand why people come out with such garbage, as did the cab driver when I told him whom I was going to meet.

"Just talk to Dr. Terán, grandpa. Don't let those other bastards fool you. Some of them even say it wasn't Villa who killed the Chinitos. Shit, think about it! Who the fuck else could it have been? Just go talk to the doctor, grandpa. He knows what's up. And he owns every frigging museum in Torreón. He's got around eight of them."

I'm surprised by the number of historical errors Terán had been capable of packing into thirty pages. While he does in fact acquit Villa, he says there were two thousand Chinese in Torreón, when it is unlikely their number approached even half that figure; he confuses Lim's country chalet with Foon-chuck's house; he claims the existence of a section within the Ministry of War that ensured the incorporation of a group of paramilitary Chinese into the 1911 defense: that, more than an error, is calumny.

But he's likable. Very likable.

●●●●●

It is not only wrong that Pancho Villa took part in the massacre: it is also a lie that there were Asiatic mothers to be bayoneted in La Laguna. A document cited by Carlos Castañón mentions only four Chinese women named in the 1910 census in Coahuila. There was, of course, Lim's sister: the only one about whom there is reliable evidence. But the vast majority of the members of the community were male.

Neither is it credible that there were many minors: according to official records, two seventeen-year-olds, a boy of fourteen, and another of twelve perished in the incident. They were all shot.

"There must have been women," Silvia Castro had insisted when I visited her at the Museo de la Revolución. "Where else did the children come from?"

Perhaps the twelve-year-old victim crossed half the planet without his mother. Or maybe that mother was Mexican; there is a great deal of documentary evidence of mixed marriages. Of all the possibilities, this last one seems to me the worst: that a bunch of killers takes their hatred of you out on your children, never giving you the chance to shoulder the burden of the hate the world metes out on those children because their skin is a different color from yours, a different color from their executioners'.

OBLIVION OF LOVE

You better run,
You better take cover.
"Down Under," Men at Work

I think: there is a place where what is closest to you, what you pretend to possess, is called by another name. It's no big deal. It could, for example, have to do with your mother. So you had to learn she never was "Mom," that she had a first name and surnames. And even worse: in private, your father referred to her by a repulsive pet name. So what? Then she dies and, still raw from her loss, you have to rummage among her things in search of something or other, some document for the death certificate, and you discover that yellowed letter in which a girlfriend from high school uses a slur that destroys you, calling her a "frigging Macaque." My mother's dead body is a Frigging Macaque. From this viewpoint, from the isolation of our names, nothing is yours. Things belong to language.

I remember how indignant I felt on learning that the Nao de China, the trading ships that docked in the port of Acapulco, in fact came from the Philippines. Their real name, I heard, was something else, the name they were given in the North: the Manila Galleons. I learned this when I was a child. I was playing alone in the Fuerte de San Diego in Acapulco, and overheard a tour guide passing on that information. I spent years trying to forget it. It was my cherished illusion that the boats crossed the ocean from the port of Peking to my house in Acapulco.

The Manila Galleons were the first formal contact between Mexico and Asia. The service was inaugurated in 1565 by Andrés de Urdaneta, who discovered what would become known as Urdaneta's route, or the Kuroshio: an ocean current (also known as the Black Stream) that flows north from Taiwan, passes Japan to the east, crosses the Chinook Trough to the south of the Aleutian Islands, and gradually descends to the Pacific coast of Mexico. There is no larger stretch of water. Urdaneta's route took four or five months, but in 1521 Magallanes-Elcano succeeded in making the return voyage in just three.

The first Chinese immigrants to arrive in America may have come in the service of Spanish merchants. Some—surely very few: migration was not yet synonymous with survival for them—set themselves up as storekeepers, launderers, or barbers in segregated zones of a handful of cities in Nueva España, and particularly in the capital. They christened the viceroyalty Da Lusong (Big Luzon) to distinguish it from Xiao Lusong (Small Luzon): the Philippines.

For two and a half centuries (longer than the history of Mexico as a nation), the Manila Galleons crossed the seas once or twice a year, and provisioned the homes and imagination of the colony with exquisite products: silk, spices, ceramics, poisons . . . The trade came to an end in 1815 as a result of the War of Independence from Spain, but its chinoiserie still lived on in Mexican fantasy at the time of the massacre. Traces of it can be found in this poem by Francisco González León:

> The Chinese ship
> that came to Acapulco
> brought to the noble
> Marquesa de Uluapa
> a lacquered chest
> the color of vanilla;
> decorated with golden
> winged dragons
> and strange flowers,
> and a pair of earthen jars.
> But to me it brought
> something better:
> to me it has brought
> oblivion of love.

The Chinese ship
brought to the Viceroy,
for his daughter Pía,
the miracle that opened
out into a fan
of woven tortoiseshell;
and for his wife
the worked crystal glass
of a flask filled
with essence of roses.

But to me it brought
something better:
to me it has brought
oblivion of love.

Suffering that stands
to one side of the path;
anodyne formula
of an eastern recipe;
smoke of sorrows
seen through a telescope.

The Chinese ship
has today sent in a bill
for my weary, secret ills
a net pound of
dreams and oblivion
with a label reading:
Opium!

The brilliance of the piece lies in its anachronism: the exchange
of gazes between the graceful China of the Nao era and its terrifying counterpart, the Opium Wars.

A lovely book by Patricia Buckley Ebrey entitled *The Cambridge Illustrated History of China* begins:

Most peoples have myths about their origins, and the Chinese are no exception. Through most of the imperial period, literate Chinese had a "great man" theory of how their civilization developed. Unlike other peoples who pointed to gods as their creators or progenitors, the Chinese attributed to a series of extraordinarily brilliant human beings the inventions that step by step transformed the Chinese from a primitive people to a highly civilized one. Fu Xi, the Ox-tamer, domesticated animals and invented the family. Shen Nong, the Divine Farmer, invented the plough and hoe. Huang Di, the Yellow Lord, invented the bow and arrow, boats, carts, ceramics, writing, and silk. He also fought a great battle against alien tribes, thus securing the Yellow River plain for his people. In China's earliest history, he was labelled the first of the five great pre-dynastic rulers, the last two of whom were Yao and Shun. Yao was credited with devising the calendar and rituals. Rather than hand over power to his own less worthy son, he selected Shun as his successor, a poor peasant whose filial piety had been demonstrated by his devoted service to his blind father and evil stepmother. Shun not only became the next ruler but also married two of Yao's daughters. Despite their virtue, even Yao and Shun were unable to predict floods, so they appointed an official, Yu, to tackle this problem. For over a decade Yu travelled through the land, dredging the channels that became the rivers of north China. So zealous was he that he passed his own home several times without pausing to greet his wife and children. Shun named Yu to succeed him. Yu divided the realm into nine regions, and had bronze vessels cast to represent each one. When Yu died, the people ignored the successor he had chosen and turned to Yu's son to lead them, establishing the precedent of hereditary, dynastic rule. Yu and his son thus were the first two kings of the Xia dynasty, a dynasty which lasted through fourteen rulers.

It is impossible to summarize the history of a country whose first, almost legendary dynasty (the Xia) came to power over four thousand years ago. A country whose territory is the third largest on the planet, and is covered by ice and deserts to the north, encircled by mountains to the west, carpeted in jungle to the south, and scattered with ports to the south and east. A country that, in the eleventh century, already had ten million inhabitants. A country with a history of mourning: half the population was once lost to bubonic plague. A country that first devised a writing system five thousand years ago. A country whose dynasties (from the viewpoint of an educated man of the European Enlightenment: the Qin, Tang, Han, Yuan, and Ming) stretch back beyond the millennium: this is as dizzying as moving in a single sentence from the Crusades to Steve Jobs. It is impossible to summarize the history of a country that invented such perversely refined methods of torture as *leng t'che* (that ecstatic form of death by a hundred cuts that obsessed the writer Salvador Elizondo and the musician John Zorn), but also produced such simple, sublime poets as Li Bai. A nation made up of many peoples: the Yi, the Chinese (China means "the center"), the Manchu, the Tocharians, the Zhuang, the Hakka, the . . . A country that produced Confucianism and, over the centuries, succeeded in transforming that subtle philosophy into bureaucratic jargon: in the nineteenth century, the doctrinal examinations for entry into the civil service were so rigorous and complex, yet also so absolutely useless, they would have delighted the Talmudic mind of Franz Kafka.

It is impossible to summarize the history of a country that seems to embody otherness.

In 1644 a peasant uprising ended in the suicide of the last emperor of the Ming dynasty. After a civil war that lasted nearly two decades, an eight-year-old child named Kangxi, the first emperor to follow the line of primogeniture, ascended to the throne to rule for sixty years. He was the founder of the Qing dynasty, a Manchu tribe that remained in power until 1912. The first three monarchs (Kangxi, Yongzheng, and Qianglong) fulfilled their roles successfully: they expanded the frontiers of the realm and stabilized the economy, but the dynasty struggled against strong allegations of corruption from the eighteenth century onward. One of the most famous of these scandals had as its protagonist Heshen, a court official whom the fifth emperor, Jiaqing, obliged to commit suicide at the beginning of the nineteenth century.

The Qing soon had to confront a greater crisis in the history of this expansive empire: Dao Guang, the sixth sovereign of the dynasty—who occupied the throne from 1820 to 1850—reigned through the beginning of the end. One of the problems he faced was a demographic explosion: the imperial census of 1830 registered an increase of one hundred million in the population over a period of approximately fifty years. Corruption, high taxes, constant droughts and floods made it impossible to feed four hundred million people. Thousands upon thousands died of starvation.

The second conflict was the mercantile and military advantage enjoyed by the Western powers (France, Holland, Portugal, Spain, and especially England), which led to the Opium Wars.

A shining example of the double-edged morality of capitalism is the story of the commercial relations between China and England. For a long time, the Chinese had maintained a positive trading relationship with an expanding Europe due to the fact that while the latter desired a great number of Asian products (silk, dyes, spices), the Chinese accepted only silver in exchange. In response to this situation, the English—and after them, other Western merchants—introduced opium grown in British India into China on a massive scale; they did this with the same seriousness as, a century and a half later, Pablo Escobar would exhibit while flying Colombian cocaine into the United States. The Chinese authorities banned this trade, deeming the number of addicts to be a public health issue, but also because trafficking of the drug swung the balance of trade toward the West.

In late 1838 the incorruptible official Lin Tse Su traveled to the port of Guangzhou to demand that the opium cargo on board the ships anchored in the bay be surrendered. Captain Charles Elliot, chief superintendent of English trade, urged the traders affected by this order to yield their merchandise to Queen Victoria. He then allowed Lin to impound the opium, but immediately informed London of the destruction of goods belonging to the British Crown. The response was the dispatch of 20 warships, 4,000 soldiers, and 540 cannons. This force grew to 130 warships and 13,500 soldiers under the command of Henry Pottinger, who fought the Chinese troops and the rebellious civilian population at sea, on land, and on rivers until they were defeated on August 27, 1841. On that same day, the Treaty of Nanking was signed, with the lion's share going to the European powers; a large sum in silver to be paid in war reparations, zero import duties, the right to trade opium and any other product throughout the length and breadth of China (a prize that was extended to the Americans, who were more than happy to employ themselves as traders of the Turkish poppy), and a criminal juridical norm: notwithstanding the offense committed—even when it affected Chinese subjects—foreign residents could answer to their own consulate rather than to the local authorities. According to Juan Puig, the First Opium War cost the nation a third of its annual revenues in 1841.

Emperor Tao Kuang's successors were faced with a steady accumulation of woes. And they faced them very poorly, especially in their response to popular unrest.

With the exception of World War II, the Taiping Rebellion is the conflict that has generated the greatest loss of human life: conservative estimates speak of twenty million deaths. Taking into account the perversity of political language ("beautiful words to hide the absence of facts," as Tzvetan Todorov put it), it is no surprise to me that such a devastating, toxic social movement became known as the Heavenly Kingdom of Great Peace. The rebellion began in the southern province of Guangxi, to the west of Canton, and the starring role was played by Hong Xiuquan, a Guangzhou peasant of Hakka origins, born in 1844.

An outstanding student from his childhood, but born into poverty, Xiuquan studied for years to take the official exams on Confucian doctrine that would, theoretically, give him access to a better life in the Chinese civil service. As still happens in the poor families of many countries, everyone (parents, uncles, aunts, brothers, sisters, cousins) made sacrifices to ensure that the smart kid stayed in school: Xiuquan's failure to pass the official exams in 1836 and 1837 led to a psychotic break. Before this episode, he had come into contact with Christian doctrine through reading *An Exhortation to Perfection*, a pamphlet written by Liang Fa, probably the first Protestant pastor in China. There is also evidence that Xiuquan had some knowledge of the American Baptist missionary Issachar Jacob Roberts. Based on these experiences, and following his academic failure, Hong Xiuquan began experiencing hallucinations in which an old man, accompanied by a younger one, asked him to bring China into the fold of the Christian faith and destroy images of demons. Hong decided the subjects of these visions were none other than God the Father—whose second son he declared himself to be—and Jesus Christ, whom he claimed was his elder brother.

At first the self-proclaimed Heavenly King did nothing more than found an iconoclastic sect in collaboration with his parents, and dedicate himself to destroying every Confucian devotional image that crossed his path. Later, as he gained more apostles and began to be persecuted, he declared open war on the army of Sien Feng, the new Manchu emperor. His initially scant band of followers had grown to five hundred thousand fighters by the time they arrived on the banks of the Yangtze River. They would soon number millions. They advanced northward, taking major cities such as Wuchang and, most significantly, Nanking, which they renamed Tienching and designated the capital of their realm.

My perception of the Taipings is that they were a massively expanded, hyperviolent, and briefly successful version of the Cathars. They traveled everywhere with their wives and children, like a species of bellicose nomads aiming to devour a sedentary nation from within. Their military effectiveness depended on a single advantage that, in the long term, led to their ruin: the absence of work. As their objectives were to enter cities and fight, for thirteen years the Taipings took absolutely no interest in agriculture or any other form of productive labor. They sapped the ground beneath their feet throughout an unusually long and cruel war.

The rebellion lasted from 1851 to 1864, coinciding with the Second Opium War, and its economic and social costs were so great that, at the end of that conflict, the governments of Europe allied themselves with the Chinese Empire to fight the Taipings, fearing that the latter would eventually destroy China completely, thus depriving the West of its perks (which by then were great). For their part, between 1858 and 1860, the Taipings faced an internal rebellion that depleted their numbers, brought down or made enemies of some of their best strategists, and severely damaged their will to fight. They managed to make a comeback, defeated the regular Chinese army for the umpteenth time, and occupied new, strategic positions, but then almost immediately suffered the military reversal that marked the beginning of their downfall: the failed advance on Shanghai. From the moment the Taipings were repelled and their forces decimated by imperial troops, both the insurgents and their charismatic leader fell into a trough of despair. It is probable that by then the saintly Xiuquan had succumbed to the lust for and abuse of power. He may have—historians speculate—committed suicide. The Heavenly Kingdom of Great Peace, which by 1864 occupied significant territories in southern and central China (meanwhile, in Mexico, another strange, bloody war between liberals and liberals disguised as conservatives was being unleashed), died out not long afterward. Its leader, one of the most illustrious sacred lunatics of the nineteenth century, and the chief craftsman of the second-greatest massacre in human history, passed into oblivion in the West.

More violence followed: the war against France in 1885, which was no more than a gala updating of the favorable trading conditions already enjoyed by the English; the war against Japan, which wrested dominion over Korea from China; the Boxer Rebellion, a thrilling nationalist attempt to recoup the country on the basis of terrorism, civil war, and martial arts . . . Many other events could be added to this list without changing the outcome: China was, at that moment, Tralalá—Hubert Selby's drugged hooker whom a gang of hooligans rape to a bloody death in the backseat of a dilapidated car.

Each province faced the disaster as best it could. Some accustomed themselves to war, others concentrated their population in large cities, yet others became killing fields. Canton (Guangdong in Pinyin transcription, 廣東 in traditional Chinese) had access to the sea, and its inhabitants were born sailors. Some men—the most daring, the most desperate—took to their boats and headed for the Philippines, Japan, India, or even farther afield. Very soon, like a slowly awakening rumble of waves, the news spread through the port, then the city, then the surrounding towns, and finally more-distant regions: there, across the ocean, gold had been found. Tons of gold. Enough gold to reinvent reality.

(Or at least so thought Karl Marx, who, with his fine-honed instinct for sensationalism, declared that the discovery of gold in California would be historically more important than the discovery of America.)

And this was how thousands and thousands of Cantonese people came to abandon their homes, their meager possessions, their language, their families, and board ships to ascend the Kuroshio Current, the Black Stream, the old route of the Manila Galleons, which decades before had led to Da Lusong, in a crossing of four or five months. This time their destination was not the salubrious Bay of Acapulco, but an area much farther north: gold-fever California. It was the beginning of what is today known as the great Chinese diaspora, a phenomenon that, over a period of 101 years, hurled eight million Cantonese from their province: the equivalent of the population of Honduras.

●●●●●

Pablo Chee emigrated from 廣東 to Chiapas in 1901. He established himself as a trader and found a wife: a Mexican woman by the name of Adelina Palomegus. In 1910 the couple had a son: Manuel

Jesús Chee. Probably due to the revolutionary upheavals and accompanying xenophobia, the family relocated to 廣東 four years later. Pablo then made a disconcerting decision: he left his wife and child in his parents' care and returned to Mexico alone. He settled in Baja California and, during the next decade, made his fortune as the owner of a store, a hotel, and a cantina (and, probably, as an opium dealer). Throughout this period, he kept tabs on what was happening back home, and sent money for his Mexican son to be educated in the best British school in China. Thanks to his large fortune, he finally purchased American citizenship for himself, Adelina, and Manuel Jesús. The Chees were reunited in 1924 in Imperial Valley, California.

Lee Kwong Lun wore a homburg pushed slightly back on his head, had a neatly cut mustache and the watchful gaze of a famous gunslinger (a photograph of him is reproduced on the front cover of *The Chinese in Mexico*, a book by Robert Chao Romero from which I took this and the preceding story). He immigrated to Cuba sometime after 1850, probably contracted as a "coolie," which meant that the majority of his earnings would end up in the hands of a people-trafficking network. Lee learned Spanish, and for many years worked in the cigar industry. He then moved to California, where he set himself up as a merchant, learned English, and started a family; all this despite the fact that the Chinese Exclusion Act had just come into force. Sometime in the early years of the twentieth century, he and his family had to leave the United States due to their unofficial status as migrants, and settled in Sonora. Lee earned a living as a middleman between Chinese, Mexican, Cuban, and United States businesses thanks to his knowledge of those four countries and their three languages. After ten years in Mexico, and threatened by the revolution, the family managed to put their papers in order and returned to the United States, where they made a home in Tucson.

The similarities in these stories offer—apart from images of real people—a backdrop for understanding the transnational character of the diaspora. The United States was the main point of arrival on the American continent for the exiled Chinese, but Mexico and Cuba played the role of migratory wildcards. It could even be said that Cuba competed with California as the destination of choice: by 1870, some one hundred thousand Cantonese had settled on the island.

(It is, therefore, no surprise that the mood-indigo kid, Severo Sarduy, should dedicate a third eclogue with a whiff of ottava rima dressed up as a bolero to that race: "By the River of Rose Ashes," a profuse passage of his novel *Where Are the Singers From?*[8])

There was one difference: almost all the Chinese in the United States and Mexico enjoyed freedom of movement. In contrast, the greater part of those in Cuba were subjected to the coolie regime, which left them in conditions close to those of slavery.

The global nature of the diaspora was a nuanced phenomenon. The north of the American continent and the Caribbean were, for the Chinese, a megaterritory they could strategically cross depending on where the economic balance was most favorable and there was least antagonism to their presence. The frontiers were much more diffuse from the viewpoint of the newcomers. This partly explains the prosperity of the Chinese community in Torreón: their relationship to transnational capital (from China, Canada, and the United States) was unique in the history of Mexico.

⁕⁕⁕⁕⁕

Juan Puig observes that anti-Chinese feeling in the Americas did not emerge with the arrival of the first Asian immigrants: when the Cantonese came ashore on the California coast, the white, Protestant Democrats had already abhorred them for decades from the thorny territory of the imagination.

The first people to bring news of the empire were merchants, smugglers, and sailors. Common elements of their stories were the corruption of the immigration authorities and the lack of honor of

---

8. *De dónde son los cantantes*

many Chinese traders, who sold cargoes of tea in which the top layers were high quality, while the remainder was foul leaves. The Chinese were also accused of being, says Puig, "torturers, polygamists, enemies of progress, idolaters, superstitious, given to female infanticide, incapable of navigating the high seas and, above all, inveterate gamblers."

The second source of Sinophobia was a compound of the various European diplomatic missions, all of which pronounced the Celestial subjects dirty, uncouth, and arrogant. It seems what most offended the Westerners was that attempts were made to force them to *kao tao*: to prostrate themselves before the emperor with their arms and foreheads on the floor. In addition, John Barlow accused them of having no sense of humor. That definitely seems to me a serious imputation. But there is nothing more difficult than translating humor, that simultaneous expression of our hopes and nightmares.

(I wonder if the whole *kao tao* thing might not have been a theatrical practical joke at which Chinese officials sniggered behind their rice paper screens.)

That hatred based on fantasy soon became an editorial niche. The reports of the European diplomatic missions to the Orient were published and reprinted, not in their countries of origin, but in Philadelphia. Books about the natural ineptitude and evil intent of the Chinese grew in number with the years, paving the way for anti-Chinese sentiment in California, and provoking the solidarity and approval of the very noble and sensitive East Coast elite, who, in this particular case, turned out to be more racist than they ever were in relation to African slavery.

The nail in the coffin was hammered home by the Protestant missionaries. They were not, by any stretch of the imagination, the first Christians to spread the word of the Lord in Asia. The passage of Nestorians is attested to by a monument dating from 625. The Yuan Mongol dynasty (founded by Kublai Khan) notes the presence of a Franciscan mission between the thirteenth and sixteenth centuries. The all-terrain Society of Jesus arrived in the empire in 1582, and was notable for its pragmatism in opposing papal dictates, advocating the use of classical Chinese in services, and the adaptation of the liturgy and catechism to the traditions of the country. Nevertheless, despite the positive impression Asian civilization made on them, even the best Jesuit priests whom rationality could forge failed to introduce Christianity into China.

Their failure was as resounding as that of the nineteenth-century Anglo-Saxon Puritans: around 1842, after almost four decades of supreme effort, the number of Chinese converts to Protestant Christianity had reached the sum total of six. Puig offers the key to at least one aspect of the debacle: "There was not in the language, in Cantonese, even an old, antiquated word for the name of God, or for designating the immortal soul, or for alluding to sin, not even for referring to 'religion.'"

Nothing is yours: things belong to language.

The missionaries took their revenge for the impermeability of the Chinese by repeating and magnifying the insults heaped on them in United States. Namely—I return to Puig here—that they were

an infinite multitude of irremediable pagans, child murderers, venerators of an uncultivated, banal pseudo-philosophy (Confucianism), perverted erotomaniacs, lacking all shame, oppressors of women, insensitive as iron, cultivators of a diabolical language, small-brained savages, and, as if all that was not enough to make them detestable, willful agents of Lucifer and declared enemies of the One God, whom they delighted in hating and offending.

(The irony is that one of the few Christian Cantonese of the era was Hong Xiuquan, whose conversion to the faith of brotherly love resulted in so much slaughter.)

The United States press published those and other similar reports. Newspapers of incipient sensationalist fame, such as the *New York Herald* or the *Boston Evening Transcript*, considered insulting

Celestial subjects an essential element of their marketing strategy. And they were not mistaken: Sinophobia became a best seller. "And yet not a single Chinese person had been recorded as arriving in California," states Puig.

The diaspora began in 1848 and the problem became more acute three years later in the wake of the Taiping Rebellion: nearly twenty thousand Cantonese landed in California in 1852. According to Chao Romero, this number would reach three hundred thousand legal residents over the following thirty years (without taking into account the death rate during that whole period), with a record total of forty thousand new arrivals in 1881, the year before further entry was prohibited.

In 1878, the Chinese Empire established a diplomatic mission in the United States.

Some Cantonese immigrants headed for Oregon, Nevada, Idaho . . . But the majority remained in California, with San Francisco and Sacramento their cities of choice. A small number were traders who had brought with them the meager capital they would soon multiply. There were some women, but very few: Elmer Sandmeyer states they scarcely reached 7 percent of the total diaspora, and almost all took to prostitution. The greater part of the migrants were day laborers: workmen without families (or who had left families on the other side of the ocean), almost illiterate, and with no specialized skills. They were not, in fact, very different from the majority of Californians: between 1848 and 1849, the population of the state rose from thirteen thousand to one hundred thousand; nearly all the new inhabitants were white, single men attracted by the mines. Perhaps the only thing, appearance apart, that distinguished the Chinese from the Caucasians was their desperation: the Chinese came from a world that was falling apart, and they were willing to work harder than anyone in any job—from the toughest to the most repugnant—for half, or even less than half, the going rate.

The Chinese joined the gangs working in the gold mines until they dropped. They also found employment in railroad companies, particularly the Southern Pacific, almost all of whose tracks they constructed. They worked as dockhands in the ports, machine operators in the textile industry, when not as market gardeners, farmers, builders, and tobacco rollers. They undertook jobs traditionally reserved for women: cooks, launderers, cleaners. They had no unions. A single gray eminence—partially public spirited, partially sinister—watched out for them: the Six Companies.

New arrivals were generally subject to organizations that received them in California, put them in touch with their first employer, and helped them to settle in one of the local Chinatowns. There were six such bodies, five of which—acting separately— concerned themselves with workers from the five most profusely migratory Cantonese districts, while the sixth dealt with those from any other district or, in exceptional cases, any province of China. These six guilds were also involved—to a lesser degree, surreptitiously, and always denied—in illegal human trafficking, the opium trade, and the management of prostitution rings. They are an example of the historical proximity of organized crime and social activism.

It was not long before everyday and labor-related anti-Chinese feeling began to well up in the California unions. As always happens with mass migration, the cheapness of the Asian workforce affected local wages—the highest in the Union once gold fever had taken hold. Persecution in the media, unrest, and the appearance of anti-Chinese clubs were not long in following. One of the great enemies of the diaspora was Denis Kearney, from the Workingmen's Party of California, who campaigned for the application of special laws, and fomented a mode of thought that led to the 1882 Chinese Exclusion Act.

And then there was the press: Sandmeyer points to an article in the *Marin Journal* of March 30, 1876, that characterizes the Chinese as a threat to the working class, civilization, freedom, democracy, health, and, while they were at it, happiness. An official document made public that same year accused the Chinese migrants of sending half their wages home in remittances, and claimed that 75 percent of what they consumed on United States soil came from their homeland, thus doubly damaging the local economy. As I read those pages, and compare them with what is printed nowadays in the United States about Mexican migrants, I can't avoid a sense of unease: over a hundred years have gone by, and the arguments for excluding the other haven't changed one bit. More than a moral, social, or economic failure, I consider this to be one of rhetoric.

The half-fantasy, half-pragmatic anti-Chinese sentiment of US citizens was institutionalized through the classic electoral route: both Republicans and Democrats used it to attract votes at state and federal levels for three decades. Some politicians were masters of this practice, without the right hand knowing what the left was doing: as governor of California, Leland Stanford referred to the Chinese as "an inferior race" and called for their expulsion in his inaugural address; but as an industrialist and president of the Central Pacific Railroad, he hired them and encouraged immigration. There were also committee members like A. A. Sargent and leaders such as Governor George Clement Perkins whose objections were at least sincere and consistent.

In the hands of the authorities, Sinophobia acquired a pantomime of legitimacy. In contrast to what happened to white foreigners, the Chinese were taxed for migrating, for having a place to live, for seeking work, and for finding work. Along with what are now called the Native Americans, African Americans, and Mexicans, they were denied the ability to act as jurors in trials. In the case of suffering any form of abuse, they had no right to testify against a Caucasian: only if another white man declared in their favor could they defend themselves before the law. California held a referendum that included only one option: no to Chinese immigration. Congress ordered a detailed report on their presence in the United States—on that occasion the Chinese could count on a sympathizer, Senator Oliver P. Morton—and during the Republican presidency of Chester A. Arthur the number of discriminatory laws increased. The most important was the 1882 Exclusion Act, a piece of legislation that prohibited Chinese immigrants from entering United States territory for the next ten years.

If the diaspora continued to—illegally—enter the United States, it was because the owners of capital wanted it so. Thousands of Chinese arrived in Florida from Cuba under the pretext of being repatriated, and climbed onto trains that took them on a transcontinental journey to California. The majority of those passengers were "lost" en route. Other Cantonese immigrants traveled to the coastal regions of Sinaloa and Baja California, and so entered the United States as "wetbacks."

The general discontent of white people was channeled into demonstrations and invective. And, on a few occasions, into physical violence.

On October 24, 1871, a mob attacked the Los Angeles Chinatown and destroyed a large percentage of the dwellings there; eighteen Cantonese people died in the disturbance. In 1887, on March 18, there was another outbreak of violence in the community of Chico, California, which also ended with a toll of several killings. The most serious event was the Rock Springs massacre of September 2, 1885, when thirty Chinese miners lost their lives, and fifteen more were gravely injured.

It's no surprise to me that Rock Springs was the site of the worst massacre of Chinese people in the history of the United States: at that time, immigration was illegal. Rock Springs is an example of the fact that xenophobia, even when exhibited by a faceless mob, is linked to the norms prevalent within the society.

Not all North Americans detested the diaspora. In 1877 there were, in Oakland and San Francisco, Anglo-Saxon brigades that protected the Chinese. Their president was William T. Coleman, and at their peak the brigades had seven thousand volunteers.

●●●●●

On the American continent, the event that cost the most Chinese lives was not a massacre but a collective suicide, and it offers a striking depiction of the coolie system.

In 1854 hundreds of Cantonese disembarked on the coast of

Panama to work on a stretch of railroad. They advanced inland to a town with the sinisterly ironic name of Matachín: Killchin(ese). (The name has only an accidental relationship to the story I'm narrating, as it was already documented on sixteenth-century maps.)

Matachín is in the center of a humid, swampy, stiflingly hot region. The coolies worked on the railroad in shifts of twelve to fifteen hours; they slept one atop the other, almost in the open air, and earned a wage that scarcely covered their basic needs. The main objective of their journey—saving money to send to the families they had left behind—turned out to be a swindle. Many of them soon began to suffer from depression, thus affecting their availability for work and, as a result, their usefulness to the railroad company. It seems an executive of the deeply out-of-the-box-kind-of-guy variety had the brilliant idea of raising their spirits by including a ration of opium with their daily fare. The dreadful consequences of this lateral thinking are as follows.

An eyewitness—probably one of the gangmasters—saw something that at first seemed to him strange, and then impressive: one of the Chinese laborers in his charge straightened up, ceremoniously lifted the pointed tool he was carrying and buried it in his own throat. A number of his workmates approached the dying man, first in alarm, then in curiosity, and finally in approval. The majority stopped working. Some went to a nearby beach, smoked a little opium, and lay down in the waves. They went on smoking and drinking gulps of saltwater until they drowned. Others, perhaps the majority, took lengths of rope from the company stores, ran to the trees growing by the track they were in the process of constructing, and hanged themselves. When the company bosses came to take control of the situation, all they found was an orchard with bodies swinging from the branches like rotten fruit.

Four hundred fifteen Chinese men were involved in the mass suicide in Matachín, Panama, in 1854. Yet hardly anyone remembers it. Not only Tartary wheat for them but also a veil of opium: oblivion of love.

CAB (3)

Midnight. I had dinner with the poet Julio César Félix, his wife, two supersmart little girls, and a tweenage son constantly busy with household chores ("He's grounded," explained Julio). We roasted meat, drained a couple of six-packs, and drank hot chocolate for dessert. Félix accompanied me to the exit of the housing complex (he lives in the northeast of the city, on the old road to San Pedro, strategically located close to both the Universidad Iberoamericana—where he works—and the Santos stadium); it took twenty minutes for a cab to show up. We hugged, I got into the passenger seat of the vehicle and gave the driver the address of my hotel. I'm exhausted: I've spent a week trying to capture the scent of the regional history in the archives, in interviews, walking around. I glance over at the cab driver. He's a young man, dark, with his hair cut short over his ears and a little longer in the back; a "Buki cut," we used to say in the eighties. He looks scared. I imagine I catch something in his eyes I've seen on many other faces, and also in my own mirror; the dull molten-glass light common among meth smokers.

"Do you know who killed the Chinese?" I ask, more from a sense of academic discipline than curiosity; I'm half asleep, and it's no hour to be going around interrogating cab drivers.

The man gives a slight shake of his head. We continue the journey in silence.

When we arrive at my hotel, I get out of the car, pay, and say good night. The kid hands me my change and, without looking at me directly, murmurs, "It must have been the Zetas, right? They're the jerks that kill everyone."

NO MAN'S TSAI YÜAN

. . . cities destroy customs.
José Alfredo Jiménez

In the late nineteenth century, after the failure of the foreign policy designed to encourage European immigration, Mexico turned
to the Chinese. It was 1882; the Exclusion Act had just been passed
in the United States. The first (and only) Mexican politician to ex-
pend any energy on this new initiative was a citizen with a high
forehead and a beard, possibly handsome and, I'd guess, short in
stature: Matías Romero Avendaño.

Matías Romero was born in 1837 in Oaxaca, also the birthplace
of Benito Juárez and Don Porfirio (Alfonso Reyes, referring to José
Vasconcelos, says all Oaxaqueños are dogmatic). Romero joined
the foreign service at the age of eighteen; at twenty-five he was
secretary and legal adviser to the Mexican legation in the United
States. In 1863 he returned to his native land to battle against the
French under the command of General Díaz, who promoted him
to the rank of colonel in the blink of an eye. But Matías's talents
lay not in arms but diplomacy, so two months later he was back in
Washington, DC. From that point on, he pursued a career in the
civil service, serving as finance minister three times between 1868
and 1879, and ended his life as a plenipotentiary minister for the
United States (receiving the title of ambassador just before his death
when the Mexican mission was upgraded to an embassy). He died
in New York at the age of sixty-one, after spending twenty years
injecting a calmer tone into the dispute between three Mexican
presidents and their northern neighbor.

Matías's body arrived in Torreón on January 15, 1899, taking local
authorities by surprise: they had barely half an hour—and then only

thanks to a tip-off from a reporter—to organize a more or less worthy reception for the coffin. Ernesto and José Romero, the ambassador's brothers, traveled to La Laguna and escorted the body from there to Mexico City. That Torreón was chosen illustrates how important it had become for the Porfirian regime.

A quarter of a century before his death, Matías published an article about Chinese immigration to Mexico. In a realistic analysis uncommon among Porfirian politicians, he suggested there was little possibility of Europeans coming to the country, and claimed that the similarities between the climates of Mexico and China would favor the formation of Chinese communities. He had no difficulty with the idea of national ethnic groups mixing with the Chinese, as he considered the latter to be "the race of origin of our Indians." Based on that early text, Romero championed Asiatic immigration for twenty years: he didn't live long enough to see the fruits of his advocacy.

The global economy and bilateral relations formed a backdrop to this tangled web. After the opening of the California gold mines, the price of silver (in general, but particularly Mexican silver) had fallen, reaching a crisis point in 1891. In the meantime, the Celestial Empire, clinging to its age-old customs (and I imagine also owing to a certain resentment toward the allies who had humiliated it during the Opium Wars), refused to tender its financial backing in gold and/or the new standard silver dollar minted from ore extracted from United States mines, and continued to index its reserves to the Mexican silver peso. From the perspective of the Porfirian regime, this made China what airlines term a "Titanium Member."

Beginning in 1882, mutual interests—in terms of migration and silver—led to attempts to negotiate the first of a number of Sino-Mexican treaties. At that time, there were no formal relations between the two nations, so, in the purest of Mexican (and Chinese) styles, the negotiations were bureaucratized in a manner now inconceivable, including several yards of ink-stained paper, distractions caused by the countries' respective internal problems, and a diplomatic blunder made by the Asian nation, which sent an official communiqué intended for Mexico to the government in Washington, DC. The treaty was finally signed in 1899: seventeen years after the initial negotiations, and a few months after the train carrying Matías Romero's body passed through Torreón.

The number of Chinese in Mexico would never, even by a long stretch, approach those in the United States or Cuba. By 1895 the figure was only 900, and in 1910 it was 13,000. Following the dynamic of the global migratory phenomenon, the Chinese who came to Mexico actually had their eyes set on the United States: 7,855 lived in border zones, while there were 667 more in Sinaloa, with its close ties to northern culture. Of the thirty-two Mexican states, just seven (Baja California, Sonora, Sinaloa, Chihuahua, Coahuila, Nuevo León, and Tamaulipas) were home to two-thirds of the total diaspora in the country. Outside these regions, only the Federal District of Mexico City (1,482) and the Yucatán (875) had Chinese communities exceeding 500 inhabitants. The other states had sometimes a couple of hundred, sometimes only dozens. There were 5 in Querétaro, and 3 in Quintana Roo. The presence of Chinese immigrants dwindled as the observer moved from west to east: only in Sonora (where, to cap it all, the most intense Sinophobic political discourse would be unleashed) did the figure reach 4,486: a third of the national total. The number decreased uniformly along the northern fan until it dwindled to 213 Cantonese in Tamaulipas. In Coahuila there were 759, and between 70 and 80 percent of those were in Torreón.

They worked as railroad laborers, launderers, cooks, salesclerks, shoemakers, traders . . . They brought their love of fishing to Sonora, were recognized as skilled cultivators of fruit and vegetables in La Laguna, and an enterprise undertaken by the Chinese in Sinaloa, about which nothing has been written (because there is no documentary evidence), was the introduction and cultivation of poppies for the production of opium.

In June 1911 five men (Hom Hing, Ah Fong, Lee Lock, San Seu, and Leu Lin) sailed from Canton to Ensenada, where they were met by a pair of coyotes: Francisco Ríos and Antonio Solís. The immigrants paid the Mexicans anywhere between 120 and 450 dollars to guide them across the frontier to the United States, dodging the border patrol. The group crossed at San Ysidro, traveled on to El Cajón, near San Diego, and stayed there for five days, hiding in a pile of straw adjacent to the Riverview train station. Then the laborers and their coyote guide dogs climbed into a wagon of the Santa Fe Railroad and tried to hitch a ride to Anaheim, where representatives of an employment network for illegal workers awaited them.

At around three in the morning on July 8, the immigration officer Harry H. Weddle checked a freight train and discovered seven men in one of the wagons: five Chinese and two Mexicans. After taking them into custody, he reported his discovery to Ralph L. Conklin. The two officers interrogated the Mexicans, who denounced their Californian counterparts' involvement in a vast human trafficking business. After that, the Chinese disappear—as if they were merchandise—from the documentary account.

What followed was one of those undercover cop stories so beloved by Hollywood. Weddle and Conklin recruited George Placencia from Santa Ana, California, to take the place of one of the Mexican smugglers. The mission was to dismantle a Chinese-American network of traffickers that, according to the coyotes, paid 150 dollars per illegal head. Sheriff Placencia traveled to Anaheim under the name of Francisco Ríos, and introduced himself to Ngan Fook, who asked him to wait a few hours for the arrival of the leader of the gang—Chin Tung Yin, a well-known Los Angeles businessman—with whom he could close the deal.

The meeting took place in Anaheim's Chinatown, from where Placencia, Ngan, and Chin went to a garden on the edge of the city, under the constant surveillance of the border police. The undercover officer succeeded in getting the traffickers to incriminate themselves before leading them to a blackberry hedge, behind which federal agents were hiding. Ngan Fook and Chin Tung Yin were arrested—I like to believe after a frantic chase on foot—but they never came to trial. Neither did the coyotes. The district attorney's office dismissed the charges due to an irregularity in the investigation.

●●●●●

One traditional argument used against the diaspora—both in Mexico and the United States—was that the Chinese did not integrate: they consumed goods imported from their home country, hired only their compatriots, and tended to live on the margins of Western societies. The latter is a half-truth: in part, their segregation was due to local bylaws. In California marriage between Chinese men and white women was prohibited until 1968. And by "white women," the law meant "Western women." What is ironic is that it was only in relation to the Chinese that the vague concept of *white women* was applied to African Americans, Native Americans, and those of mixed race.

In Mexico, however, the case was different: arguments against interracial marriage appeared *after* many Chinese had married local girls. Taking the examples of Pablo Chee and Rodolfo Ley—the latter went on to lead a prosperous life in Mexicali—Chao Romero demonstrates that the Mexican wives offered the immigrants a network of relatives and friends, thus helping them to flourish financially and incorporate themselves into the culture of their adoptive country without abandoning their traditions. This is a real-life refutation of Spencerian theory.

●●●●●

Most historians—including both the most scrupulous, such as Chao Romero, and the less rigorous, for example, Juan Puig—take for granted that in Mexico there was a clear correlation between attitudes toward the diaspora and social class. They establish the notion that Sinophobia arose informally among the poor after the Torreón massacre in 1911. They then theorize that ideology evolved, became formalized, and contaminated the middle class through a sort of anti-Chinese conference (attended mostly by small-business men) that took place in Magdalena, Sonora State, on February 5, 1916. Romero suggests these developments were never supported by the ruling class.

This reading of the situation systematizes the historical discourse but does not reflect reality. Its first fallacy is that a minority ideology, originating among the poorest people in the country, ascended the social ladder at a speed greater than that of any other revolutionary concern (democracy, agrarian and constitutional reform, and so on); I don't find this particularly convincing. The description also implies that the transnational dimension of the diaspora had no Mexican equivalent: that the anti-Chinese sentiment of the East Coast middle and upper classes and California labor groups did not take root in Mexico during the final third of the nineteenth century. That seems implausible. Many of the first engine drivers to cross López Velado's "Sweet Nation" ("the train rolling along the track / like a child's Christmas toy") were white, English-speaking, and unionized (and very well paid: they earned 200 pesos a month—between ten and twelve times the minimum wage in La Laguna, and equivalent to approximately 20,000 pesos at current rates). Influential Mexican families (some represented by rich agriculturalists, such as the Maderos in La Laguna, and also the Creels, the Lujáns, the Terrazas, the Mendirichagas, the Gómez Palacios, and the Lavíns) sent their offspring to study in the United States, showing a particular predilection for such cities as Philadelphia, New York, and Boston. In 1896 Coahuila gave scholarships to five graduates of the state teacher training college to undertake specialist studies in Bridgewater, Massachusetts. At least one of those youths—Gabriel Calzada—was from La Laguna, had lived for a time in Torreón, and was extremely close to Francisco I. Madero: some of the letters he exchanged with the spiritualist president have been preserved, and oral tradition has him as the style editor of Madero's *The Presidential Succession in 1910*.

I'm not speaking of facts but degrees of separation; it is by no means unreasonable to conclude that some members of Mexico's middle and upper classes must have adopted the anti-Chinese prejudice of the leading United States citizens of the day. The influence can be inferred from the reiteration of certain accusations leveled at Asians—that they were filthy, carriers of disease, lacking in intelligence and a sense of humor, arrogant, ungodly, and so on and so forth—that appeared in Mexican discourse years before the labor-related prejudices.

I believe that what happened was precisely the reverse of the narrative offered by Juan Puig and Chao Romero: Sinophobia in Mexico echoed the geopolitical scheme of its expansion in the United States. What first developed was a more or less fantasized intellectual, middle-class version of the phobia; that prejudice was reinforced by provincial, then by federal governments, and, years later (after 1906), the ideology fitted in with the pragmatic xenophobia of the working class.

Perhaps the oldest anti-Chinese text published in Mexico has its origins in an article that appeared in Coahuila in 1882, the year of the Exclusion Act. It is an article in the state newspaper, the *Diario Oficial*, which Sergio Corona Páez cites in his *Chronicle of Torreón*.[9] Among other things, it says:

> We have already stated that immigration is a problem that will affect the future of Mexico, and we now add that the extent to which the measures adopted by the authorities in this respect benefit our interests and institutions will determine whether that future is great and rosy.
>
> But it is not for us to address such questions today. We limit ourselves here to stating the general rightness, the pressing need for, the duty of our governors and societies to improve the

---

9. *Crónica de Torreón*

[indigenous] race, to rouse it from stagnation. . . . What is required is crossbreeding with European races of Saxon, Germanic, or Teutonic descent, never with their own Latin race, much less Mongols.

If the Chinese, for example, come to inhabit and cultivate our lands, rather than benefiting our nation, immigration will become one more evil to add to the many others we already suffer.

The ideological distance between public policy and the viewpoint of oligarchs was practically nonexistent during the Porfirian regime. I state this without any demagogic intention: the press of the day generally held the same opinions (independently of whether they condemned or applauded a given circumstance), and it is enough to listen to such well-informed testimony as that of John Kenneth Turner to understand that the editorial of an official organ at the end of the nineteenth century represented, if not the interests, at least the thinking of the Mexican upper class.

Eighteen years later, in 1900, the Mexico City satirical magazine *El Cómico* published an unsigned article about an outbreak of bubonic plague in Hawaii: "Sanitary Measures in Honolulu." It is a fictitious letter addressed to a certain Mr. Pawl H. Pawl. I transcribe the text in its entirety here because, despite the cruelty and racism, it is worth half a semester of prose.

My Dear Sir,

I beg your attention in relation to my distressing situation: I am Chinese and in need; as they say, I live a dog's life, and am the victim of the American cleanup of Honolulu, more terrible than the one that is lapping at the feet of Mexico City.

You will be aware that we Chinese have pigtails because our God uses that appendage to take us to heaven in groups of three and a bit, that is to say, three adults and a child; you will know we eat rice without use of cutlery; that in just one outbuilding

live father, mother, children, cousins, and such other depen-
dents as domestic animals, so benefiting the homeless and preventing proprietors from making fortunes; that we sew our own
clothes, speak little, don't make jests, and are even economi-
cal with our eyes, because God does not allow us to look at his
works, except through a slanting but expressive slit; we eat rats,
so preventing the spread of such delicious animals that destroy
valuable furniture, and yet despite all this, ill fortune has come
our way.

[Untranslatable oath.]

It seems we produce the plague called bubonic by the
Europeans, and the Bolivian sickness by us, because of the number of bumps it produces; it seems the rats transmit it themselves, and rats and Chinese have come to be the same thing for
the doctors there.

[Another oath, this time philosophical.]

An ingrown toenail, a gumboil, a chilblain, or any other
lump of uncertain origin, such as cysts for instance, is enough
for them to declare you a *suspicious case*, and that's the end of you.

[A scientific oath.]

Let me give you an example: a poor wretch who died
from ingesting prickly pears had a belly swollen like a sack of
potatoes.

"It's the bubonic fever," said the doctor, when he felt how
cold and rigid he was; and without another word, they put
him in the oven of a soap factory, where they burned him to a
crisp—cases must be isolated!—and any other sick person they
found, even if it was only a matter of toothache, they put in a
vat of refined petroleum, and then into steam baths, and they
were smothered in mule fat and carbolic acid, and left in the
open air for forty-eight hours to dry out in the cages that had
belonged to some circus lions. They made us evacuate all eight
blocks of our neighborhood, not even allowing us to collect our
combs.

"Strip down!"

And they pointed a piece of artillery at us, and put us in regulation summer clothing, and subjected us to a rigorous examination of tongue, nose, eyes, and other noble parts of the physiognomy.

Some people are more yellow than others, and the sanitary officers fell on them, causing them to be rubbed down with clay and vinegar to cleanse them of any germs they might have. Later, they gave us clean clothes. Some got soldiers' uniforms—and this has annoyed us greatly—others got overcoats and others jackets. Used as we are to our robes, the conical hat, the jipi, or cap, they were as much use to us as a pair of pistols to Christ.

[There follows a passage impossible to print since it would lead us to Bedlam along Bucareli.]

"Right, Smith, you cut the pigtails, because that plait can activate the *bubonic agent*."

A great clamor rose from all present: our braids are as precious to us as theirs are to (the bullfighters) Minuto, Fuentes, and Algabeño; our braids are our playthings; our braids are our second mothers; our braids are our religion; our braids are our braids.

And they cut them off with horse shears; heavy tears fell on the pile of braids that were shuddering in their death throes.

"Now march."

They gave us a few cents a head (women and children half pay) and loaded us onto large canoes headed for Quarantine Island, where we would stay until all suspicion was past.

Then they set fire to our hovels and twenty blocks were burning; the pigs went into hiding; the goats were prancing about in pain; the rats fled in terror; the officers were swinging their truncheons left and right to disperse curious onlookers approaching; there was a smell of burned hair: our pigtails.

Only the Buddha knows how I suffered!

We are on the island, without any covering but a loincloth of antiseptic lint; they fumigate us the whole day long; they've hung cowbells around our necks, and we are tied by one leg to numbered stakes.

As soon as they suspect someone is a *case*, whether or not it is bubonic plague, they apply five or six good doses of carbolic air with a foot pump, which causes many explosions.

I want to come to you. I'll be a waiter, cook, child minder, acrobat, chamber servant, kitchen assistant, gladiator, whatever you like. But I can no longer bear the terrible ordeal of hygiene that is killing so many of my compatriots, and I am in danger of being taken as a case, and that will be the last straw, because it will finish me off.

Yours affectionately,
Re-Kon-Li

The article is quite simply a comic description of a pogrom.

Can such a text shed light on the massacre? "The unconscious is outside," wrote Slavoj Žižek: I doubt whether such an elegantly malign satire could be produced in the heart of any society that does not encourage active hatred of Chinese people. I am not accusing the author of the article of inciting the masses to commit the long series of murders, but am referring to something subtler: the way in which good writers (particularly satirists) are capable of capturing the zeitgeist. Jonathan Swift didn't have to eat a child (or at least I hope not) to describe the immorality with which the Irish of his day perceived poverty and hunger.

Killing in the name of racism—always justified through negative emotions: hatred, contempt, and objectification; a degree of farce—is not, in the liberal-romanticized West, a spontaneous practice. First the violence needs to be *represented* to the point where it becomes denatured, until it is converted into a solemn discourse, a sort of law.

Mexican anti-Chinese sentiment did not begin with the slaughter in Torreón, nor did it end with that event. Before the small genocide, the fantasy of annihilation had set up camp in the press, in coffeehouse conversations, jokes, laws, segregation, public demonstrations, and vituperation until things came to blows. The first murder of a Chinese man by a mob in Mexico occurred in 1881: the

Exclusion Act was on the horizon in the United States, and negotiations for the Sino-Mexican Treaty of Amity, Commerce and
Navigation were about to open.

What emerged from the 1911 Torreón massacre was not repen-
tance, or even self-criticism, but a symbolic acceptance of trans-
gression: any further ill treatment of the Cantonese now had a
historical precedent that not only justified but excused it, since it
was less serious than that canonical outburst of violence.

This is how the economy of cruelty functions.

•••••

The earliest articulation of anti-Chinese sentiment in Mexico was
the work of the middle-class and the ruling Científicos, and came
from the seat of the federal government. Although it was published
in 1911, both its origin and fundamental ideology date from 1903;
scarcely four years after the signing of the Sino-Mexican Treaty of
Amity. This text is called the Romero Commission Report.

On October 17, 1903, Porfirio Díaz created a special commission
to look into the impact of large-scale immigration from China. He
did this, to quote Chao Romero, "in response to fears expressed by
the Mexican citizenry." Two questions occur to me. First: If there
was no anti-Chinese campaign in existence in 1903, where did
the president of the republic get the gruesome idea that such fears
had in fact been expressed? Second: from historical experience,
and based on such creditable testimony as J. K. Turner's *Barbarous
Mexico*, whom exactly did the regime see as that "Mexican citizenry"
whose fears had to be taken so seriously? It's my conviction that the
term refers to the financial elite that had already begun to be concerned by the extremely generous perks foreign residents enjoyed.

The commission was composed of five men: Genaro Raigosa,
José María Romero, Eduardo Liceaga, Rafael Rebollar, and José
Covarrubias. Their task was to answer four questions. (1) Does un-
limited immigration of Chinese and Japanese citizens benefit
Mexico? (2) Are the effects of the immigration of Chinese nation-

als the same as those of the Japanese? If not, should different policies be adopted for each group? (3) Should norms be established discouraging Asian immigration, notwithstanding the agreements in place with China and Japan? (4) What constitutional, legal, and diplomatic reforms does the commission consider appropriate in relation to this topic?

None of the questions addresses the Magonista Sinophobic agenda, and since this had not even been formulated in 1903, it is chronologically impossible for the tacit anti-Chinese sentiment of the Romero Commission to have had its roots in the working classes.

The final 121-page report—published in 1911, written by José María Romero—established that Chinese immigration, whether at an individual or group level, was not to the greater benefit of Mexico. Rather than offering pragmatic reasoning to support its conclusions, Romero closely followed Herbert Spencer's eugenic theories. He concluded that the Chinese were "undesirables" because they took the place of, and inhibited the immigration of more "desirable" ethnic groups: white Europeans whom the text claims were the architects of economic development in Argentina, Brazil, and Australia (as if geography, history, climate, and internal policies played no role in the situation). He added that the Chinese were incapable of integrating, had irreconcilable differences in their relationship with Western culture, tended to form secret societies, were opposed to the mixing of races, considered themselves superior, planned to return to their country with whatever gains they made rather than settling, and, in general, represented a barrier to the noncoercive integration of Mexican Indians in the general climate of crossbreeding with whites.

The anti-Chinese feeling of the working class did not take long to surface, in the voice of the social reformer and anarchist Ricardo Flores Magón. In 1906 the Mexican Liberal Party Plan clarified its position:

The prohibition of Chinese immigration is, above all, a protective measure for workers of other nationalities, principally the

Mexicans. The Chinaman, disposed in general to work for the lowest wage, submissive, petty in his aspirations, is a great obstacle to the prosperity of other workers.

On April 10, 1911—thirty-three days after the slaughter—the Mexico City newspaper *El Tiempo* published a letter by José Díaz Zulueta refuting a proposal by David Thomatis, which had previously appeared in the same organ, to support Chinese immigration into Mexico. Although the findings of the Romero Commission had yet to be published, Díaz Zulueta endorses them, which suggests it was, among others, the landowning businessmen of La Laguna who were behind the Sinophobic rhetoric. Before resorting to the usual arguments, the letter declares:

> I am very sorry to find among Señor Thomatis's very good intentions the notion of bringing over Chinese immigrants, which, far from benefiting us, would be highly prejudicial. Take the cases of Ecuador and Peru, where such immigration has become a veritable plague. I believe that in order to cultivate the amount of cotton we need for our own consumption and for export, we have no need of the Chinese, and our present cotton producers, the most progressive of Mexican agriculturalists, would not improve their reputations by making greater profit in the short term at the cost of bringing a veritable plague into the country, or so I would say for, at least, the cotton producers of Mexico.

I'm sure Díaz Zulueta speaks on behalf of the large hacienda owners of La Laguna when he identifies (twice in the same paragraph) the Chinese as the source of the plague: this could not be more racist, because plagues, naturally, have to be eradicated. At that time, La Laguna was the principal cotton producer in Mexico, and the polemicist is expressing himself with the confidence of one who has the backing and approval of the social group he defends.

After four paragraphs of deploring what he considers to be the stupidity of the Chinese, Díaz Zulueta finishes with:

Let our enterprising, progressive cotton producers say if all this [the iniquities mentioned above] is what they want for this rich and fertile region, where cities that do us honor are already under construction.

Let foreign capital, most particularly English, come in good time to do its part in adding to the fruitfulness of our grateful regions, and we will welcome it with open arms, and give the investors all kinds of guarantees, but do not bring us Chinamen, since they themselves will not welcome them into their beloved *Home* [the English word is used in the original—trans.].

Here, the diatribe appears to allude to the burgeoning cities of Torreón and Gómez Palacio, and the reference to "our grateful regions" makes me think the Porfirist gentleman might have been from La Laguna; I did not, however, find any solid facts to support this supposition.

This is sufficient evidence to cast doubt on the declaration of Chao Romero—and many other historians—that those with power and influence in La Laguna did not hold Sinophobic feelings a month before the small genocide.

On April 21, Chinese representatives in Mexico sent a letter to *El Tiempo*, politely rebutting Díaz Zulueta's accusations. Twenty-four days later, the bodies of 303 Chinese people lay strewn along the streets and in the market gardens of Torreón.

●●●●●

I spent my childhood in Ciudad Frontera, a city that in 1982 had approximately forty thousand inhabitants—the same number as Torreón in 1911—and which is no distance from Monclova. That "no distance from" is literal: halfway along the gates of the Hidalgo lumberyard, there used to be a metal plaque announcing the division between the two municipalities. You could hop from one to the next.

I graduated from the Ferrocarriles Nacionales elementary school, barely two blocks from the train station. Between my sandy playground and the iron road were the remains of a crimson building: the Hotel Internacional. Among its nooks and crannies, galleries, and paths, girls and boys in my class used to throw stones at small animals, hide porn mags, or exchange wet kisses on the pretext of playing spin the bottle.

Then I heard that, while it was still a going concern, the decadent ruin whose grounds we enjoyed temporary possession of sheltered an opulent secret: inside, it had harbored a salon for opium smokers. *Such French elegance!* What I didn't know then was that the former proprietor of that now derelict hotel would be a character in the book I'd be trying to write thirty years later: Foon-chuck, the businessman who breathed life into the Chinese community of Torreón.

Wong Foon Check, alias Foon-chuck, was born in February 1863 in Hoy Pung. The other day I had coffee with Bernardo Chuck, one of his great-grandsons, who assured me that the village (he had gone to visit it years ago in search of his roots, and found that the poverty-stricken location his aunt Celina used to speak about had become an enormous, prosperous city) was on the mainland, to the southwest of Hong Kong, and so very likely Cantonese.

At the age of twelve, Wong ("The word doesn't exist in Chinese," Don Manuel Lee Soriano explained. "It should be pronounced something like *Wah*") ran away from home and boarded a ship for America, arriving in San Francisco in 1875. He learned English in a mission school, and was taken in as a servant by a certain Dr. Lummis, in whose employ he remained for two years. He was then hired as a waiter in the Hotel Jackson, on California Street, but couldn't accustom himself to the routine and returned to his adoptive home, where he stayed three more years. Bernardo Chuck says that the Lummises are venerated in his family, not as masters, but as surrogate parents of his great-grandfather.

In 1881 *Wah* Foon Check, alias Foon-chuck, traveled to China for several months to visit his parents. On his return to America, his ship was detained in San Francisco, and none of the Cantonese passengers were allowed to disembark; the Exclusion Act had come into force. Foon-chuck managed to escape from the ship—probably by jumping overboard—and so returned to the United States. He found work with the Southern Pacific Railroad Company, which was at that time constructing the line from Los Angeles to San Antonio, and so went to Texas for the first time. He worked as a cook in El Paso for six months, then moved to San Antonio, and later to Del Rio, across the border from the Coahuila community of Las Vacas (now Ciudad Acuña). For a while, he settled in Eagle Pass, on the frontier with Ciudad Porfirio Díaz (now Piedras Negras), where he learned Spanish, again found work as a cook, and entered negotiations to buy the Hotel Central. In conjunction with this, he set up a curio store and a laundry.

He was twenty-two.

In 1886 Foon-chuck transferred ownership of his hotel and crossed the Rio Bravo, following the tracks of the Ferrocarril Internacional south, and selling cheap chinoiscrie to perplexed townsfolk. Then in San Buenaventura, he made friends with a man who would be the cornerstone of his future in Mexico: Miguel Cárdenas, a lawyer, congressional representative, and cattle breeder.

When the Ferrocarril Internacional arrived in Torreón in 1888, Foon-chuck came with it; his aim was to obtain the franchise for a hotel about to be opened next to the train station. It is not clear if this desire came to fruition, but if it did, it wasn't for long: in 1889 he set sail for China, where he stayed for ten months. He returned to Mexico in 1890 and—now twenty-seven—started to work for the Coahuila Coal Company in San Felipe as a foreman in charge of four hundred Cantonese laborers. He stayed in that line of work for three years, until the dangers of coal mining led him to try his luck once more in the hotel trade. In 1893 he finally secured a five-year concession on the Torreón Hotel del Ferrocarril through a joint agreement with the Central and Internacional railroad companies.

He was by then thirty, and the most successful Chinese immigrant in the region. Two years later, he married a young Tamaulipeco girl named Cristina Vega Domínguez. They set up house in Eagle Pass and—after the birth of their first baby—moved to Piedras Negras, where they had nine more children.

Foon-chuck's hotel business rapidly expanded. Ferrocarril Internacional granted him franchises to at least six establishments (one of them the ruined building in which I played as a child) throughout the Coahuila region. Considering this sudden prosperity and the decadently opulent opium-smoking salon in Ciudad Frontera, I wonder if the young entrepreneur had taken part in the transport of the drug. However, the growth of his fortune also coincided with the height of the political career of his friend Miguel Cárdenas, who, by 1893, was a junior minister, and soon would become governor of Coahuila, a post he held for fifteen years. I doubt if this was mere chance.

Foon-chuck's fortune did not come entirely from hotels. Part of it was the product of the Asociación Reformista China, founded in Torreón in 1903, and the Compañía Bancaria y de Tranvías Wah Yick, a railroad and banking company created in 1906. Both these businesses were linked to an illustrious Chinese thinker, a personal adviser to the Guangxu monarch and spreader of slanderous rumors about the Empress Cixi, a Buddhist academic and leader of political coups, a messianic investor and utopian xenophobe, a short-lived minister of foreign affairs and unrepentant collector of donations: Kang Youwei, the reformist.

•••••

He was born on March 19, 1858, to an influential aristocratic family in the district of Nanhai. From an early age, his intelligence and calligraphy were outstanding. One of his uncles noted his talents and urged his parents to send him to study the classic texts of Confucianism in one of the schools where young people were prepared to take the complex, useless doctrinal examinations for entry into the civil service (the same exams Hong Xiuquan, leader of the Taiping Rebellion, had failed in 1836 and 1837 with dire consequences for humanity).

Even as a teenager, Kang Youwei was at odds with contemporary trends in academic thought, and very soon showed himself to be a born iconoclast. As a complement to his study of Confucian doctrine, he took up Buddhist meditation, a practice considered heretical by his conservative tutors. Going against the grain of official discourse, he interpreted the work of Confucius as reformist rather than reactionary, and asserted that some recently discovered versions of classic Confucianism were mere modern inventions aimed at shaping the tradition to fit a bureaucratic mode of thought. Even more shockingly, when he had yet to take the regulation examinations, he proclaimed himself to be in favor of a constitutional monarchy and state reform.

Kang easily passed the provincial examinations, and took their metropolitan equivalents in 1882. He failed. He tried for a second time, in 1889, and failed again. On this occasion, he decided to write to Emperor Guangxu—at that time a boy of sixteen—and in this excursus made a strong appeal for greater participation of the erudite classes in the formation of imperial policies. The document never reached the hands of the monarch, but many of the officials who had access to it agreed that the views of the thirty-year-old Cantonese man were worthy of being heard.

In May 1895 Kang Youwei became one of the thirteen hundred learned men who met in Peking to take (in his case for the third time) the metropolitan examinations. He was by then thirty-seven, and had devoted thirteen years to writing his magnum opus, *Da Tongshu: The Book of Great Unity*.

His rebellious attitude was not so far removed from the general discontent felt throughout different strata of Chinese society. In 1861 the defunct emperor's five-year-old son had ascended to the throne, with his mother, the Empress Dowager Cixi, as regent. Tongzhi assumed full power at sixteen, but died of smallpox (some say syphilis, because he was given to frequenting prostitutes) two years later. Cixi continued as regent, and succeeded in having her nephew, Guangxu—only three years old—named emperor. Toward the end of her regency, in 1894 (by which time Guangxu was twenty-one, but still enslaved to his aunt, who must have been one of the most charismatic, experienced women of her time), China suffered a serious setback: the military defeat by Japan and subsequent loss of Korea, plus the humiliating burden of tributes and obligations set out in the Treaty of Shimonoseki.

In 1895, the thirteen hundred entrants to the metropolitan examinations sent Emperor Guangxu a manifesto written by Kang— the postulant who had become their leader—challenging him to move the court from Peking, reorganize his military forces, and refuse to ratify the treaty with Japan. They advocated for state reforms in such areas as education, technology, public administration, and international relations. This document did not reach the sovereign's hands either: it was intercepted by an entourage of censors. But it was obvious, even within the Celestial bureaucratic elite, that it would soon be impossible to brush the arguments of those pacifist, petit bourgeois revolutionaries under the carpet.

Kang Youwei wrote a third letter to Guangxu (who was surely by then weary of the furious scheming of his aunt-regent) in 1897. This time the arrow hit its mark: the young monarch read the text and identified with its ideas. The criticisms and proposals of a new, educated generation became imperial policy.

When Guangxu initiated the Hundred Days of Reform in 1898, the Dowager Empress Cixi and her conservative retinue withdrew from the political arena, harrowed by the memory of their military defeat by Japan (the Treaty of Shimonoseki had by then been ratified), and by the scorn of the lower classes resulting from Western penetration. Kang's disciples (mainly youths) founded study groups, organized discussion forums, and printed and distributed on a massive scale the three political proposals of their intellectual leader, plus a great number of other documents, manifestos, and reports written by an emerging, optimistic political class. On June 16, Kang, then in his forties, was appointed minister of foreign affairs for the empire by a twenty-five-year-old sovereign.

The age-old entry requirements for the civil service were abolished. The Eight-Legged Essay—as far as I can tell, it would have made Antonio Vieira's exposition on the excellence of Christ and Sor Juana Inés de la Cruz's *Carta Atenagórica* look like child's play—was replaced by examinations in science and technology, based on Western academic disciplines. The bureaucracy was cut back severely; the army was disbanded and reconstituted; a ministry for raising public funds and controlling spending was created; the subsidy enjoyed by natives of Manchuria due to the mere fact of being fellow countrymen of the ruling family was suspended; entities for the development of railroads, mining, agriculture, industry, and commerce were created; individuals in the various guilds were urged to found chambers or professional bodies; the Society for Self-Strengthening came into being and, a few weeks later, its Translators' Department would form the University of Peking.

It is possible that this pacific revolution would have triumphed if it had taken into account one of the great threats to the human race: the incapacity of the majority to feel and communicate empathy with the new. The conservative circles of the dowager empress's salons had little to do but wait. As soon as the reforms came into effect, increasing numbers of subjects at all levels began to experience a nostalgic longing for the return of those who had destroyed their peace through wars, corruption, and starvation. It was a nostalgia that went hand in hand with the absolute hatred of the people who had proposed to introduce Isaac Newton into their curricula.

On the 103rd day of the reforms, there was a coup. Emperor Guangxu was put under house arrest, and if he did not die at the hands of his aunt's henchmen, it was due to the intercession of the Japanese government. But there was no such mercy for the political class that had dared to defy tradition: one by one, the reformists were executed. At Cixi's decree, Kang Youwei—the greatest of the monsters—was sentenced to a singular form of death: the subtleties of *leng t'che*, the form of lethal torture consisting of dismembering the condemned man by means of a long, slow, painful process involving the finest and sharpest steel knives, and which culminates in a horrendous expression of mystical ecstasy. The sentence was never carried out, because, possibly alerted by some kindhearted spy, Kang fled to Peking before the coup, and managed to find asylum on the island of Hong Kong.

The perilous existence that is exile began. Kang traveled between Canada and the United States, from where he advocated in favor of respect for human life and the immediate liberation of the emperor. He founded the Protect the Emperor Society, which in Mexico (and specifically in Torreón) would be known as the Asociación Reformista China: a political studies circle, center for the dissemination of ideas, and an arena for combating conservative imperialism and a new emerging enemy: Chinese republicans, headed by Sun Yat-sen. In Vancouver, Kang Youwei also founded—with the aid of the brothers Liang Chi Chao and Liang Chi Tien, both financiers—the Commercial Corporation, a business aimed at administering, reinvesting, and deploying donations received by reformists in exile. In addition, he spent time writing: the first two chapters of *Da Tongshu* were published in Japan in 1900.

Da Tongshu—the definitive edition appeared in 1935, seven years after Kang's death, and fifty after he began writing it—is a monumental philosophical project that can be compared on the one hand to Thomas More's *Utopia*, and on the other to Karl Marx's *Capital*. It proposes the creation of a new imperial society, based on geographically rectangular, self-governing units of population that would answer to an enlightened despot with global authority. The family is seen as a mechanism for the oppression of women (Kang is perhaps the first Asian feminist) and must therefore be dissolved: early child care and the education of children would be the responsibility of the state, while marriage between men and women would become a contract entered into by mutual consent, legally binding for a year. The work describes capitalism as an inherently perverse system that should be regulated and replaced by socialist and communist institutions in the service of the emperor. Although some of these ideas were inspired by Western thinkers—Kang explicitly cites Charles Fourier—many others come from Chinese folklore and tradition.

Da Tongshu is a deranged work that displays evidence of some of the most mule-headed prejudices of traditional communism, and puts our left-wing, do-gooder ability to read to the test: while its defense of the rights of women is overtly stated, the age-old Chinese taboo regarding sexual preference is also a constant presence, so there is no mention of the role of homosexuality in this dream of a future society. Neither is there any place in this utopia for black- or brown-skinned people: the author proposes we should be exterminated or, at best, our features gradually integrated into the grand corpus of a single normalized race. Such ideas paradoxically and in a slightly macabre manner coincide with the Porfirian school of thought that would have such a fatal impact on one of the practical projects Kang Youwei supported: the Chinese community in Torreón.

Kang's end is a warning to any revolutionary intellectual: a mixture of pathos and intelligence going up in flames. After having figured as a leading light of renewal and freedom in the Chinese political landscape, Kang Youwei moved increasingly to the right of Sun Yat-sen and the other twentieth-century Chinese republicans. When it wasn't just a failed lobbying group, the Asociación Reformista became a stronghold of hard-line conservatism in exile. Possibly infuriated by the memory of having been condemned to death, Kang spent the last decades of his life spreading base rumors about Cixi. In response, the dowager empress's ideological champions caricatured him as a tightfisted petit bourgeois who had used his five minutes of imperial fame to live the high life at the expense of the diaspora.

In 1912, when the Chinese Republic had triumphed, and only a few months after the massacre in Torreón, Kang returned to his native land. During the following five years, he opposed the new republic; this time he was a reactionary, not a radical. In 1917 he fomented an unsuccessful coup to reinstate Puyi, that beautiful child who emerges from behind the silk curtains in Bertolucci's *The Last Emperor*. He then retreated to a mansion in Qingdao, where he died—some say by poison—eleven days short of his sixty-ninth birthday.

But in 1906, two decades before his death, Kang Youwei, one of Asia's most brilliant politicians and philosophers, still in full possession of his passion and senses, descended the steps of a railway carriage in a Mexican town on the point of being elevated to city status: Torreón, Coahuila. His arrival gave rise to excitement in the local Cantonese community, which came en masse to greet him. Kang was accompanied by Foon-chuck and several Chinese residents of Piedras Negras and Monclova. His passage through Torreón received enthusiastic coverage in the Mexico City newspaper *El Popular*, which not only was aware of his arrival in the newly appointed city, and his intention to found a shipping company there that would connect the ports of Hong Kong and Mazatlán, but also would later report on his journey to the capital and his interview with Porfirio Díaz, an act in which the former Celestial minister was accompanied by Dr. J. W. Lim, who provided moral leadership to the Chinese community in Torreón.

I would estimate that few people of such illustrious lineage set foot in La Laguna during the first half of the twentieth century, and I know of no Lebanese, North American, or German philosopher who visited Torreón before 1911. However, the arrival of Kang is an event of little interest to the Torreónese, or Mexicans in general. Even today, there is no plaque in La Laguna, or even a museum document, commemorating such an extraordinary event: the meeting of a professional utopian from Asia and a pragmatic utopia recently born on the American continent.

●●●●●

So why did Kang Youwei come?

It is impossible to say when exactly the businessman Foon-chuck and the philosopher Kang met, but it must have been long before the latter's journey to Coahuila's Mayrán desert, because the Asociación Reformista China was founded in La Laguna in 1903. Foon-chuck was a personal friend of Hop Lee's, a San Francisco capitalist whose investments in the United States formed an empire that extended from restaurants to mines, agricultural land, and banking institutions. Hop Lee was involved in the reformist movement, and this could have been the route by which these two personages came into contact. The truth is that there is no reliable map of the transnational economy of the diaspora.

The leaders of the Chinese community in Torreón might initially seem to have been only distantly involved in politics, and more interested in staying in the Americas than in returning to the empire. J. Wong Lim had become a Mexican national, and Foon-chuck (in addition to being linked to the Asociación Reformista) had founded the Yue Mae School in Monclova, where the children studied Spanish, Cantonese, and English, and wore Kuomintang-style uniforms. Evelyn Hu-DeHart reads this detail (the uniforms) as a political statement: Foon-chuck identified with reformist pedagogy.

In La Laguna (where the typographers' guild had grown at lightning speed), a press using ideographic characters was very soon set up, thus encouraging written communication between different Asian communities. It is relatively simple for businessmen to agree about economics, but Kang's project always had an additional intellectual component. So what was the link between that aspect of reformism in exile and the Cantonese community? It is likely that the connection was a practically unknown figure: Woo Lam Po, whom I suppose (there is insufficient evidence to definitely affirm it) to have been a sort of delegate of Kang's.

Woo Lam Po was the founding secretary of the Torreón branch of the Asociación Reformista, yet, barring matters relating to the slaughter, his name scarcely appears in the annals of La Laguna: not only is there little documentary information about him, but he is also absent from oral tradition. Nevertheless, his leadership is clear: in the days before the capture of Torreón, it was he who wrote and circulated a message in ideographic characters warning of the possibility of an armed attack on the Cantonese. Sergio Corona Páez has translated and published a note that situates him as the official spokesperson of the community to the international press. Moreover, there is a communiqué in which the United States secretary of state authorizes Consul George C. Carothers to offer Woo Lam Po the run of his office in Torreón in order to initiate an investigation into the massacre. Neither Foon-chuck, the magnate, nor J. Wong Lim, the moral leader, received preferential treatment from the United States government. For these reasons, I imagine it was Woo Lam Po who, in 1906, welcomed Kang and his retinue at the railroad station.

Kang appeared in Torreón, together with the Liang brothers, his Sino-Canadian advisers. Soon after his arrival, he tested the waters with the purchase of a block (one of those divided into perfect lots by Federico Wulff) for 1,700 pesos. A few days later, he sold the same land for 3,400. He then bought a house for 2,400 pesos and again sold it for double the initial price. He was impressed: the frenetic development of Torreón allowed for fortunes to be made in real estate speculation by those with timely information and sufficient liquidity. He had the latter. The former was the responsibility of local Chinese businessmen. It was for these reasons that Kang Youwei decided to create a Mexican affiliate of the Vancouver Commercial Corporation with the joint capital from the Lagunero Chinese community and investors in a New York transportation company. The formal name of the new company was the Compañía Bancaria y de Tranvías Wah Yick, S.A.; in La Laguna it was simply called the Banco Chino. The headquarters of the undertaking were (or supposedly were: it remains to be seen what Silvia Castro has to say on the subject) at the junction of Juárez and Valdez Carrillo, on the southeast corner of the Plaza de Armas, where today stands—what else?—an Oxxo store. Many of the lots purchased by Youwei to the east, in the area known as El Pajonal—now the site of the city's middle-class residential estates: Torreón Jardín, Nuevo Torreón, La Rosita, and San Isidro—were originally resold or offered as concessions to other Chinese businessmen, who converted them into farms specializing in the cultivation of vegetables. Juan Puig states there were at least seven sizable market gardens in the zone, the largest being the Do Sing Yuen (owned by Foon-chuck), adjoining La Rosita ranch. Another two important farms were Lu Zoc Yuen and Tai Sing Yuen, some of whose employees would be the first victims of the small genocide in 1911.

The banking activities of the Cantonese community were under the supervision of Foon-chuck, while management of real estate holdings was given to a doctor from Mexico City by the name of Huang Jih Chuck. Despite the fact that Kang mentioned to the reporter from *El Popular* his intention of setting up a shipping company with its administrative headquarters in the Wah Yick building, there is no proof that this project ever got off the ground.

Leo M. Dambourges Jacques notes the construction of eight miles of the Wah Yick streetcar line along Avenida Morelos, and Silvia Castro told me that she had once seen certain papers describing its route to the east, toward the market gardens in El Pajonal. On the basis of oral testimony, Manuel Terán Lira claims that the aim of the company was to construct a branch line extending to the neighboring municipality of Matamoros. These streetcar lines definitely existed and, if only briefly, functioned in La Laguna; I have not, however, been able to find a single photograph of the system. There are many images (some picturesque) of the Lerdo–Torreón streetcar, but of the Wah Yick, nothing. It's difficult not to be intrigued by this lack of technological sympathy on the part of Torreón photographers, who were accustomed to registering on their plates anything that signified progress.

The vision of the La Laguna Banco Chino was to become a credit agency servicing all members of the diaspora living in Mexico. Torreón was a large banking center: nine such institutions coexisted there. Why not set one's sights on the sum capital of an extraordinarily thrifty migrant group, 70 percent of whom were concentrated in the border zone? Due to the transnational nature of its resources, the Torreón representatives of that group formed the most powerful (although not necessarily most numerous) Cantonese community in Mexico. It was capitalist in essence, and the only one to compete openly with the Mexican and US upper classes in 1911. I find it hard to believe that that fact was irrelevant to other businessmen in La Laguna. In this respect, there is one significant datum: when the Wah Yick company (whose list of directors includes the names Woo Lam Po, Walter J. Lim, Foon-chuck, and Kang Youwei) was set up, the Chinese community decided not to complete the formalities in Torreón: they found a public notary in Matamoros. This might have been because some of the investors knew the notary. Or it might have been because they wanted to employ the greatest possible discretion in revealing the nature of their alliance to the rest of the Torreón business sector.

⬤⬤⬤⬤⬤

For Juan Puig, what must have caught Kang Youwei's attention was the fact that the local Chinese community had settled in Torreón rather than migrating seasonally. For Dambourges Jacques and Silvia Castro, on the other hand, it was the high level of investment made by the Asociación Reformista in La Laguna that created the conditions for that community to flourish. I'd go along with the latter. The census shows that there were few Chinese in Torreón in 1900; their complete absence from the business directory compiled by Jacobo M. Aguirre indicates that their resources were not significant. In 1905, however, the number of their advertisements in the *Directorio Comercial y Industrial de La Laguna* had already increased, and their presence is highly visible in the *Directorio Profesional de Arte y Mercantil de La Laguna 1908–1909*.

The Torreón Chinese community was not merely prospering: it was becoming powerful. And if this irritated the poor, the rich would have felt the threat more strongly. In 1907 Mexican businessmen founded a Chamber of Commerce with the overt intention of combating both the influence of the Banco Chino and the growth of United States companies, which were thriving due to the tax exemptions they had been granted. Wealthy Mexicans published a manifesto in *El Nuevo Mundo*:

We cannot compete with the foreigners in the business arena. The sad, lamentable fact is that the prostration of our national commerce has created a situation in which Mexicans are replaced by foreign individuals or companies that monopolize the market and behave like the conquerors of a vanquished country.

They also made official complaints to the Coahuila government. While none of these messages contained anti-Chinese statements, this does not mean that local prejudice was not expressed by other means. On August 17, 1907, the magazine *La Iberia* drew attention to a note published in a Torreón newspaper:

ENTREATY: The Chinese community in general begs the enlightened public of this progressive city to be so kind as to abolish the word CHINK to refer to those of us who belong to the Chinese community, since we do not know the meaning of that word. It can be assumed we would understand CHINESE better than CHINK, which means nothing to us. We therefore kindly beg you to erase that word from your language, and accept our most sincere good wishes. Woo Lampo.

The entreaty is not as revealing as the response from the Torreón newspaper: "We would advise Woo Lampo to stop his foolishness, and smoke 'Flor de Lis' cigarettes, made with Mexican tobacco, to cure his hypochondria."

With respect to this matter, Sergio Corona Páez reflects:

How can those print media . . . deal with the information so irresponsibly, offending a whole sector of the Torreón community? Such blindness is inconceivable unless there was in fact a "racial agenda" that carried political benefits for the newspaper in question.

Another critical event, which took place at the beginning of April 1907, was the arrival in Torreón of Antonio de Pío Araujo, a Magonista leader. In a letter dated May 18, de Pío Araujo informed Flores Magón that a group including Orestes Pereyra and Manuel "El Chino" Banda—future generals in Pancho Villa's army—was ready to carry out an armed uprising in Torreón. A number of the rebels were from the middle and upper classes, and had access to financial resources. It would be malicious not to admit that anti-Chinese sentiment was part of their ideology.

On June 11, the *Mexican Herald* published a report detailing how real estate speculation in Torreón, for which the Banco Chino was largely responsible, had resulted in a housing shortage. Rents had soared and, in consequence, many newly arrived workers were homeless or living in overcrowded conditions. The tension led to strikes among the Mexican railroad boilermakers and engine drivers. The strike by the latter was broken by scabs.

The proclamation elevating Torreón to city status was published on September 15, 1907. Three months later, the Banco de La Laguna was founded with franchises granted to Juan Brittingham, Luis Gurza, and Praxedis de la Peña. It was clearly meant to compete with the Banco Chino: the seven other financial houses in the city were all subsidiaries, so that only those belonging to the Chinese and Mexicans were purely Torreonese. The new bank had a capital reserve of 6 million pesos, set against the bare million of its Chinese counterpart. The Lerdo–Torreón streetcar company was also given additional backing, and as a result acquired six new passenger cars and a two-hundred-horsepower engine to vie with its Wah Yick competitor.

The year 1908 was one of great upheaval. The Magonistas rose up in the Coahuila town of Viesca, attacked the municipal government offices, and managed to gain control for a few hours before taking to their heels. When skirmishes broke out after dark in a number of residential areas of Torreón, civilians were advised to arm themselves, and to support the militia movements and the government against the rebels. In June, Orestes Pereyra and Enrique

Adame Macías (both of whom would later participate in the capture of Torreón) were arrested along with other members of the
Mexican Liberal Party (PLM).

The economic crisis, which seriously affected the value of Wah
Yick shares, produced a confrontation between Foon-chuck and
Dr. Huang Jih Chuck: the former decided to stop investing in the
streetcars, in spite of the Mexican government's threat to rescind the
concession. Notwithstanding, the Chinese community continued
to prosper: scattered throughout the whole downtown were such
businesses as El Puerto de Shanghai, El Pabellón Mexicano, El
Puerto de Ho Nam, and La Plaza de Armas. There were also large
grocery stores like Wing Hing Lung and the house of Yee Hop. In
the enclave where today stands the rundown Hotel Calvete was the
splendid Lavandería de Vapor Oriental, a steam laundry employing twenty launderers, which had a large wood-burning vat, and
a dining area and chef exclusively at the service of the employees.
There was a wealth of restaurants like the one owned by Chon
Lee. The market (nowadays the Mercado Juárez) was packed with
stalls where the Chinese sold fruit and vegetables. A few streets
to the west, the Asian staff of the Hotel Internacional attended
to the needs of a constant flow of clients. On the top floor of the
Compañía Wah Yick, the rooms of the Asociación Reformista ac-
commodated newly arrived Cantonese migrants, hosted political
study groups, and/or generated strategies for employing an ever-
expanding workforce.

It must have been a lovely sight: all those single men with their
peculiar clothes and long pigtails participating—alongside laborers in huge sombreros, international cowboys, and professionals
in frock coats—in the construction of a city that was part Sam
Peckinpah movie and part Tower of Babel. The Chinese christened
Torreón with a name whose sweetness was expunged from history
at rifle point: Tsai Yüan, the Vegetable Garden, a ghost town that
would live on, hidden in the clefts and crannies of a modern city.

On October 12, 1909, ten thousand Torreón inhabitants congre-
gated at the railroad station to greet Porfirio Díaz when he passed

through en route to Ciudad Juárez, where he was to hold talks with US president Taft. Díaz, however, snubbed the crowd. The train stopped for only a few minutes, and the old general did not even deign to wave at the multitude from his window. Perhaps by that time Don Porfirio was beginning to notice that Torreón—once the apple of his eye, the irrefutable proof that the policies of the positivist regime were capable of performing urban miracles—had betrayed him. By then it was a hotbed of subversion. Not only had it shown a preference for the reforms proposed by Bernardo Reyes, it was also one of the places where Magonismo had the most supporters and, still worse, was the leading light of a region that had given birth to Francisco I. Madero, the most popular opposition candidate in the republic. Torreón, the artificial pearl of the Porfirian regime, had become the retina of an upheaval. Perhaps this was not so much because the Torreonese were revolutionaries (as local history suggests) as that all other Laguneros—the excluded, those reduced to near slavery: the peasant farmers and sharecroppers of Chávez, Cuencamé, Tlahualilo, and Matamoros—had had enough of the regime. They are eyes that once were pearls.

On September 15, 1910, heavy rain fell on the city, and the program of events to celebrate one hundred years of independence had to be modified at the last moment. The original plan was for the Centenary School to be opened in the morning, and then in the evening, Dr. Leopoldo Escobar (who had been elected mayor seven months before) would address the crowd in Plaza 2 de Abril from the balcony of the Casino de la Laguna. The downpour forced the authorities to postpone the inauguration of the school and relocate the mayoral speech, the Grito, to the interior of the Teatro Ricardo de la Vega.

The venue was packed by eleven that night; at least half those who turned out had to stand in the street. Dr. Founier's octet played an overture, and the academics Carlos E. Suárez and Emilio G. Saraiza gave speeches. The national anthem and other patriotic pieces were then sung and, finally, Dr. Escobar gave the traditional cry of "¡Viva México!"

When the ceremony was over, the various city guilds marched through the streets carrying standards. Although not mentioned in the press, it is likely that stones were thrown at some premises belonging to the Spanish community that night: Urquizo says this was a well-established local custom after the Grito. In his official correspondence, Carothers states that some Chinese businesses were also attacked that day.

The festivities lasted four days. On September 16 there was a parade; on the seventeenth the Spanish community presented the Centenary School with desks and chairs; then, on the eighteenth, the Cantonese community provided fireworks. I daresay that by that point significant quantities of alcohol had been consumed by the revelers. As the nights progressed, the cry of "¡Viva México!" began to be substituted by another in the streets of Torreón: "¡Viva Madero!" Tension rose in the face of this festive challenge to authority. Eduardo Guerra notes that someone shouted "Death to the Chinese!" Certain establishments were stoned for a second time. There was looting, but nothing more serious occurred.

At least not that night.

PEDESTRIAN

And I found no thing on which to lay my eyes
that was not memory of death.
Quevedo

Sunday. I go for a walk, but haven't taken thirty steps before I regret the decision. Cities like Torreón, sculpted with white light, are unwelcoming to the person traveling on foot: you melt in the summer. I hail a cab and ask to be taken to the Plaza de Armas. The car goes straight along Independencia, crosses Colón, skirts the historic downtown, turns left at Valdez Carrillo, passes my two favorite cantinas from way back—the Gota de Uva and the Reforma—and drops me at the corner of Morelos, next to the Palacio Real, the hotel where I regularly stayed in the early nineties because it was considered second-rate. Nowadays it's not even third.

I find the plaza surrounded by squads of federal police: people seem unfazed. It's a permanent deployment, aimed at containing the drug cartels, who, not so long ago, took pleasure in converting the former center of Porfirian power into a shooting range. The presence of the Julias (named after the woman who first lent her car to a local police force) is ominous, but it seems to work: at the southern end of the plaza, the pedestrian areas of Valdez Carrillo and Cepeda are packed with people buying roast corn on the cob, oven-baked gorditos, strips of crispy pork rind with pico de gallo, and fruit squashes, and then sitting to enjoy the cool—cool?—under ultramodern shade sails installed by the city authorities. I'm not sure how much I like them. The La Perla underground passage—one of the last vestiges of the region's former status as the Promised Land—is closed. The signs say it is under repair.

I continue along Valdez Carrillo. The sidewalk to my right looks like it's taken more hits than the other three surrounding the plaza.

There's absolutely nothing there: an empty lot, another used for parking, a Popsicle store called La Michoacana: absolutely nothing. I take a shortcut across the infamous expanse of concrete that is the modern Plaza Mayor, and head east, parallel to Avenida Juárez. Three buildings make up the entire southern side of the plaza: the Banco Chino, the facade of the casino (designed in 1910 by the French architect Louis Channel), and the Banco de La Laguna. The construction of the last began on June 16, 1911—exactly a month after the Chinese community lost everything—and the bank opened on November 20, 1912.

I turn counterclockwise and explore the eastern side of the plaza. On the corner where the Pathé cinema and theater used to stand are the remains of the building that took its place: the Hotel García, which was once one of the finest establishments in the city, but now only partially functions, and on which are hung large canvas banners advertising a price of 160 pesos for the clients of the prostitutes. The whole of this side is lined with stores selling denim clothing, trinkets, and hosiery, all probably manufactured cheaply in China. About halfway down is a small, depressing Chinese restaurant whose menu is handwritten, with spelling errors, on sheets of glossy paper.

Turning toward the north side of the plaza, I pass another building; I don't know what it used to be, but it now houses the municipal treasury: a small institutional triumph over the traditional Torreón refusal to locate public offices around the main square. I'm back at the Palacio Real. I retrace my steps along Cepeda to reach one of the most spectacular buildings of the historic downtown: the Arocena gallery.

The Arocena building is one block southeast of the Plaza de Armas, at the junction of Hidalgo and Cepeda. It was constructed in 1920 by the family whose name it bears. The facade is grandiose: terra-cotta walls and white moldings—the lower sections of the balconies simulate open fans—that contrast with the spare lines and monochrome design of the majority of the surrounding edifices. There is a strange chinoiserie about the roof garden dome,

which crowns that squat corner, and has led certain people to believe the building once housed the Banco de Chino. This is untrue:
the Arocena didn't even exist during the Chinese community's
most splendid era. Everything in Torreón is so new, and so old, it's
hard to relate the city's history to its architecture.

Between the Arocena and the Banco de La Laguna is an extremely peculiar structure: the new entrance to the gallery, constructed not long ago on the site of the former Casino de La Laguna.
I'm not too sure if I like the facade of this section of the Arocena,
the work of architect Abby Aguirre Garay: a Latin American version of those ultramodern European designs that manage to live
in harmony with historic buildings, but which here seem to indicate pretension rather than a sense of space. That impression
may be due to the fact that the original layout of the downtown
is too tightly packed to allow pedestrians the opportunity to enjoy
a building with features that are artfully fluid compared with the
usual Torreón attitude to construction, and the city's tough character. Be that as it may, the section of Calle Cepeda between Juárez
and Hidalgo seems to me delicious in architectonic terms.

I walk along the pedestrian zone for the third time until I come
to a halt at the southeast corner of Hidalgo and Cepeda. What's
there? Once again, nothing: a modern, rectangular construction
in a bad way: I mean it. But another question presents itself. Silvia
Castro is certain that the real Banco Chino was once housed in this
building, not in the older edifice on the Plaza de Armas, at the opposite extreme of the adjacent street. It is her comment that has
brought me here this Sunday.

The question arose from my research. In a passage of *Between
the Perla and the Nazas Rivers*, Juan Puig gives the original address of the bank as Juárez and Valdez Carrillo. But then, when
listing the many Chinese businesses in Torreón, he offers a different headquarters for the Wah Yick banking and railroad company: a building on Avenida Hidalgo. Which address was correct?
Silvia Castro asked this same question ten years ago and, in com-
paring statements by Woo Lam Po with other documents in the

Estrada archive, discovered that the Banco de La Laguna was installed on the first floor of the Banco Chino before the attack, and not *afterward*, as Juan Puig suggests. This contradicts both popular lore and accepted historical accounts, which for decades identified the wrong building as the focus of the massacre. In reality, the events occurred on a different corner: a hundred yards farther south, and a hundred yards to the east, where today stands a very ordinary Coppel store.

I continue along Hidalgo, and try to imagine what was once to be seen here: dozens of corpses, people running down the sidewalks, laden with looted goods (many of which were no use to them), men crying and begging for mercy, drunken trigger-happy mobs, bodies dragged behind horses, blood . . . I try to imagine all this without being melodramatic, without even fantasizing: I appeal to history, to its stoic assimilation of facts. I can't do it. Torreón is no more than what you can see: a Sunday in June 2014, sweating pedestrians, traffic and car horns, stores. It's always easier to destroy memory than re-create it. And that's a tragedy, but also a blessing. After all, biological impulses are deaf and blind, and don't have language: they are pure present. It is we humans who set ourselves the task of escaping The Real through language and memory. Forgetting is closer to nature than we are.

NUMEROUS BANDS

(Fugitive slave route)

As far as your eyes can see—your eyes, passing reader—everything is mine, I bought it from the devil for a blind hen. If you arrived here on your own two feet, along this fugitive slave route, you know very little of yourself. Arriving doesn't mean being here. Setting foot on this moorland hill can be confused with the drying up of a spring. Listen to me then with your far-hearing ear. Come, cheer up, whatever you say you are, I am a little like you, with a few too many canaries perhaps. Together we make words, the act of silence, the virgin's desert. What I want to say has no commas: my emotion is a sleeping eye. That is why I know your children are chasing a soap bubble in the cemetery.
Ernesto Lumbreras

Numerosas bandas is a book by the Jaliscan poet Ernesto Lumbreras in whose pages coexist Rilke's angels, the tattered remnants of Russian acmeism, idiomatic language, the anarchist aesthetic, a railroad station manager who casts his mind back over his deceased lovers, an Argentinian prostitute who, in her younger days, was like a ring found in the mud of the road to the cemetery . . . *Numerous Bands.* The title makes me think of the nomads of the desert where I live: Guachichiles, Borrados, Cocoyomes, and Yoricas, who traveled these parts for centuries before being wiped out by my tribe. *Numerous Bands*: an appropriate description for the earliest revolutionaries, the innumerable groups of ten to fifty guerrillas who assaulted La Laguna at the beginning of the twentieth century, until they slowly merged into the army (there are people who speak of five thousand, or seven thousand men; but it is most unlikely that army ever numbered more than two thousand) that arrived at the gates of Torreón in mid-spring 1911, under the command of a twenty-three-year-old rebel.

William K. Meyers has written an essay on this topic, which I will attempt to summarize here.

La Laguna is an example of what *modernization* means in Mexico: Porfirian policies generated increased production and an economic boom, but also a social abyss. While development occurred in Torreón, Gómez Palacio, and Lerdo, and landowners and businesses amassed fortunes, outside these urban centers the four subregions formed by the river basins were sunk in poverty. In less than 150 years, large local companies did to La Laguna what had taken the inhabitants of Mesopotamia various millennia and three civilizations to achieve. However, says Meyers, "even with large profits, the elite managed to find one complaint or another." Another problem was that, in addition to jointly participating in diatribes against the central powers, industrialists and speculators continually argued among themselves, as had been the case since the time of Benito Juárez and Leonardo Zuloaga.

Meyers states:

> From 1884 until Torreón's fall to the region's popular classes, Díaz devoted a great deal of attention to handling the disputes of the region's divided elite as they battled over everything from water rights to the price of soap. In the early 1880s, planters in the lower river zone armed resident workers and sent them into the upper river zone in Durango to destroy dams in order to obtain more water for Coahuila.
>
> The ensuing battle between armies of agricultural workers created a major incident between Durango and Coahuila, prompting Díaz's intervention to prevent private wars.

The oldest subregion is Cuencamé, to the southwest, on the Durango side. This had always been an agricultural area, and it was the only territory in La Laguna where the rural protests Calixto Contreras and Severino Ceniceros headed starting in 1905 took on communal aspects; a sort of Norteño Zapata movement (although they never managed to ally themselves with Zapata). Cuencamé was the sole bastion of regional unrest to have a group of indigenous people in its ranks: the Ocuileños. While their Maderismo was better defined than that of other groups, and their uprising occurred on the date stipulated by Madero, the Ocuileños didn't take part in the original assault on Gómez Palacio. Their greatest defect was their unwillingness to move beyond their own territory, stubbornly waging war on home ground.

Calixto Contreras was known as "El Indio." He was born in the fall of 1867, in San Pedro de Ocuila. It is quite possible he was able to read, as he had three or four years of elementary education. At the age of twelve, he left school to contribute to the family income, working in a mine. His politicization came later: the first mention of his existence is when, at thirty-six, he protested against the plundering of his tribe's arable lands by the owners of Sombreretillo. For five years he fought a legal battle against the regime and the hacienda. When legal avenues ran out, he responded to Francisco I. Madero's war cry. At one point, he was a candidate for the leadership of the regional revolt. The command, however, fell in the end to Jesús Agustín Castro, which wasn't particularly to Calixto's liking. It may be for this reason, or for an error in military coordination, that his troops arrived late to the capture of Torreón.

At the northern extreme of the second Durango subregion in La Laguna lies the town of Tlahualilo, seat of one of the most important agroindustries of the Porfirio regime. At the center of this subregion is the northwestern town of Real de Mapimí, twelve short miles from Bermejillo, an obligatory point of transit between the states of Durango, Coahuila, and Chihuahua. Mapimí—"High Hill" in the Cocoyome language—was founded in 1598. Decades before the revolutionary era, the settlers had wiped out the nomadic Indians of the region, and what was left was a mining and agricultural trading center attracting thousands of seasonal workers. And also bandits: two *corridos*—"The Two Friends" and "Four Mounted Men"—tell their story.

Jesús Agustín Castro, the leader of the guerrilla forces in the northwest of La Laguna that eventually captured Mapimí and made it their center of operations, was not born in a rural environment: he was from Lerdo, one of a trio of rich cities. As a young man, his talent for strategy, his charisma, or courage must have been exceptional. While it is true that Madero headed the first stage of the Revolution on the political front, it was Jesús Agustín, a Durango streetcar employee, who set the military campaign in motion.

Castro was short but sturdy, and had a bronzed complexion. A militant constitutionalist, he wore a waxed mustache, turned up at the ends, that gave him a slightly comical appearance. Urquizo recounts that during the first months of the uprising, "he sported a Moorish beard, and resembled a Bedouin from the Moroccan desert." Although he came from a poor family, he managed to stay in school until the age of fifteen; there is no doubt that he completed his elementary education. From 1902 he was employed in a variety of roles in the Durango and Chihuahua mining industries: store clerk, paymaster, carpenter . . . When Madero issued the call to arms, Castro was working as a streetcar conductor and living in Gómez Palacio. He joined the conspirators. Since La Laguna was the birthplace of Francisco I. Madero, and Torreón one of the greatest exemplars of Porfirian power, attaining the presidency of the municipality was a natural aim of the movement.

On November 3, 1910, Francisco I. Madero sent a personal messenger bearing a copy of the Plan of San Luis Potosí, which was handed directly to Manuel N. Oviedo, leader of the local Anti-reelection Club, along with a series of verbal instructions. At a clandestine gathering, Oviedo read out the plan with an oratorical tremor in his voice, and assured those present, perhaps indiscreetly, that on November 20 he and between one thousand and six thousand men would seize the city hall. He never turned up: the authorities came after him and he was taken into custody.

The second option was to gain control of Gómez Palacio. Mariano López Ortiz, former assistant to a superintendent of police and

Oviedo's second in command in his capacity as vice president of the Anti-reelection Club, was appointed to undertake this exploit.

On November 16, López Ortiz withdrew to a safe house with Castro, Orestes Pereyra, Sixto Ugalde, and a number of his fellow ringleaders. On Monday the twentieth, at six in the evening, the contingent went to the nearby former hacienda of Santa Rosa, where machetes and Mausers were distributed. But the Torreón rebels were destined—at least in that first bid—to doubt: realizing they had only twenty-one rifles and eighty-eight men, López Ortiz resigned his leadership. The person who took the reins was Jesús Agustín, the youngest of all the rebels.

At two in the morning of the twenty-first, Castro's men attacked police headquarters. Chief Ruiz and the four officers who were with him opened fire, but soon ran out of ammo and took to their heels through the back door. The conspirators occupied the building, destroyed the archives, and freed the prisoners. Some of the troops split off and marched to the local treasury with the intention of claiming 10,000 pesos. They found only 800.

The number of rebels grew: before dawn there were over two hundred.

In Ciudad Lerdo, at around half past two in the morning, the retired colonel Carlos Abundis heard distant explosions while drinking coffee, and presented himself before his local political boss, Colonel Zuñiga.

"The rebels are taking Gómez," said Abundis.

Zuñiga sent Félix Chávez, the head of the Rurales—his local police force—and sixteen men to the neighboring city, where they advanced on police headquarters. They rode on horseback down the center of the street without realizing that their objective was by then a rebel stronghold: shots rang out. One horse was killed in the first salvo. Some of the gunfire was coming from the rooftops, where Castro had positioned snipers. Taking advantage of the darkness, the Rurales fell back and managed to take refuge in the adjoining streets. The second confrontation occurred soon afterward, near the market. Officer Rosales was killed by a bullet, and his colleague Leandro Zermeño suffered machete wounds. A couple of hours later, the Rurales and Maderistas had a third encounter on the streetcar line connecting Gómez Palacio to Torreón in which Chávez, head of the Lerdo contingent, fell. The insurgents searched the body, and, in an act of grossness, relieved him of the 400 pesos in his billfold (no small sum: a little more than the annual wage of the average worker). The rebels then marched to the bridge connecting the area to Coahuila. They had no idea what awaited them on the other side.

In Torreón, Mayor Escobar took precautions to ensure his own survival: fearing a mob would free his political rival, Oviedo, he fortified the prison and ordered the warden, Félix de la Garza, to kill—in cold blood, without legal process—the inmates in their cells should an assault on the premises occur. He then urged Enrique Sardaneta, his local commander in chief, to attack the Maderistas. Sardaneta marched on Gómez Palacio at the head of the Twenty-Third Cavalry Battalion, led by Captain Arnulfo Ortiz, and the Eighth Infantry Battalion, commanded by First Lieutenant Juan Zorrilla Guerrero. The force consisted of a total of fifty uniformed men.

It was daybreak.

The government troops opened fire in a calm, disciplined manner—as they had been taught during their exhausting hours of training—from the opposite bank of the Nazas River. Their cannons caused significant losses in the ranks of the enemy, who were packed onto the narrow track of the Puente Negro railroad bridge. Disconcerted, the inexperienced Maderista troops retreated along the Lerdo road, while enemy fire continued to thunder behind them, bringing down riders. According to popular tradition, Jesús Agustín Castro dismounted, found a protected position, and covered the retreat of his fellow rebels with a hail of bullets from his Mauser. Some of his comrades in arms—among them the veteran anarchist Orestes Pereyra and the ringleaders Gregorio García and Antonio Palacios—joined him; others did not. But that simple demonstration of initiative confirmed the twenty-three-year-old streetcar conductor as the leader of the revolt. And although in the coming months he had great difficulty gathering more than fifty men around him, while the number of soldiers under Contreras, Moya, and Lavín grew, it was finally he who headed the army that would take Torreón: the youthful leader who united numerous bands. No one—neither veteran overseers like Ugalde, nor ranch bullies like Benjamín Argumedo, some of whom were twice his age—challenged his right.

The Gómez Palacio insurgents escaped northwest toward the mountains of Mapimí. They did not then know it, but they had just supplied the Revolution with the best of fuels: foolishness.

The third subregion in La Laguna was made up of the municipalities of Viesca and Matamoros, on the Coahuila side of the Nazas River. In both this zone and in Mapimí, the uprising acquired a foundational status in a climate of seasonal banditry. For years, around December and January—when the cotton harvest was over and the ranks of the unemployed swelled—some peasants would hole up in the Sierra de Durango or the Desierto de Mayrán (territory they knew better than La Acordada) to make a living rustling livestock or ambushing payroll wagons, fleecing gamblers or kidnapping virgins and young women. This criminal tradition had been in existence since the nineteenth century, and there was even a popular female character associated with it: "La China" Apolinaria, who led a gang of highway robbers. She became famous because, after holding up stagecoaches, she would bare her breasts to the dismayed passengers with the cry of "Look who you're losing out to, you idiots!"

By 1908, Viesca had become a minor capital where firearms were the ruling power.

A primary cause of rural discontent was sharecropping, a system rooted in feudalism in which large landowners allow peasants the use of parcels of land in exchange for a high percentage of their harvest. This system left the majority of sharecroppers in poverty, and hampered the development of the local small-business community, an agrarian middle class, distanced from the governing powers and gradually beginning to feel solidarity with the popular struggle.

The conjunction of seasonal banditry, sharecropper unrest, and the indignation of the owners of small farms was the match that lit the first fuse: the uprising in 1908 of representatives of the PLM in La Laguna, with the aim of taking Viesca by force of arms. This assault marked the beginning of the regional rebellion, and the appearance of its first leaders: Mariano López Ortiz (who headed an attempted revolution in Matamoros in 1909), Orestes Pereyra, Enrique Adame Macías, and Sixto Ugalde.

Orestes Pereyra was from El Oro, Durango, and, before the Revolution, was a tinsmith. The future general and novelist Francisco L. Urquizo, who served under him in 1911, describes him thus:

> He was missing an ear, and to hide this defect used to wear his hair long, which artfully covered the lack of an outer ear. . . . He had the look of the heroes of 47: he was never seen without his federal sword and spurs, even if he was walking around barefoot and wearing cheap everyday pants.

It seems that Orestes had little education. The first time he rose in revolt was in an attack on Viesca in 1908, when he was forty-seven. He was captured in Torreón, but reappeared as a free man at an unspecified date before the Maderista rebellion. It is unclear if he escaped from prison or was acquitted, and neither is it known why he had such good luck; the majority of his companions—and even some innocent civilians—were sent to the gallows or imprisoned in San Juan de Ulúa after the uprising.

After the failed attempt to take the municipal government headquarters in Gómez Palacio in 1910, Orestes spent several months at the side of Castro in the mountainous region of Mapimí. Later, sometime around April 1911, he moved to the Tlahualilo area to recruit troops.

Another participant in the 1908 Magonista uprising was a twenty-four-year-old former miner named Enrique Adame Macías. He was taken prisoner with the veteran Orestes Pereyra and also later freed. Or did he escape? The odds for that seem low to me: months afterward Enrique had a more or less stable job with access to gossip, serving in a cantina in Matamoros; as they say, within a stone's throw of Torreón. It is possible that both Pereyra and Enrique negotiated a pardon in exchange for informing on their fellow rebels, but if that were the case, they would have sacrificed the trust of others of their persuasion in La Laguna. It would be more realistic to imagine that someone—I mean someone with political and financial power—interceded on behalf of the two men at the time of their arrest in 1908. This wouldn't be the first time social mobility expressed itself in an exchange of favors. The enigma of the release of Orestes and Adame Macías offers a glimpse of just how much we do not know about the personal relationships between the rebel ringleaders and the various strata of Porfirian power.

Enrique Adame Macías was born in Villa de Cos, Zacatecas, in 1884. Urquizo disrespectfully described him as short and plump, and eccentric in his dress: he used to wear a gray canvas suit, a gigantic coffee-colored, animal-skin sombrero, miners' boots, and his ostentatious colonel's insignia on a sash across his breast. His favorite weapon was never the revolver or Mauser, but—miner that he was—dynamite. With a stick of the explosive in hand, he joined the Maderista movement, took part in the uprising in San Pedro, and, in April 1911, attacked Parras de la Fuente, where he wreaked havoc by planting bombs in several buildings, including the parish church. It was his explosive intervention that persuaded the federales to surrender the main square without a fight. He was present at the taking of Torreón in May, and it is possible he was also there—as an active participant—during the massacre of the Chinese community.

Very little information now remains about Sixto Ugalde. What is known is that he was a native of Matamoros, took part in the attack on the municipal government offices in Gómez de Palacio under Castro, was close to both Orestes Pereyra and Benjamín Argumedo (eventually his sworn enemy), was among the first of the ringleaders to enter Torreón in 1911, and may possibly have participated in the spilling of blood. There is also this brief portrait by Urquizo:

> Don Sixto Ugalde still wore the uniform from his time as a steward in a cotton-growing hacienda: a white straw hat and a corduroy suit. His chubbiness and rosy complexion gave him an air of perfect goodness. When positioning his men during combat, it was as if he was walking around the hacienda, as he used to, apportioning tasks to the hands.

The fourth and last subregion of La Laguna that Meyers describes is located in the center of the lower area of the Nazas River. The most important town is San Pedro de las Colonias, a free community founded in 1869 by republican volunteers who, after being discharged from the army, took to farming on a small scale. Although San Pedro is called the Cradle of the Revolution, it joined the struggle late in the day and timidly. Adame Macías and Benjamín Argumedo did in fact attempt an uprising there, but were forced to make an immediate retreat, not due to resistance from the federal army, but because several members of Madero's family were still in the town, and mounting an attack there would have been a sad task. It was not until April 1911, when Emilio Madero negotiated with the federal troops for the peaceful surrender of the main square, that it fell under the control of the revolutionaries. The town's situation was paradoxical: it was symbolically essential but, once the uprising had begun, became a stone in the shoe of the revolutionaries.

Emilio Madero was an accidental insurgent: a man of business caught up in a time of rebellion. His power derived from neither his actions nor his ideology, but from the particular situation of being the sibling of a charismatic leader. He was barely thirty (almost ten years younger than his brother Francisco) when the fighting broke out. During the first months—from November 1910 to March 1911—his family commissioned him and his uncle Salvador to manage their immense patrimony; he had no time to get mixed up in politics. On April 22 (less than a month before the fall of

Torreón), he was imprisoned by the Porfirian authorities of San Pedro de las Colonias. The town's military detachment went out to confront Sixto Ugalde's troops, who were camped in San Lorenzo, and the peasants took advantage of this to rebel—armed with sticks and machetes—against the municipal leaders. Under the pretext of the ascent of his brother Francisco, Emilio was freed in order to rescue the well-to-do inhabitants from what could have been an outbreak of lynching. This fortuitous event converted him in one fell swoop into the leader of the rebels. When Sixto's men advanced on San Pedro after defeating the federal forces, Emilio was again commissioned (not by the insurgents, but by the aristocracy) to negotiate the surrender. He had absolutely no military experience when his brother made the decision to award him the rank of major (and later the vague position of army chief) so as to unite the numerous different bands in La Laguna. The appointment simply fell into his lap.

The Madero clan had been landowners in Coahuila and Texas from the days of Nueva España. Its origins can be traced back as far as Alejo Bernabé, who was born in 1706. At the beginning of the nineteenth century, José Francisco Madero Gaxiola, great-grandfather of the man who would be honored as the Apostle of the Revolution, founded the town of Liberty, Texas. One of José Francisco's sons, Evaristo, was a successful businessman in La Laguna: he was an agriculturalist, owned a textile mill, was involved in transportation, and was a partner in the local metal smelter, in addition to being the governor of Coahuila from 1880 to 1884. His property extended from the municipality of Parras de la Fuente in the southeast to San Pedro de las Colonias in the north, thus constituting one of the mammoth establishments that are traditional within La Laguna. Patriarchal, efficient, and tough, Evaristo was the embodiment of regional Porfirismo. He had eighteen children, and died in Monterrey in April 1911 at the age of eighty-three. His death coincided with the attack by revolutionary troops on Parras de la Fuente, where to this day still stands the green-and-white shell (all whitewashed walls, and long terraces trellised with vines) of his finest hacienda, on whose paved patios ran, as a child, the architect of the civil war Don Evaristo abhorred to his dying day.

Francisco Madero Hernández was a less interesting and vigorous man than his father or his eldest son. What follows is an excerpt from a letter he sent to his firstborn in January 1909:

> It is hardly to be credited that a man like you, who considers himself a good son, exposes the committed interests of your good father to failure, and I will not hide from you the fact that although you publish that text [*The Presidential Succession in 1910*] against the wishes of me, your father, and it is all your own creation, they cannot believe we have not taken an active part in that publication, because we want and intend to obtain positions for which you commit us all; through carelessness, you are the cause of your father's ruin. . . . Of course, you have a number of companions who praise you to the heavens because you bell the cat, and they will tell you that you do so as one of the best of reformists, keeping your head in the clouds, and comparing you to the great Demosthenes, and you don't realize they are laughing at you. . . . By becoming involved in such serious affairs as this, it is hardly to be credited that a man like you, who should be helping his father to put his business on a firm footing, should be an obstacle to that end, and even contribute to his ruin. It is clear you are a child who does not think, or wish to consult anyone. . . . Whenever I reflect on your conduct, I fear you have lost your wits, because you do not even consult the opinions of sensible people, and I feel you have gotten in over your head. . . . You are one of the many who have gotten your father into difficulties, and instead of helping him to survive them, you contribute to his downfall.

Francisco I. Madero, the recipient of the above missive, was born in Parras de la Fuente in 1873. A man of very short stature, he spent long stretches of his childhood and youth in the United

States and Europe; he enjoyed swimming; even as a boy, he was interested in homeopathy and spiritualism. He began his militancy at the age of thirty-one, when he founded the Anti-reelection Party and published the above-mentioned tome, which had an enormous influence on Mexico's history, and could bore anyone to tears.

My favorite photograph of Don Panchito—as the ordinary people of La Laguna call him—was taken in Parras before 1880. The future statesman must have been about six, and stands with an arm around his younger brother, Gustavo, who was already by then an inch or so taller. They are dressed identically: ankle boots, white socks, striped cropped pants, ties, and elegant jackets unsettlingly similar to those worn by the Kuomintang students. Gustavo is perched on a stool that is covered with a floral-patterned cloth; his left arm is around his elder brother's waist. Francisco's right hand rests on Gustavo's shoulder; his left arm hangs at his side, the hand clenched in a fist. What is most disquieting is the future president's face: he is looking at the camera with a slight frown, with that painfully serious expression that accompanied him throughout his life.

⁕⁕⁕⁕⁕

Sparks flew that fall. Numerous bands of ten to twenty men roamed through La Laguna, dismantling railroad tracks, ambushing convoys, stealing weapons or grain, harassing ranchers . . . This done, they retreated into the mountains or the desert. Although they paralyzed the regional economy, they were never able to form a unified force. They were few in number, lacked any central organization; they called themselves Maderistas, but had no common military strategy or political objectives, except for the determination to make Porfirio Díaz resign the presidency. Tulitas Jamieson says that one of the insurgents, when questioned about whom he was fighting for, replied to Federico Wulff that "he thought it was for one Don Luis (probably referring to Madero's Plan of San Luis Potosí)." Meyers reports that Graham, the British consul in Gómez Palacio, described them in this way:

I do not suppose 10% of the insurrectos have any definite objective in view: they are simply having a good time at the expense of those who were formerly their masters; in short they have for the first time in their lives a good horse, a good rifle, and the pleasure of "bossing" instead of being "bossed."

Although idealized, and a little more in-depth, Francisco L. Urquizo's description is not dissimilar:

Those of us who were in the hills, carrying our arms, were very far from defeating the federal forces. True, we were mostly country people accustomed to the unpleasantness of the hard life on haciendas or in the mountains. We were men who lived on horseback, toughened in the weariness of constant, daily labor; we knew how to handle weapons, and to take care of our personal needs. . . . But for all that, we lacked military experience, discipline, and skill; we knew nothing of the art of warfare. We had no leaders, and those we thought of as leaders were really only so in name and appearance. . . .

There was only one battle cry, and that was unfailingly given by the head of each faction as he galloped at full speed toward the enemy, firing his rifle: "If you're a man, follow me!" More than an order, it was a kind of vague invitation to risk your neck. . . . No one considered himself to be among those people with a definite obligation to fight; we were there to "help."

"Whose side are you on?" someone was asked.

"I'm helping Don Sixto Ugalde."

That is to say, it was Don Sixto who was under the obligation to fight, not the person affiliated with his band.

The outlook began to change in December. The end of the cotton harvest also saw the end of much of the seasonal work, a phenomenon that neither Madero nor the federal army had accounted for in their calculations. The newly unemployed immediately enlisted in the ranks of the malcontent. By January 1911, both the number of bands and of individual guerrillas had grown. The principal leaders started to delegate authority to subregions and groups.

The federal army had no idea how to respond to guerrilla warfare. They were not trained for this form of combat and, more importantly, didn't know the ground under their feet. What use was it to ride off at a gallop behind Madero's men if, at the first hill, the first stretch of wetlands, you lost all trace of them? After many tantrums and a great deal of wasted time, the Porfirian militia chose to pursue a defensive strategy: protecting the urban centers without harassing the rebels. This attitude angered the landowners and increased Madero's popularity. Haciendas were abandoned. The wealthy took refuge in Torreón.

One factor that influenced the sense of cohesion within the rebel troops was the rise of leaders from among the privileged classes whose positions were not the result of popular assemblies, but were based on better education and the financial power they represented.

Luis Moya Regis was a well-to-do rancher from the north of Zacatecas who had expressed opposition to Porfirio Díaz from the turn of the twentieth century. He joined Madero's political campaign in Chihuahua and, at the outbreak of civil war, fought in Jiménez and Parral with troops paid from his own pocket. Due to his background (it seems he was a good reader and had theoretical knowledge of military strategy), he didn't limit himself to controlling the immediate terrain, but advanced in a southerly direction with a band of men that initially numbered thirty but had grown to two hundred by the time they passed through La Laguna. Moya attempted to work in coordination with the many other local bands—Meyers believes he was on the point of consolidating his position as a regional leader before Castro—but as his military dynamic was different from theirs, he decided to continue south and got so far as to continue his operations in Aguascalientes and Jalisco, some three hundred miles from La Laguna. The only photograph of him I know of shows a serene, slightly severe man with a long graying beard, a Samuel Beckett gaze, and a hat that is so perfect it was surely custom-made. Rather than a Mexican revolutionary, he looks like the classic dandyish gunfighter of a Western novel by Marcial Lafuente Estefanía. He was fifty years old in 1910. He might have become a prominent figure in the Madero movement if he hadn't met his end on May 9, 1911, in his hometown of Sombrerete, while fighting General Trucy Aubert's forces.

Another wealthy man who joined Madero was Pablo Lavín, son of the founder of Gómez Palacio, and one of the heirs to a large agricultural establishment known as Perímetro Lavín.

A photo published in the newspaper *El Siglo de Torreón* in April 2012, with the caption "The Lavín Brothers," portrays—from left to right—the sons of Don Santiago, a Spaniard by birth and one of the richest men in prerevolutionary Mexico: Alejandro, Gilberto, Benjamín, and Pablo. The boys are flanked by two individuals, each holding a Derby hat; they must be hacienda stewards. Gilberto is the eldest brother: he has a neatly trimmed mustache and is holding a tome or bound notebook in his right hand. Alejandro and Benjamín seem to be straddling adolescence and adulthood. Pablo, the youngest, probably about seven, is sitting on a low stool. At his feet is a miniature dog, so elegantly tense it could be made of porcelain. You can tell a mile away that the boy is bored, but even so, he is the only one looking directly at the camera.

Pablo Lavín took up arms at the end of March 1911. He was still very young. Some historians (and many revolutionaries) have speculated that his motive for becoming involved in the revolution was opportunism: to take part in a struggle, on the side his relations predicted would come out on top, and so later protect the family patrimony from the ranks of the victors. There is no firm foundation to this supposition, but neither is it beyond belief. Pablo's troops played an important role in the (peaceful) capture of Gómez Palacio and Lerdo, but they were not officially involved in the attack on Torreón, despite having been summoned there by Castro. On the other hand, a curious incident had occurred weeks before: when an altercation broke out between Pablo's men and those of Juan Ramírez (another of the rebel leaders occupying Lerdo), Lavín sent a message to the federal troops asking for their intervention to prevent a riot.

Pablo Lavín headed an enormous, well-armed contingent, but the men lacked discipline and did not always respect their chief's orders. One cannot help but note in this relationship a resemblance to the private (or paramilitary, or mercenary) armies the land-owners maintained for decades in La Laguna, and whose ideological affiliation was never very far from what in the twentieth century was christened the far right.

*****

Francisco I. Madero did not immediately understand what was going on in the region of his birth. His head filled with the advances in Chihuahua, it was March before he noticed how deeply entrenched the uprising was in La Laguna, and became aware of the pressing need to provide leadership for the numerous bands. This was not only a matter of military and financial urgency: the fields would very soon be ready for sowing, and the conjunction of a paralyzed economy and lack of agricultural production would bring about irreparable losses (as happened with the Perímetro Lavín estate, which never recovered from the war). Madero negotiated with the rebel leaders through emissaries and letters with the aim of transforming the troops from a destructive looting force into the new guardians of a prosperous middle class.

On February 9, Sixto Ugalde brought different groups together in an attack on Matamoros; they occupied the city for a number of hours, freed prisoners, stole weapons and money. At the end of March, Luis Moya and Calixto Contreras's troops threatened Lerdo and Gómez Palacio. A month later, various guerrilla groups occupied Matamoros, Viesca, Mapimí, Lerdo, Gómez Palacio, Nazas, Velardeña, and San Pedro. In an official letter to the government dated May 1, the United States consul, George C. Carothers, declared that the only thing stopping Madero's forces from taking

Torreón was the absence of "any revolutionary leader strong enough to unite the different bands."

Such leadership presented itself in the form of a two-headed entity: Emilio Madero and Jesús Agustín Castro. While Emilio took on the military command, Jesús Agustín possessed faculties that located him in a gray area between the bosses and the rebels: he came from a poor family, but he was fair-skinned, more or less educated, and had grown up in an urban environment. On May 9, 1911, he was designated commander in chief, with only Emilio as his superior. Perhaps with the intention of justifying this rank, that same day Castro took it upon himself to attack Torreón. There was little point in this maneuver: his forces were inferior to those of the defending general, Emiliano Lojero.

Meyers presumes some of the rebel leaders may have been against Castro's appointment, but did not dare show their dissent openly because gaining control of La Laguna was becoming a matter of urgency: they needed to disband the troops and set them to planting cotton at the earliest possible opportunity. On May 12, Castro sent dispatches containing his orders to each of the rebel chiefs under him: Ugalde in the east, Pereyra and Lavín in the west, and Calixto in the south. Castro marched his own army southwest from Gómez Palacio.

Inside the besieged city of Torreón, there were fewer than seven hundred federal troops. General Emiliano Lojero ordered the construction of barricades in the streets. All points of entry into the city were covered by volunteers, military personnel, ditches, and barricades. The first assault would occur in a few short hours.

1

On February 29, 1916, Benjamín Argumedo gave evidence before the court-martial in Durango that would sentence him to be executed by firing squad the following day. They had brought him there from El Paraíso, Zacatecas, on a stretcher, "wrapped up like a firework." The charge was rebellion. Having been on the run for some time, after suffering one military reverse after another and abandoning his troops due to ill health, he was close to confronting a destiny he had always despised:

"Better to go out fighting than to face the firing squad, and be laughed at and humiliated by our victors," he once said.

When he came before the judges, he was suffering from fever and explained:

"I am not trembling from fear. It's malaria that's killing me and causing this chill."

He was forty years old, and five of those years had been spent in the ranks of the revolutionary forces. The combatants who came to know him gave him a variety of nicknames: El Zarco, El León, or El Tigre de La Laguna, El Orejón . . . And also El Resellado (The Switcher), because of the great number of factions in which he served: he was a Maderista, Orozquista, Huertista, Convencionista, and, when Venustiano Carranza's men arrested him, he had just spoken to Juan Bautista Vargas Arreola with a view to establishing an alliance with the man who had been, until then, his greatest enemy: General Francisco "Pancho" Villa.

As he was too ill to stand, he was executed sitting down.

Benjamín Argumedo was born on January 3, 1876, on the Hacienda de Guadalupe, then to be found between Congregación Chávez (now the municipality of Francisco I. Madero) and San Pedro de las Colonias. He was the son of Albino Argumedo and

Tiburcia Hernández, country folk native to the region. His father owned a small amount of land in the area of El Gatuño. Benjamín had at least one brother, Miguel, who also joined the insurrection and died in combat in 1912 in Huejuquilla, Jalisco State. Two women are named as his spouse: the first was Valeria Soto, whom it seems to be certain he did marry (there is a sworn statement by one of the daughters they produced), but where and when is unclear. The second was María, the woman the moribund Argumedo introduced as his wife to General Vargas Arreola during their conversation: El Tigre was lying on a camp bed, and the girl was nursing him through a pulmonary infection resulting from a gunshot wound. He had at least two daughters: Dolores and Julia, who at different times (1920 and 1940) asked the secretary of war for their father's contribution to the military campaigns to be officially recorded.

Argumedo used the rank of lieutenant colonel when he joined the former Magonista Enrique Adame Macías in the uprising in San Pedro, but it was in the first attack on Torreón that the Maderista movement formally accepted him as a captain under Sixto Ugalde. He would rise to be a general with Pascual Orozco in the irregular army, and was finally recognized as a permanent brigadier general in the cavalry during Victoriano Huerta's presidency (1913–14). His various fellow rebels and enemies gave him another title: "Valiant among the Valiant." The novelist and political activist Paco Ignacio Taibo II recounts that when Villa took Zacatecas, Argumedo— who was defending the main square on the Huertista side—dressed himself in a splendid black Mexican cowboy suit ("a beautiful uniform to die in"), took up his machete, went out into the street, and walked like a poor-man's samurai straight through the ranks of the enemy troops to the city gates.

I have no doubt at all that he was a sociopath.

When his executioners asked him what his job was, Benjamín said he was a tailor. This sparks the imagination: a quiet little country tailor who wakes up one morning a warrior ("I killed six in one blow"), one of the most ferocious men in the Revolution; the man who always hit his mark when defending the rear guard of his (almost always defeated) factions, crying, "The fallen have fallen!" Before becoming a soldier, he had also worked in agriculture, but the picture of him that remains in the popular imagination is that of a harness maker, since he "made reins and covered buttons, dressed saddles, and cut and decorated leather for spurs," as his biographer, Jesús Sotomayor, vividly puts it.

What he enjoyed most was riding, and he not only rode horses but also broke them. He was very fond of dancing, and was capable of galloping miles just to do a polka. There are those who accuse him of having been a heavy drinker, and even a braggart, but José Santos Valdés—one of the first people to offer a portrait of him—rejects this accusation, adducing he was for many years a close friend of his father's, Pedro Valdés Rosales, who was abstemious and had no time for drunkards.

In the oral tradition of La Laguna, it is still a matter of debate whether Argumedo had anarchist affiliations at the time of the Viesca uprising of 1908. No hard evidence is available to confirm these ties, although, two years later, his sympathy for Orestes Pereyra and Enrique Adame Macías was unmistakable. But what is a fact, documented by the Ministry of War, is that he joined the Maderista revolution on November 18, 1910, under Sixto Ugalde.

Benjamín Argumedo is one of the principal protagonists of both the first occupation of Torreón and the small genocide. In his testimony to Macrino J. Martínez, he admits it was he who gave the order to open fire on the Chinese. In the words of the military judge, he adds, "If he had not been convinced that the Chinese were firing on his troops, he wouldn't have ordered the attack, because he had instructions to respect all foreigners, except in such a case."

This declaration would become a headache for Benjamín, to the point of being—according to his own testimony before facing the firing squad—one of the reasons for his revolt against the Madero government. In August 1912, a warrant was issued for his arrest for robbery and homicide.

Did Benjamín have personal reasons for hating the Chinese? A witness to the events, Aurelio Olivares, accused him, along with Cresencio Soto and Lázaro Sifuentes, of being "one of the most ferocious in killing the Chinese." Argumedo was not only valiant: he was a corpse-making machine, a man who was always fearless, and never compassionate.

Ironically, as I have mentioned, oral tradition insists, to the very limits of idiocy, on attributing the massacre to Pancho Villa (a man who had absolutely nothing to do with the event, and who was El Tigre de la Laguna's bitterest enemy). And if you do assert that Argumedo was the guilty party, there is no lack of people in La Laguna ready to come to blows in defense of his memory.

2

On June 17, 1911, the English-language *Torreon Enterprise* published a classified advertisement that went more or less like this:

DR. LIM'S ANTIALCOHOLIC SPECIFIC
A SPECIAL HERBAL TONIC FOR ALL
ALCOHOL-RELATED NERVOUS AILMENTS

This splendid infusion, composed exclusively of vegetable matter, provides a fast, radical cure for the habit of drinking liquor. Many experiments carried out on victims of alcohol have had highly satisfactory results, and for that reason I believe that, in putting this product on the market, I am offering a great benefit to families who will be able to help any of their members who have acquired this terrible vice return to normal life.

DR. J. WALTER LIM

offers his services in his office at
Calle Cepeda No. 226, in the main square, Torreón, Mexico.

Information concerning Lim is scant. It is known that he arrived in La Laguna in 1895 from California, and that with him came—or possibly they met up at a later date, it's hard to be sure—his sister: the only Chinese woman whose presence in the city in 1911 is not in doubt. That this sister was married (there is no evidence to say whether this happened before her arrival, or if the couple met here) to Ten Yen Tea, an agriculturalist and employee of Lim's. That the couple had three children: a girl of fourteen at the time of the capture of Torreón, and two younger boys. That the doctor had deeply assimilated US culture; it is probable that he was a Christian of the Protestant persuasion, and his medical degree was awarded by a California university, which makes me think that, like Foon-chuck, he landed in America as an adolescent, and was perhaps adopted by a devout Anglo-Saxon family. That he adapted very well to life in Mexico, and intended to remain there: he became a national in 1889. That he lived in the center of the city and offered his services on Plaza 2 de Abril. That he owned a redbrick house east of town, on the road to El Pajonal, between the Alameda and his compatriots' market gardens. That in addition to his medical practice, he was involved in Foon-chuck's businesses and the Asociación Reformista. That he was, according to oral tradition, much loved in Torreón, probably due to his affable nature, his fluent English and Spanish, and because, unlike other members of the Cantonese community, he had adopted a Western lifestyle. That he was not a representative of the Celestial Empire: he himself stressed this in his testimony to the district attorney, Ramos Pedrueza, in August 1911. That in May, the military judge Macrino J. Martínez forced him to sign a document full of libelous statements. That in the days following the massacre, he spent his time assisting the survivors. That he felt respect for a revolutionary soldier named Sabino Flores, whom he described as "a man of honor, and a gentleman." (He was wrong: Sabino may have spoken well of the Chinese to Lim in private, but to Ramos Pedrueza, he repeated exactly what he had declared to Martínez: he and his followers had killed a number of Cantonese people because they were armed and had been harrying them since May 13.) That Lim's misjudgment of Sabino's character shows him to have been a guileless man. That the massacre ruined his life.

It is also known that JW went on living in Torreón until at least 1919. I don't know when he died. He has no descendants in La Laguna.

3

At the age of seventeen, Emiliano Lojero went through a baptism of fire that proved his destiny for greatness: on May 5, 1862, under the command of Ignacio Zaragoza, he fought the French army in the Battle of Puebla. He was then a second lieutenant. Five years later, in June, the newly promoted twenty-two-year-old captain was appointed member of the war council that would condemn Archduke Maximilian of Austria to death.

Lojero was born in Querétaro in 1845. By the time the revolution broke out, he was a gray-haired general with proven skills in a wide variety of areas, ranging from open warfare to repression. He was sixty-six and was renowned for being an upright man, which is why, in 1911, the Porfirian regime entrusted him with the defense of Torreón, one of its main centers of power, and a hotbed of rebellion and discontent.

There will be time later to speak of what Lojero did and failed to do between May 13 and 15 of that year, three days that would link his name with genocide. What is certain is that, after the episode, everything he touched went badly. General Juan Manuel Torrea, witness to and analyst of the Ten Tragic Days preceding the assassination of Francisco I. Madero, situates him as being loyal to democracy, or at least in a position of neutrality that would have enabled him to mediate between the military and President Madero if only the latter had named him minister of war in January 1913. But the appointment never materialized, and, in February, Lojero witnessed the detention of his friend Felipe Ángeles, and the assassinations of Madero and his vice president, José María Pino Suárez. In March, Victoriano Huerta appointed him head of the Third

Military Zone, based in Nuevo León. The veteran general had the mayor, Nicéforo Zambrano, arrested and sent to Mexico City for execution or imprisonment, along with other known opponents of the regime. Lojero didn't appear to have been happy with this commission, since he retired from the army a few months later.

Humiliations soon followed; Venustiano Carranza's triumphal Carrancismo movement was unable to forgive his loyalty to Huerta. Salvador Alvarado recounts that the by then senile Emiliano Lojero attempted suicide in February 1918 due to his much reduced financial circumstances. He died in 1923, at the age of seventy-eight. Except for the story of how he abandoned Torreón, history has forgotten him. Such is the glory of a man who made his military debut defeating an unbeatable army, and who later permitted himself the luxury of sending the younger brother of an emperor to the firing squad.

4

The second time Federico Wulff came to La Laguna, Andrés Eppen offered him a job that seemed to have been conceived in a high fever: to draw up the plans for a modern city to be constructed around a solitary railroad station in the middle of the desert.

Two things distinguish the project Fred designed on that occasion. One, it is precise; in spite of the rough terrain, which, to the west, formed a complex bottleneck between the river and the hills, the architect-engineer managed to trace a grid of perfect squares for almost all the blocks. Two, it is spacious: it's said Wulff's measurements were in the English imperial system, but those charged with the task of making the plan a reality used the decimal system. That is why the streets and sidewalks of Torreón are less claustrophobic than those of almost any other Mexican city.

Federico took up residence in the conurbation he himself had invented, and grew rich designing irrigation systems for the cotton magnates. He also undertook projects for mining companies and constructed buildings such as the Hotel Salvador—where Emilio Madero would put up after the first capture of the city—and the

Porfirian municipal building. A number of his original drawings are now scattered around La Laguna. People—I witnessed this myself among the miners of Ojuela—treasure them as relics.

In 1901 Wulff bought the land at the top of a rocky outcrop near the present-day Duragueña neighborhood, and built a chalet there of gray Durango stone in a mixture of neoclassical and German Schloss styles. It had fifteen rooms and a cellar, a laundry-basket system running between the bathrooms on the first and second floors, and both the interior and the terraces had wooden floors made from California oak with Italian tiles. The mansion was finished in 1905, and the people of La Laguna dubbed it La Casa del Cerro—Hill House. It is now the home of the city's museum.

On May 13, 1911, probably armed with a pair of field glasses, Federico went up to the roof of the chalet. From there, at different times over three days, he witnessed the battle for Torreón. His makeshift observation post gave him a panoramic view of the massacre of the Chinese community.

5

José María Grajeda was an herbalist who made himself out to be a doctor. He had a stall in the marketplace, where his cries alternated with those of the Chinese fruit and vegetable sellers. Puig thinks his jealousy of the immigrants was rooted in the reputation for reliability enjoyed by the remedies they sold. The fact is, we know almost nothing of him: it is not even certain Grajeda was a member of the Maderista army before the taking of Torreón. He could just have been some infuriated local on horseback. No one knows why he hated the Chinese.

6

Hartford Harold Miller Cook was an American businessman and photographer who arrived in Torreón in 1905 and stayed for thirty years. His camera registered some of the most photogenic moments of the La Laguna utopia. He illuminated everything (the word *il-luminate* is very nice: it unites poets, painters, and photographers): from the revolutionaries who rode their mounts into the Casino de la Laguna to the opening of a steel bridge over the river. His photographic gaze is profound—spiritual, it could be said. He styled himself an "amateur photographer," but that title doesn't do him justice. He had an uncommon instinct for being in the right place at the right time, as demonstrated by his best revolutionary plates: eleven cavalrymen outside the Torreón smelting works; federal soldiers standing around a plane so fragile it seems to be made of paper. He also had a kinetic sensibility, not in itself pure, but truly fresh, something that can be seen in the passage of horsemen—to the left—and young ladies—to the right—along Plaza 2 de Abril in 1907. The solidity of the male bodies in dark clothing with their backs turned to the viewer in the foreground is like a weighty object about to plummet. In contrast, the group of approaching maidens, almost all in white, seems to float in space. It is, in its extremes and inconsequence, a lovely image.

Miller documented the 1911 massacre. His photographic plates are in the Archivo Municipal Eduardo Guerra in Torreón. One of the best known shows a print worthy of Ingmar Bergman: on a muddy avenue, a *guayín* (way-in), a sort of proto–station wagon, is pulling away with its load of corpses.

7

It seems to me that bureaucratic rhetoric was more straightforward in the early twentieth century than it is today. I found an extreme example of this in the official communications the interim president of the republic sent to his secretary of foreign affairs in the aftermath of the mass killings of 1911. The messages, three or four lines long, are signed with a terse "León de la Barra."

Alejandro Rosas says Francisco León de la Barra, born in 1863—descendant of an Argentinian aristocrat and a young high-society lady from Querétaro—was nicknamed the White President for his breeding, refinement, and Catholicism (and, I would add, because, unlike Díaz, he wasn't a mestizo). In my opinion, however, he should be known as the gray president: nothing remains of the almost six months he governed Mexico. I don't believe this was due to any lack of ability on his part (in his time he was a recognized expert in international law), but to the circumstances surrounding any interregnum.

Francisco studied law at the Universidad Nacional and rapidly became involved in politics: at twenty-eight he was already a federal representative. He was what might nowadays be considered a career diplomat, starting as a legal adviser in the Ministry of Foreign Affairs, and then joining the official diplomatic corps in 1896 to serve first in South America, before moving to Holland and Belgium. He was the Mexican representative at the 1907 Hague Peace Conference, and in 1909 was appointed ambassador to the United States, a post he still held when the revolution broke out. Díaz recalled him to Mexico to take charge of the MFA, perhaps thinking of the importance of US backing for his government. On May 25, León de la Barra took on the position of interim president after the resignation of Don Porfirio.

Although the massacre occurred before his time in office, it fell to the gray president to confront it in judicial terms. In this respect, de la Barra showed himself to be every inch the diplomat: active, well informed, respectful, energetic, and incapable of managing his way out of a paper bag. It is fair to say, nevertheless, that he made an outstanding decision in naming a jurist of the standing of Antonio Ramos Pedrueza as district attorney for the case. That is a great deal more than can be said of any Mexican president so far in the twenty-first century.

8

A charismatic glutton, George C. Carothers is the embodiment of one of Mexico's favorite variations of the *pinche gringo*. Many of the stories that surround him clearly demonstrate his sense of humor and pragmatism, his negotiator's instinct, the speed with which he attended to his duties, his ironic resignation in the face of what he considered the defects of the Indians and mestizos (in a letter cited by Dambourges Jacques, he declares that Mexicans could be "worse than savages when they are beyond control"); but it is also clear he felt a real empathy for Mexico, to the point of considering himself an adoptive son. If only distantly, the destinies of those living in poverty mattered to him.

He was born in San Antonio, Texas, in 1878, but as his father, a doctor, lived intermittently in Saltillo from 1868 onward, George spent long periods of his life in Mexico. At the age of seventeen, he turned up in Torreón as cashier of Ferrocarril Internacional. At twenty-two, he figured as the owner of a dry goods store. That is when he was appointed consular agent, a post he would hold until 1913, when he became a representative of the United States to Francisco Villa's government, and then, in 1914, a mediator between Wilson and Venustiano Carranza during the diplomatic crisis of Veracruz, after what became known as the Tampico Affair. Previous to that, in 1905, Carothers had set up a couple of import businesses in La Laguna. He also owned a mine, and was elected secretary of the Chamber of Commerce. In addition, he found time to act as a theatrical impresario. His wife, Clara, who had ash-blonde hair and was reputedly a beauty, used to complain to her bridge group that she had "a face like an unbaked pie."

The best-known portrait of George Carothers shows a chubby-cheeked but attractive man with a calm expression, a cleft chin, blue eyes behind round spectacles, a very short neck, and, on his wide brow (he was going bald), a correct Peña-Nieto pompadour.

Carothers was thirty-three when the Maderistas arrived at the gates of Torreón. The tone of his official correspondence before the attack gives the impression that he was vaguely sympathetic toward the revolutionaries, and while his later declaration to Ramos Pedrueza expresses condemnation of the massacre, it would

not be long before the consular agent would return to his former
enthusiasm for the armed movement through the person of one of
its most enduring characters: General Francisco Villa.

9

William Jamieson (or Billee, as his wife affectionately called him)
came to La Laguna at the turn of the twentieth century. He was born
in Ottawa, the son of a pharmacist, studied medicine at McGill
University, and practiced in Oklahoma before moving to Torreón
on the recommendation of his childhood friend Tom Fairbairn.
The arrival of his passenger train coincided with some form of re-
union with ample supplies of alcohol: there wasn't a single sober
doctor in the town that day. The beautiful Clara Carothers had
gone out in urgent search of help for George, who was suffering
from a throat infection, when she ran into a stranger in the street
who was obviously not Mexican.

She looked him over, and asked,

"Aren't you Dr. Jamieson?"

He nodded, and she continued,

"Are you drunk?"

"I don't think so."

Clara took his arm and led him to the room where her husband
lay on his sickbed. A close friendship blossomed between the doctor and the consular agent.

Just as soon as he had established himself in practice, Jamieson
decided to court Gertrudis (or Tulitas, as her parents nicknamed
her, or Dalla, as he would call her in his letters), a girl of seventeen
whom he'd met—"wrinkled, dirty and generally awful-looking"—
one winter morning at the railway station. Linda, Tulitas's mother,
was against the match: a white Canadian doctor was not good
enough for her; she would have preferred her daughter to wed a
German. And so the engagement dragged out over the course of a
year. During that time there was a minor scandal that almost put an
end to the relationship: in 1905, on the occasion of a ball cohosted

by Federico and Linda Wulff and a newly married Mexican couple, who offered to provide the wines. But the alcohol had been adulterated, and some of the guests began to show symptoms of poisoning. Accusations soon began to fly: someone got up on a chair and shouted that the gringos were trying to do away with the Mexicans, while a foreign resident claimed just the opposite. Fortunately, there were no deaths. The young Mexican—also a doctor—who had contributed the alcohol was formally charged with the attempted homicide of his father-in-law, with whom he was on very bad terms. There was no lack of rumors about subversion: an attack against the middle class by the common people. The suspicions of criminal intoxication grew in the region with the passing years, and had their sequel in 1911, when the Maderistas accused the Chinese community of trying to poison them with cognac.

Billee and Tulitas were married in 1906, and during their time together in Torreón had two children, the youngest of whom died in 1910. In April 1911, with an attack on the city imminent, Billee accompanied his wife and the little Evelyn to San Antonio. He returned to Torreón after an eventful journey lasting 125 hours: over five times the usual duration. At the end of May, Jamieson wrote a long letter to his father telling him of that and other vicissitudes, and also recounting his experience as a Red Cross volunteer during the first capture of Torreón. It is one of the most touching extant testimonies of the small genocide.

10

Herbert Ashley Cunard Cummins was born in England in 1871. He spent the first decades of the twentieth century in Mexico, and came to be an important diplomat, despite the disdain and ill will he showed toward the country on not a few occasions. In *The Worm in the Wheat*, Timothy J. Henderson describes him thus:

[He] was fifty-two years old in 1923, a large, ruddy-faced man with a receding hairline, white mustache, and a pompously stiff bearing that befitted a self-proclaimed champion of private property and the unimpeachable rightness of all that was Anglo-Saxon. He had graduated from Christ College at Finchley and had been made a knight of the Order of St. George and St. Michael, and had become an officer in the Order of the British Empire. Rosalie Evans's passionate ethnocentrism found a hearty echo in Cummins. "I like to help you," he once told her; "you are a credit to us and show what fine English-American blood can do."

The politician and general Plutarco Elías Calles made a somewhat exaggerated, immortal statement about him that could be inscribed on his tomb: "Cummins knows as much about Mexico as I do about cricket."

When he arrived in Mexico City, Cunard (as his friends called him) created a scandal in bourgeois society by openly cohabiting with his mistress. Later, in the 1920s, he became an eccentric bachelor, living a secluded life, attended to by a butler and three Chinese servants in a house with a garden filled with canaries, peacocks, and exotic snakes. He became a headache for the Mexican authorities owing to a much commented upon diplomatic conflict: his official support for the demands of Rosalie Evans, a notoriously racist English widow whose agricultural lands had been requisitioned by a branch of Zapatismo. An enemy of agrarian reform, and determined to make no concessions to the new political order, in August 1924 Evans would be tragically murdered in a street neighboring her home—almost certainly by revolutionary elements.

In a number of his public pronouncements, and also in private, Cummins expressed views of Mexican governments and the country in general that were not far short of insulting. His attitude would seem to me unjustifiable if I did not know that he—at that time British vice-consul in Gómez Palacio—was the ad hoc gravedigger who took pity on the massacred bodies while the Maderista troops were marching through the city in triumph.

11

There is a cocky photographic record of Francisco Luis Urquizo Benavides's debut as a revolutionary. The handwritten date situates it in 1910, but I believe that is wrong: according to his own testimony, the future novelist joined the revolt on February 7, 1911. But whatever the case, the photograph is an impeccable farce: Urquizo and his companion in the pose, Manuel H. Reyes Iduñate—both of them would eventually be generals—are freshly washed, clean as two new pins. They are pretending to take cover behind a fountain, possibly in the center of an urban patio, since in the background the brick facade of a house, several potted plants, and a tall bougainvillea can be seen. It is Urquizo himself who really gives the game away: he is sporting a gigantic mustache, holding his rifle unconvincingly, and has a dubious, ham-actor smile on his face; he seems to be making an effort not to look at the camera. It wouldn't surprise me if the photo had been taken after the victory at Torreón.

Urquizo was born in San Pedro de las Colonias. His parents were farming people from the Durango side of La Laguna, and he spent part of his childhood in Torreón, which gave him a clear image of the town in all its intrigue; few authors have described it so precisely. As a child he had hoped to pursue a military career, but his father, a practical man, forced him to desist in this vocation, and sent him to the capital to study commerce. Urquizo was orphaned, and returned to La Laguna with the intention of taking charge of the family's small farm, but lack of money and dreams of adventure encouraged him to join the revolution at the age of twenty. There is no doubt that he took part in the first capture of Torreón, and it is almost certain he joined the ranks on the western front under Orestes Pereyra.

The footprint he left in relation to the attack is not military but aesthetic. His novel *The Old Troops*[10] (1937) narrates the events from the reverse viewpoint of the testimony: the first person voice

---

10. *Tropa vieja*

of the fictitious draftee, Espiridión Sifuentes, a defender of the city. The scenes that show this strategy at its best are the battle for Cerro de la Cruz, and the retreat of the federal troops along the Huarache canyon, two incidents that express with simplicity and pathos the novelist's compassion for the men on whom he had once opened fire. The general's prose style is not, by far, the best of his era: all Mexicans know that privilege belongs to Martín Luis Guzmán. Nevertheless, the focus at the end of the first part of the novel seems to me a strange, majestic moment of literary realism in Mexico.

12

Jesús Flores was a stonemason; his life was lived in an urban setting. The *Torreon Enterprise* describes him as managing public affairs (maybe as a sort of interim mayor) in Gómez Palacio in May 1911. It is likely he had been opposed to the Díaz regime for years, during the rise of anarchist tendencies within the PLM. Despite his lack of formal education, he was eloquent, had command over his troops, and wielded political authority. I say this to qualify the depictions of him offered by Juan Puig and Delfino Ríos, who describe him as an ignorant factory hand without ethics or ascendency over the masses. The mere fact that his brief period of authority and death at the front line has been noted by journalists and historians of diverse backgrounds demonstrates that he was a revolutionary figure with regional influence during the days of the attack.

On May 5, 1911, the Maderistas marched through Gómez Palacio and held a civic ceremony to commemorate the Battle of Puebla. Among the inevitable xenophobic speeches (after all, it was a matter of celebrating the mythical defeat of a foreign army) was one by Jesús Flores, directed at the Chinese: he accused them of taking Mexican jobs, supplanting Mexicans in some of their *natural tasks*—cooking and washing clothes—and proposed a complete ban on Chinese immigration to Mexico as one of the goals of the Maderista movement.

Weeks later, in an article published in the local press, Professor Delfino Ríos stated that Flores's speech had been an incitement to the populace to kill the Chinese. But Ríos wasn't present at the May 5 ceremony. On the other hand, the British vice-consul, Cunard Cummins, was. Cunard testified to Ramos Pedrueza that Flores's speech was confined to the political aspects of the situation, without any attempt to threaten the Chinese militarily.

13

The Chinese community knew it was in danger.

Shortly before the attack, Colonel Francisco del Palacio, the city's political boss, convened an assembly of businessmen, traders, and foreign residents. The meeting took place in the Sociedad Reformista China headquarters, in the presence—according to Juan Puig—of Woo Lam Po and Foon-chuck. I'm not particularly convinced the latter was there: he lived in Piedras Negras, and there are no firsthand reports or any trace of documentary evidence attesting to his presence in Torreón during the days of the fighting.

Colonel del Palacio's objective was to ask the business community and migrants to allow mercenary *guardias blancas* to cover the rear of the federal army, and tackle the problem of guerrilla infiltrators (as was later seen, these formed a relatively important contingent). The majority of those present refused to participate in the defense of the city. Miguel Robledo—who owned a dry goods store opposite El Puerto de Shanghai, and who would days later reveal himself as a Maderista activist—was enraged by the proposal. The Chinese leaders held their tongues.

There is no doubt that well-to-do inhabitants formed patrols in defense of the regime. At least one photograph (included in Terán Lira) shows a barricade of tree trunks in one of the streets. The majority of the people in that shot are in civilian clothes, with narrow-brimmed hats, some are wearing suits, and to the far right of the image, a well-dressed woman in a bonnet can be seen. Terán identifies the group as the "'Defensa Social,' composed of Porfirian society gentlemen, and headed by Colonel Carlos González." Another image in the doctor's collection—badly burned, almost impossible to decipher—shows a column of horsemen. The caption reads: "Colonel Carlos González formed a body of Rurales called the Chaquetas Amarillas (the Yellow Jackets) made up of overseers and hired guns from the haciendas to fight against the Maderistas in defense of Porfirio Díaz."

Professor Delfino Ríos is perhaps the first author to identify this group as the Voluntarios de Nuevo León, also known as the Amarillos de La Laguna. They appear in Urquizo's novel *The Old Troops*, where they are described as an elite squadron whose hatred of the revolutionaries surpassed the ill will of the federal army: they not only confronted the enemy but also hunted them down, dragged men behind their horses through the prickly pears, inflicted dozens of gunshot wounds, even after they were dead, dismembered them, hung them from telegraph poles at the roadside so they would learn respect . . . Their practices were not so dissimilar from those of paramilitary groups today.

The fact that the Amarillos were ferocious combatants in the defense of the east of Torreón, where the Chinese market gardens were located, may have stoked the Maderistas' Sinophobia: it would not be the first time a linguistic misunderstanding has fueled a massacre. There is not, however, a single piece of positive proof that La Laguna's Chinese community was interested in fighting the rebel troops. In fact, after the meeting with the political boss Francisco del Palacio, Woo Lam Po made public his stance in relation to the approaching storm. The lobbyist had a flyer printed in Chinese characters that was distributed among the community starting on May 12. Evelyn Hu-DeHart includes the English-language translation of the flyer Woo gave one of the committees that later investigated the events:

> Brothers, attention! Attention! This is serious. Many unjust acts
> have happened during the revolution. Notice have [*sic*] been received that before 10 o'clock today the revolutionists will unite

their forces and attack the city. It is very probable that during the battle a mob will spring up and sack the stores. For this reason, we advise all our people, when the crowds assemble, to close your door and hide yourself and under no circumstances open your places for business or go outside to see the fighting. And if any of your stores are broken into, offer no resistance but allow them to take what they please, since otherwise you might endanger your lives.

Despite its prophetic nature, it is probable that the flyer reached the market gardens too late: the number of Chinese corpses mounted after dusk the following day.

CAB (4)

I've just arrived,
I'm not a stranger.
Charly García

My suitcase is packed. I scan the room to make sure I haven't forgotten anything. Hotel rooms are entities of passion; they are beings in their own right: you can inhabit them for six hours or a weekend, enjoy what they offer in terms of emptiness, novelty, ardor, or superficiality. But if you run aground on their comfort for a couple of weeks, the walls are likely to begin to devour you, as if provisionality were a praying mantis of the mind.

I pay my bill at the desk, request a cab, and ask the driver to take me to the bus station. I'm not going very far. I'm what is known as a partisan: someone close, someone capable of loving La Laguna in the backlight of a small drop of poison. I'm not a stranger.

As the car moves along Diagonal Reforma in the direction of Juárez, I mentally review my journey. I smell the coffee in Adriana Luévano's house; the whole place stank of pigeon droppings because a flock had gate-crashed the patio on a permanent basis, claiming their natural status as the world's expropriators. I smell the dense mix of clean air and stagnant water as the draftees sing at dawn along the tracks of the Venustiano Carranza woods: "This little step, this tiny little step, this tiny little step is going to last." I recall the endless malls, the escalators, the diffuse feeling of the air-conditioning like asphyxia in motion. I savor the tasteless, imported Black Angus meat at the Tony Roma's, and the exquisite whimsy of the small local restaurant with plastic tables the poet Félix took me to. I smoke happiness that is nothing: a cigarette offered by a stranger inside Revistas Juárez, as if we didn't live in the grouchy, reactionary, healthy twenty-first century. I hear the treble voice of the boy selling

155

cheese curd gorditas from a bicycle in front of the García de Leona library. I lose consciousness in a tiny, deserted, snobby bar in Plaza San Isidro, where they gave me a couple of single malts on the house for having come there in the company of illustrious locals.

The cab passes the Central Market.

I recall other journeys: the groovy dive I once sang in wearing pajamas, like the front man in a rock band, the rapid verbal contracts with street corner dealers, the sotol in Jimulco, the mezcal in Nombre de Dios, the shacks in La Alianza, the good-looking fifty-something woman whose slow orgasm left me with bloodied knees, the basketball court where I was humiliated at the age of twenty-one by the poet and wizard Carlos Reyes, the Hotel Palacio Real and its three hundred hookers, the dressing rooms in the Teatro Nazas, the ice-cold beers I drank with Paco Amparán—now dead—in *botanero* bars, the night I turned up unexpectedly, accompanied by a blonde woman who was taller than me and covered in sand from the Dunas de Bilbao, at Marco Antonio and Susana's Buddhist home, the best bookstores in the old north of the country, Miguel Morales's mestizo virulence, Santos games with fans singing "We don't win, but boy we have fun" to plastic-bottle percussion, the droplets of liquid opium known as monkey piss, the tales of ghosts, sex, drugs, and cumbia music, the deafening noise of the engines of the ancient buses on the route to San Pedro, Madero (formerly Chávez), Viesca, and Matamoros, the boarded-up stores, the humorless graffiti, the joy and beauty thrown to the ground and kicked along by Reality . . .

We take a left at Juárez. The cab driver talks about something I neither understand nor am interested in: he says he's from Durango and that there used to be a mining company there that destroyed a whole hillside in ten years.

"Do you know anything about the Chinese who were killed here?" I ask.

He shakes his head. Then, after a pause, he looks at me in the rearview mirror.

"Do you?"

"Do I what?

"Know anything about them?"

THE HOUSE OF THE PAIN OF OTHERS

Saturday, May 13, 1911

Early in the morning, Benjamín Argumedo passed a scarf under his chin, pulled it upward, and tied it loosely in a double knot at the crown of his head. Then he put on his sombrero.

"An' what's that for?" asked one of his men.

"So the flies don't get in."

Years later, Benjamín would declare, according to the Victorian—that is, Huertista—prose of an unknown secretary, "Flies disgust me, because I've many times been horrified to see how they gather around corpses, attracted by the wounds and the stench, and then they come out in a swarm from the mouth."

Benjamín's troops took up their positions to the south and east of the city, a few miles from the Alameda, by the Continental Rubber Company, and on the edge of the Chinese market gardens. They consisted of a few hundred horsemen, among whom were perhaps Sabino Flores and Plácido Orduña. All of them were under the orders of Sixto Ugalde.

Although Pablo Lavín refused to fight, it is possible that elements of his clan joined the siege: they occupied Lerdo, a few miles from Torreón, and Jesús Agustín Castro's authority gradually asserted itself—added to the lust for robbery—among the members of other factions. Five days after the massacre, Sabino Flores told J. Lim that the first soldiers to occupy the market gardens came from Lerdo. It's not impossible that Pablo's people were among them.

The Maderista headquarters, where the young Castro was stationed, were in the La Rosita ranch house. Three Mexican flags fluttered in the breeze on the rooftop, representing the triumvirate: Sixto, Jesús, and Orestes. On the western boundary between Durango and Coahuila, Pereyra attacked the superior position held by the federal army (behind fortifications in the hills), his men widely spread out. His objectives were to flank Calabazas's line of defense and Cerro de la Cruz, occupy the southern extreme of Torreón through the gullies, and climb the hills in La Constitución and La Fe. This would allow him to combat the enemy from within the city, at the same height, and from the rear.

Every single inch of the outskirts of Torreón was patrolled by rebel forces. As federal lookouts would later determine, the least fortified area was the Huarache canyon. The reason for this could be that the Ocuileño Indians, commanded by Calixto Contreras, reached the hillside late: the fighting and slaughter were over by the time they got there.

Poorly trained infantry battalions swarmed along all the fronts. Behind them was a mixture of camp followers, curious onlookers, and not a few common thieves: poor civilians looking for a chance to loot, vent their anger, and do business. They were the spongers at the "festival of bullets."

From Gómez Palacio, and along the breadth of the rear guard, the self-confessed racist and British vice-consul, Herbert Ashley Cunard Cummins, took on the task—as had been agreed in advance with the young commander Castro—of organizing the doctors, nurses, and volunteers to set up Red Cross posts, rolling up his sleeves and going in person to retrieve the fallen. He did this with the discretion and sense of self-esteem that emanate from his portrait.

Everything indicates that, in the meantime, Emilio Madero was comfortably ensconced in a Gómez Palacio hotel, far from the events of the day.

The bustle of preparations was no less intense on the Torreón side. General Emiliano Lojero ordered Colonel González Montes de Oca's Amarillos to the eastern front line. Half the squadron (it seems there were sixty of them in total) lay belly down, carbines at the ready, beside the railway track, with the hospital behind them. The rest were positioned on the roof of the barn of the Do Sing Yuen market garden belonging to Foon-chuck. More defenders took cover in huts in other cultivated areas as well as in irrigation channels. Snipers were positioned on the highest roofs of the city: the Casino de La Laguna, the Banco Chino, the Asociación Reformista headquarters, the Lack and Buchenau department stores, and La Prueba, the Oriental steam laundry . . .

While the federal soldiers occupied the rooftops, another force was dispersing through the lower floors: urban guerrillas, whose task consisted of harrying the elevated positions of Lojero's men.

There are two photographs—Terán Lira includes both in his book—of the federal defense to the northwest of the city. In the first, taken on Cero Calabazas, the artillery is in full view. There is a bugler who stands head and shoulders above the troops in a relaxed pose: he seems out of place. At his side is an undernourished officer (the only one with decent boots), and to the right of him, a clump of draftees, a cannon, conversations. Behind this, in the center of the photograph, like some prehistoric beast, stands a topographical engineer; his image, almost lost in the surrounding landscape and the spindly instruments of his trade, is like a steampunk spider.

The second photograph is stark: it depicts four federal infantrymen defending Cerro de la Cruz. The two on the right are kneeling to fire at the enemy. The third lies flat, his rifle aimed in the same direction. The fourth man, recklessly standing upright, also has his rifle aimed at the enemy. A white mist hangs in the air behind them. It is not an ideological moment; it is morbid and tragic: an instant, halfway between Zola and the tabloid press, when someone is going to die.

Perhaps the hospital, whose location in the east of the city would surely have constituted a danger for wounded defenders, was evacuated before the attack. Three centers offering medical attention were set up: Dr. Alfonso Mondragón's, to the east, on Avenida Morelos; Dr. Salomé Garza Aldape's, at 1615 Avenida Hidalgo, and Dr. José María Rodríguez's, also located downtown, but a little farther southwest.

At ten in the morning, seven mounted men—perhaps one was Benjamín Argumedo—galloped, Mausers and revolvers blazing, along the railroad line to the east of Torreón. On the other side of the embankment, the *guardias blancas* responded to the hail of bullets, firing blindly. From a hillside to the south, a lookout signaled the precise positions of the enemy to the attackers. Successive waves of Maderista cavalry—no longer just seven men but hundreds now—continued to sweep through until after one in the afternoon, the columns charging from the southeast to the north, opening fire to their right.

From the rooftops in the center of the city, Lojero's snipers and machine gunners made a dent in the insurgent forces. The federales had better aim, were well positioned, and possessed a number of mortars, but they were also few in number and short on ammunition. Moreover, urban guerrillas were firing from the lower floors of some of the houses in the center, limiting the effectiveness of the defenders.

At around three in the afternoon, approximately a hundred revolutionary horsemen appeared behind the hospital. They had slipped in through an irrigation channel, flanking the Amarillos. Simultaneously—from the south, by the offices of the Continental Rubber Company, and from their headquarters in the La Rosita ranch house to the northeast—mounted columns attacked the front in a well-coordinated operation, taking the defenders by surprise and forcing them to retreat on horseback. The Amarillos did not even have time to respond to the assault before a contingent of a hundred horsemen, charging from the hospital, appeared to their rear. In the middle of a Mayrán desert dust cloud—like fog, but with the taste of phlegm and suffocation—the Voluntarios de Nuevo León galloped disconcertingly back into the city, taking refuge in houses around the Alameda.

This ferocious, terrifying attack gained a number of positions for the rebel army, which by dusk was occupying the terrain around the market gardens. Fear drove some of the defending volunteers away from their posts, as proved by the later discovery of seven rifles abandoned in a waterwheel.

One small group of insurgents managed to get as far as the Alameda, and caught the Amarillos between the crossfire with the urban guerrillas. But the Yellow Jackets were made of stern stuff: they regrouped, repelled the forces to their rear, and managed to force the advance rebel cavalry to retreat to the market gardens. And although—to judge by their only occasional mention in other chronicles—the military zeal of the Voluntarios de Nuevo León eventually waned, Castro's and Ugalde's troops paid dearly for their victory: by nightfall, the Maderista losses were far greater than those of the defenders of the city.

In the center of Torreón, the first day of the attack seemed unrelenting. Billee Jamieson narrates in *Tulitas of Torreón*:

Viva Madero and *Viva Porfirio Díaz* were heard on all sides. All day long the firing was an almost continuous crash. Bullets whistled up and down the streets. I was in the emergency hospital in the center of town (Garza Aldape's drugstore). Presently the wounded began to come in. The first man was a *pelado* (lower class Mexican) who, while crossing Morelos Avenue, was shot twice through the right leg, breaking the tibia in four places. The next one was a curious man who stuck his head out from the corner of the street to see what was going on. He found out, but the information did him no good, for a Mauser bullet went through his brain. All day long we worked, and when night came we had to wait, as the rebels took the electric light plant on the edge of town and shut off all the current.

We did not dare to stir, for the Federals were firing at every shadow. They fired constantly at the Red Cross, although they had promised to respect it. All night we sat in the drugstore, Drs. Gerkins, Lim, Garza Aldape and I, besides the stretcher bearers and young Carlos Gonzalez, who had volunteered for Red Cross work. The mosquitoes, the heat, the cries of the wounded whom we were unable to send to the hospital, made it a night of distress for all.

Lim gives a more sober description of the day. He says that at about four in the afternoon six people—two Mexican civilians and four soldiers, all of them wounded—arrived, and then, some two hours later, he and Garza Aldape had to go out into the street, to the corner of Acuña and Matamoros, to bring in two more casualties: a carpenter and a drunk. As he remembers it, those eight victims were the only ones to enter the drugstore; the following day, the establishment closed its doors.

.   At more or less the same time as Castro's men were flanking the Amarillos, Carothers was stationed behind one of the large windows of the Casino de La Laguna, sportingly observing the fight on the eastern front through a pair of strong field glasses. Someone soon came with the gossip that they were taking a gringo to one of the aid stations: a stray bullet had hit him in the abdomen. George was frightened. He immediately left for his own house—nearby, next to the Hotel Central—and locked himself up securely there for forty-eight hours.

Taking first- and secondhand oral testimonies as his basis, Terán Lira reconstructs the experience of the attack from the viewpoint of the poor:

> Absolutely no one had any desire to leave his house for fear of being wounded or killed by a stray bullet, and ending up as one of the great number of bodies left for days in the middle of the street, where no one dared to collect them, whether they were federales, or revolutionaries, or civilians, who from rashness . . . were killed, and thrown into the gully until merciful people came and covered them with lime.
>
> You have to remember that, at that time, most families had farm animals in their houses, sacrificing first the birds, hens and cockerels, wild turkeys, and doves, putting the pigs out in the street to forage for food, because, given the situation, there wasn't even enough for the humans to eat, and so in the streets you could see the poor beasts, hungry dogs and pigs.

There is no historical record of what occurred to the west. But there is indirect testimony: chapters thirteen and fourteen of the novel *The Old Troops*. Even though the narrator is a fictional character, and the viewpoint expressed is not Urquizo's, the clarity with which events are recounted, the veracity of the anecdotes, and the fact that the author's participation in the battles is beyond doubt, all make the story viable. According to the novel, combat in the western sector began much later: at the same time as the Maderistas were flanking the Amarillos. Before that, the federales had seen only sporadic groups of horsemen passing in the distance, and these, en route from Gómez Palacio or Lerdo, headed south through the gullies or rode toward the market gardens. The Porfiristas fired on them, but less as an act of open warfare than as target practice.

When Pereyra had infiltrated his people into the hills, Lojero's men must have broken ranks; they dismantled the artillery and relocated it behind their original position: they were eventually firing cannons on the city they were defending. Castro's commandos made no attempt to dominate the Nazas River. Their objectives were to establish a defensive position bordering this body of water to the east, and integrate into the El Pajonal squadrons. It is probable that these strategies confused the defenders.

One tactic employed on the western front line and the conquered positions to the south was to wait for nightfall and then terrorize the drafted soldiers with gunfire. The Maderistas were not great marksmen in daylight, but at night they at least had the advantage of outnumbering the enemy: "There was a whole world of people coming to attack us" are the words Urquizo put in the mouth of Espiridión Sifuentes, the hero of the tale, a fictional private earning a miserable wage of 35 centavos a day. Urquizo allows Espiridión to speak in another paragraph that more than fable feels like testimony:

There was unease all around; maybe even fear: that's what always happens when a battle's about to start; the first bullets are the ones that raise goose bumps. After a while, worse things come along but it feels like they are unimportant, the most natural thing in the world. The man who says he's never been afraid in a battle isn't telling the truth; we've all felt that cold shudder in our spines, even if only when the fighting starts. When the first bullets begin to whistle past, there's not a single man who doesn't hunch up and bow his head. You feel you have to piss, and some impatient people do just that in their own underwear. "Fear is family," and anyone who says otherwise is lying. Some confess to it, and others pretend to be real machos, but everyone feels it, even if they don't say so. Those bullets flying above your head, going *tzin*, *tzin*, pass by, but they have the privilege of making the flesh of those who hear them crawl. Those flashes you see coming from distant carbines, when you don't know where the bullet they're firing will end up, bullets that might find their mark in your own body, make you cringe, whatever the braggarts or those who make themselves out to be hardened to gunfire say.

One of the missions of the Maderista forces was to sabotage the electric plant. The man chosen to blow it up was Colonel Adame Macías, who, with the help of his squadron, had previously stolen a cargo of explosives in (believe it or not) the town of Dinamita, Durango. The electric plant burned: Torreón and Gómez Palacio were in darkness before sundown.

Conscious of his situation, General Emiliano Lojero (the fictional Espiridión calls him "the old man") ordered machine guns to be placed around the perimeter of the plant: there were at least two on Cerro de la Cruz, one more close to the Alameda, and yet another on the road to the Huarache canyon. And those were probably not the only ones. In order to prevent a night attack, which could have been definitive, Lojero had the machine guns constantly fire broadsides into the darkness. This discouraged a Maderista incursion, but also used up precious ammunition, the lack of which finally resulted in the defeat of the defenders.

According to the indirect testimony of *The Old Troops*, the revolutionaries took advantage of the shadows to enter the houses at the foot of Cerro de la Cruz, within the city limits, cutting this sector off from the rest of the army. As the stockade—a hundred years later it is still a strategic point in the wars between the narco gangs—was the main bastion of defense, control there had to be maintained at any cost. The federales replenished their ammunition and descended the hillside, firing at anything that crossed their path. It was one of the worst moments of the battle. Lojero's troops repelled the enemy, killing many of them, but not without suffering their own quota of losses and causing a significant number of civilian casualties among the poorest people in the town, who that night were sleeping in nearby shacks with their children.

Jesús Flores, the stonemason and manager of public affairs in Gómez Palacio who had given an anti-Chinese speech the week before, decided his five minutes of fame on the podium were insufficient: he wanted heroism in combat, and charged—apparently alone—the machine guns in the Huarache canyon. And there they found him: lying in the dirt with six bullet holes in his body. There was no lack of people willing to carry his remains, with full honors, to Gómez Palacio.

Perhaps because of the intensity of the gunfire during the day, as darkness fell a vague calm also descended on the eastern front. Sporadic exchanges could still be heard, but the gunfire was not as heavy as in the south and west. Castro's and Ugalde's men were occupying the Chinese market gardens and shacks. There is clear evidence that among this first contingent were Captain Benjamín Argumedo, the ringleader Sabino Flores, and Private Benito Mercado. Others who may have been present at that time were Plácido Orduña, Cresencio and Manuel Soto, and Lázaro Sifuentes. Some soldiers were crouched in the market gardens and on the banks of the irrigation channels, awaiting the early morning arrival of the camp followers from the Durango rear guard, bringing them tacos and news and, who knows, even a little hurried sexual relief. Lighting fires, or even a cigarette, was not allowed: they were within range of the snipers, for whom *downing* enemies in the middle of the night was less a duty than a form of entertainment: a talent contest in the dark.

The sky clouded over. Shadows diffused into the gloom. So began the slaughter.

Deeply rooted in the oral tradition is the notion that the Chinese were so stupid they didn't know how to respond to the military passwords: "Viva el Supremo Gobierno" for the Porfiristas, and "Viva Madero" for the rebels. To the question "Who goes there?" they would answer, "You say first," a reply whose insolence earned the person in question a broadside from a Mauser. Put in its proper context, this anecdote is revealing. On the night of May 13, frightened by the fierceness of the combat, a number of the market gardeners attempted to walk to the urban area of Torreón, crying "Viva Madelo" from time to time. Perhaps they had not seen the flyer Woo Lam Po had had printed, and even if they had, it's reasonable to suppose that very few could read. What is likely is that in the confusion they had identified themselves as unarmed enemies to the sentries of one band or the other in poor Spanish. If that is so, the first victims of the small genocide had thrown themselves into the cracks of language.

The rain started before midnight, falling solidly in one of those downpours that earned La Laguna its designation as a district of lakes. Many of the revolutionaries ordered the Cantonese workers to provide them with potable water, food, and shelter. It's almost certain they obeyed these demands without demur: nothing in the behavior of the Cantonese community in Torreón would suggest any other form of action. What's more, they were unarmed. This passive attitude encouraged abuses by some of those laying siege to the city, who made off with their savings, farm implements, and personal effects. Both the witness statements compiled by Ramos Pedrueza and oral histories reinforce the conclusion that the Chinese agricultural workers suffered assaults on at least three occasions: a revolutionary patrol from Lerdo arrived and took produce and tools, then another from Gómez Palacio divested them of clothes and cash, and finally, a third column from either Matamoros, Viesca, or Mapimí stripped them naked, then whipped and punched them because they had nothing left to give: because, in a few short hours, they had become the most vulnerable people in the Land of Lakes. The easiest to kill.

Some did put up resistance and were shot, but the majority of Celestial subjects were executed for the hell of it: out of racial hatred, financial envy, sadistic cruelty, and to entertain the troops. Several dozen died that night. Their bodies lay in the furrows in fields, piled in barns, barefoot at the doors of their adobe-walled rooms . . .

A couple of days later—and bearing in mind the political problems that were closing in on them—triumphal Maderismo collected the bodies, sending some to a mass grave by the cemetery, while others ended up under the waterwheels of El Pajonal.

Sunday, May 14, 1911

María Antonia Martínez was nicknamed La Urraca, the Magpie. She was from Durango, and no one, herself included, knew her age; Macrino J. Martínez calculated it to be about thirty. She was a camp follower who had arrived on foot at the eastern front line on Sunday morning to bring food to a couple of friends. While passing through the market gardens, she spotted a party of armed Maderistas surrounding a group of Chinese people. One of the prisoners was wounded.

María Antonia came across Private Salvador García, who escorted her through El Pajonal and showed her those who had fallen in battle the previous day. There were a great number of Cantonese corpses. The Magpie declared to Macrino that she saw twenty in just one room. She also related that among the "advance payments" taken from the homes was a case of cigars.

It's quite likely the news had already spread through the ranks that, in addition to attacking the city, some Maderistas had implemented a pogrom against the Chinese. What is unlikely is that neither Jesús Agustín nor Castro nor Sixto Ugalde had heard any rumor of this.

The battle soon recommenced. The fighting was, perhaps, less intense than the day before: both armies had suffered losses, and a lack of ammunition had begun to affect the federales' morale.

Tulitas retains a letter in which her husband, Billee Jamieson, writes:

Early next morning I started out to hunt some breakfast. The firing had ceased about 3 a.m., but I had not gone more than a block when the whine of two Mauser bullets which passed close to me made me reconsider my determination to break my fast, and I returned muy damn pronto to the hospital to chew the cud of reflection and meditate on the horrible way in which war interferes with a man's digestion or rather his getting something to digest. The cud of reflection proving poor substitute for ham, eggs, and coffee, Garza Aldape [went] home, as he had not seen his family for 24 hours and was anxious. He lives near the Alameda, which was the very center of the firing. He left Gerkins and me at the corner of Rodriguez and Morelos, and I watched him go to the bend in the street at Acuña street. Then he suddenly wheeled around and came back on the run, saying *"Muchas balas."* The battle had opened up again.

Somehow or other he got home, but he couldn't get back again. I worked until 11 a.m. Sunday, then went to bed until 5 p.m.

The indirect testimony that imbues *The Old Troops* suggests that the western front line experienced a brief lull in the morning. The foothills were carpeted with the bodies of the dead, and from time to time the report of isolated shots could be heard: they were the bullets of the snipers and deer hunters of the two bands, who, for fun, were laying bets with their colleagues to see who could hit some random target.

"The fighting was like a gust of wind that stirred a wasps' nest now and again," declared Espiridión Sifuentes.

Apart from Cerro de la Cruz, all the hills and hollows were under the control of Pereyra's men. Castro's troops were occupying Tajo del Coyote. Ugalde's had the market gardens, where gunfire

was still heavy. The Amarillos attempted to retake their former positions in El Pajonal, but were once again forced to retreat toward
the Alameda. It was there that the most violent confrontations
of the day continued well into the afternoon.

A new wave of Maderistas—Sabino Flores told Lim this contingent came from Gómez Palacio—occupied El Pajonal. Just as
the night before, the soldiers behaved brutally toward the Chinese.
According to eyewitness and secondhand testimonies compiled
by Macrino J. Martínez, Antonio Ramos Pedrueza, Owyang King,
and Delfino Ríos, on this occasion the troops were not content with
just firing at chests or heads: there were horsemen who decided to
drag Celestial citizens across the fields behind their mounts or, even
worse, tore their bodies apart by tying their extremities to each of
four horses and galloping in opposite directions. Other combatants rounded up the workers from various market gardens on open
ground and, for the fun of it, opened fire randomly, wounding some
of them. But the rage swelled and the Chinese fell dead en masse.
The executioners walked around looking for anyone still alive to
finish him off with a shot to the back of the head. When a farmer
named Francisco Almaraz lost his temper and demanded that members of the Maderista army act with decency and good sense, they
killed him and left his body on the pile with the remains of the
migrants.

The declarations that speak of greatest cruelty don't come from
eyewitnesses but hearsay; yet they are so numerous, appear at such
an early stage, and coincide in so many details, it would be ir-
responsible to discount them. Some are probably exaggerated, but
it's also indisputable that many of the Chinese were humiliated
and mutilated. Official documents recognize eighty-four homicides
committed in the market gardens between Saturday and Monday.
Thirty-five of the victims worked on Do Sing Yuen's property;
nineteen on Luc Su Yuen's. Some others were employed by Tay
Sing Yuen, and at least eleven by other proprietors.

They waited the whole day for federal reinforcements from
Monterrey, but in vain: at dusk, they saw dust rising to the west,

indicating it was the rebels who were shedding fresh blood. This further demoralized the defenders. To make matters worse, Billee states that the last consignment of ammunition was found to be full of duds: the cartridges had "wooden maneuver bullets instead of steel." Supplies might last through the night, but would not suffice to confront the enemy at dawn. General Emiliano Lojero, the youthful hero of May 5 and harsh judge of a naive emperor, could have chosen then to do the only honorable thing: surrender the main square to Emilio Madero, and request guarantees of safety for the civilian population. His self-esteem, however, got the better of him. He ordered his officers to ready their men to evacuate Torreón, taking with them as much ammunition as they could carry. They stripped the dead of their equipment, disabled the artillery, removed the bolts from carbines without owners, buried what was left of the ammunition, and, in general, pulled off a ruse that would prevent the enemy from enjoying the spoils of victory.

Weariness and impatience started to take their toll on the rebel leaders. They knew the fight could not go on much longer. Perhaps assuming (wrongly) the city would surrender the following day, both Jesús Agustín Castro and Orestes Pereyra decided to follow Emilio Madero's example, and retired to sleep in Gómez Palacio. They left the troops (who had, in any case, already initiated the massacre twenty-four hours before) to their own devices. The only authority figure left in the city was Sixto Ugalde.

The federal army's evacuation of the city began immediately after midnight on Monday. The greater part of the men moved stealthily toward Huarache canyon, while their allies on the front line—Rurales, Amarillos, infantry and artillerymen from Cerro de la Cruz—covered their maneuver with a thick curtain of gunfire. Urquizo imagines them breaking through the enemy ranks from the viewpoint of the vanquished:

> In a moment we went down to the houses, onto the long straight street they called Avenida Hidalgo. We proceeded along the sidewalk, hardly making a sound, not firing our guns, but ready to repel any attack; we wanted to advance as far as possible with-

out being spotted. The way out was through the smelting works, where heavy gunfire could be heard. . . .

In a moment we were on the outskirts of Torreón, and opened fire to force our way through.

Never in all my life have I seen death at such close quarters. It was like a landslide in which men fell as if they'd unexpectedly stumbled, never to rise again. A hail of bullets the like of which I'd never even imagined. Bullets whizzing around everywhere, our path marked by explosions in the dark night, and men buckling over or racing to find salvation. . . . If the world ever comes to an end, it will be something like what we passed through that night.

At around four in the morning, police officers knocked at George C. Carothers's door, and the consul opened it a crack.

"Señor Villanueva wants to see you."

Carothers asked for time to dress, and was still at it when they knocked again: Villanueva himself—the tax official and former city mayor—had come to inform him that the federales had withdrawn from the main square.

"What do you advise?"

It would seem that neither Mayor Escobar nor del Palacio, the political boss, were still present at that time.

Ignoring Villanueva, Carothers turned to the police officers and ordered, "Throw away those guns and take off your uniforms before you're killed."

He then offered the tax official refuge and attempted to convene a meeting of prominent city residents by telephone.

It was already too late: the streets began to fill with the sound of galloping horses, cries, and guns being fired into the air.

Monday, May 15, 1911

The first detachment began to stream in at five in the morning with a mix of caution and recklessness: they galloped down a few streets, fired off guns, and shouted Madero's name, before returning to the

Alameda, fearing a counterreaction. However, they soon noted that the only armed men who responded to their cries were of the same mind: the urban guerrillas. Hundreds of horsemen—among them Benjamín Argumedo, Sabino Flores, and Plácido Orduña—then made directly for Plaza 2 de Abril along Matamoros, Morelos, Juárez, and Hidalgo. Behind them came the foot soldiers, camp followers, and ordinary folk.

With less than an hour till daybreak, this vanguard set fire to the municipal hall and burned the archives. The troops then moved on to the adjoining building, which housed the jail, and freed those incarcerated there. In the cells, among the political prisoners and crooks, was the alarmed Professor Manuel N. Oviedo, who six months earlier had fostered the illusion of becoming the first military caudillo of the Mexican Revolution.

The building also housed the Second Civil Court, and there, in a corner of the room, lay several bottles of cognac the police had impounded after they were found to be adulterated. A rebel group opened the poisoned bottles and drank their fill. Drunk as lords (three sheets to the wind, we might say today), some of the men made their way to the cellars of the casino. Others opened the bars of hotels: the Ferrocarril, the Central, the Iberia, the Francés . . . Yet others kicked down the doors of cantinas in search of liquor. The harder the better.

Just before six, as the sun was coming up, the engineer and architect Fred Wulff went up onto the roof of La Casa del Cerro to check on the progress of the occupation. He saw a rider spurring his horse along the station side of the railroad tracks. He was carrying a Mexican flag, which he waved gloriously, shouting, "Kill the Chinese, boys!"

Wulff recognized the man: it was the herbalist José María Grajeda, who owned a stall in the market.

A short time afterward, Dr. Lim left his home to go to Garza Aldalpe's drugstore. He found it locked, and when he knocked no one opened up. He then went to Dr. José María Rodríguez's dispensary. It was open and bustling with activity, so he set about assisting the wounded. He stayed there for over two hours.

The sun rose above the horizon. The cognac from the civil court was wreaking havoc: those who had drunk it were vomiting and feverish. Several Torreón residents (including two vegetable stall holders in the market, and possibly a middle-class restaurant owner by the name of Espiridión Cantú, whom Lim later denounced as a Sinophobe) accused the Chinese of trying to poison the victorious troops.

Members of the urban guerrilla force and other civilians (principally the poor) joined the violent dawn carousals. When Sixto Ugalde's cavalry inquired where the gunfire was coming from, the people of Torreón didn't point at the buildings that had served as observation posts for the Porfirian army, but simply at those they wanted to loot. The accusations were marked by avarice, but also racial hatred and envy; the majority of the rooftops they indicated belonged to Chinese businesses. One of the first stores to be attacked was La Prueba, belonging to Tomás Zertuche Treviño. Another was La Suiza, owned by Guillermo Peters. These were then followed by those under Asian ownership: Yee Hop and Wing Hing Lung's stores, El 2 de Abril, La Ciudad de Pekin, Zaragoza, El Nuevo 5 de Mayo, El Vencedor, the store belonging to Quong Shin, and even a tiny rundown establishment called Las Quince Letras Chinas.

An armed group burst into the restaurant owned by Park Jan Long and, without uttering so much as a word, opened fire on the proprietor and his employees, killing them all. They also attacked El Puerto de Ho Nam, located in a two-story brick building that still stands on the corner of Matamoros and Blanco. The Maderistas forced the employees up to the second floor at gunpoint, and it is probable they were swiftly executed, with a single shot to the head or heart. They then sacked the store. Another establishment left in devastation was El Pabellón Mexicano, a leather goods store owned by Mar Young: they stole the stock and tied up the owner, his nephew, and the staff. On this occasion, the Chinese were beaten, thrown out of the premises, and slaughtered in the street. The mob moved on to King Chaw's store; they succeeded in destroying it, but had found it deserted: both the owner and his workers had fled. Next up were Yee Lip's premises, where they discovered thirteen Chinese in hiding. They were dragged into the street and butchered with axes and machetes.

Puig offers the following description:

As they were looting, they sought out the Chinese and shot them in their hiding places—and some, apparently, were killed by machete blows: many of the corpses were mutilated—or pushed them roughly into the street and shot them there. In addition to portable articles, they took out the frames and glass of windows, disconnected the oil lamps and crystal chandeliers from ceilings, tore out the bathroom and kitchen fixtures, took up the floorboards, and removed objects that could not even be considered furniture. The corpses of the Chinese storekeepers and their employees were dragged outside, or thrown over walls and left lying in the street. One witness of the slaughter [the trader Charles W. Enders] declared he had even seen two corpses fall on the heads of some young Mexican children.

One of the statements given to Manuel Terán Lira came from Apolinar Hernández Sifuentes, who was nine years old in 1911. Apolinar states that the most serious looting took place in the open market, and was carried out by rebel soldiers, inhabitants of Torreón, and others from Gómez and Lerdo, including women and children. Terán doesn't openly state it, but it seems very likely that Apolinar was one of those children who participated in the genocide.

Urquizo employs cruel humor to describe the reaction of certain Torreón residents:

In that store [García Hermanos, owned by Spaniards], Benito worked as an assistant, and as soon as he realized the gunfire was dying down, he ran into the street, grabbed a rifle from the first body he came across, and got ready to fight. There were no federales left, because they had fled, but there were several hundred Chinese who they said had taken part in the defense of the plaza, and he went after them. . . .

From that moment, Benito declared himself a rebel, and when the ruckus finished, he went marching smugly triumphant through the main streets, boasting of his feats.

"How many shots did you fire?" his many friends and acquaintances asked the popular Benito.

"Just ten, but not one of them missed its mark. . . . A bullet a Chinaman!"

From then on, Benito was known as "A bullet a Chinaman."

It was not yet even eight in the morning. Consul George Carothers was still locked away safely in his house, afraid to go outside. Dr. Lim was relieving pain, suturing wounds and treating them against infection at his post in the Red Cross station: he hadn't heard news of what was going on.

Juan Puig says:

Someone discovered that many of the Chinese carried cash— undoubtedly their savings—in Mexican and American bills hidden in their shoes. This news immediately spread and, very soon, as the Chinese deaths mounted, people dove for their feet, and therefore their money, which at times was no small amount.

While the urban massacre worsened, a group of fifty insurgents occupied Dr. Walter J. Lim's country house to the east of the city, halfway between the market gardens and the Alameda: a chalet with wavy tiles and redbrick walls, in the front garden of which grew two small mulberry trees Lim himself had planted a couple of years before in a fit of entrepreneurial hubris: the desire to convert a region famous for its cotton plantations into a producer of silk. The man in charge of the house was Ten Yen Tea, the doctor's brother-in-law. But Ten wasn't at home when the Republican Liberation Army appeared; the occupation had surprised him in Torreón, and he had had to hide in an apartment in the center of town with ten of his compatriots.

The band of men who came to the chalet found two young boys, Ten's wife, and the couple's eldest daughter, a girl of fourteen. Lim says that they "humiliated his sister horribly." Those who have studied the case coincide in reading this phrase as a euphemism for rape. It is more difficult to be certain about what happened to his teenage niece. In his testimony, the Chinese doctor states that the soldiers pointed their rifles at her, and forced her to promise to marry them. Whether they also sexually abused her, and the family opted to bury the crime, or the Maderistas still had an ounce of humanity left in them, and so made do with psychological torture, is impossible to ascertain. Later, Lim's family was thrown out of the building that, a century later, would become the Museo de la Revolución.

Where were Emilio Madero, Jesús Agustín Castro, and Orestes Pereyra, indisputable victors of the day, while all this was going on? I fear they had overslept. And neither is there any information on the whereabouts of Sixto Ugalde when his troops were murdering the members of the Chinese colony, although his later interrogation suggests he was already present in Torreón. Those ringleaders would never be accused of negligence. And neither would General Emiliano Lojero. It was all, according to the version favored by Mexican historians, the application of a "psychological law," a dreadful crime perpetrated by "the poor."

The climax came when various gangs (smaller, more savage versions of the numerous bands) came together in Plaza 2 de Abril, the nerve center of Torreón. They marched to the provisional offices of the Banco de La Laguna (the building now known, somewhat confusingly, as the Banco Chino), looted it, and attempted unsuccessfully to open the vault. Others went to the Wah Yick company and the premises of the Asociación Reformista China, located in the same building on the junction of Hidalgo and Cepeda. It is possible that in this faceless mass of horsemen and foot soldiers, ordinary citizens, men, women, and children, were some of the Maderistas mentioned earlier as being responsible for the crime of inciting hatred: Cresencio and Manuel Soto, Lázaro Sifuentes, and Plácido Orduña. But there is not a shadow of a doubt that—as Macrino J. Martínez's investigation established—the cavalry captain Benjamín Argumedo was among the people at the head of the crowd.

In the city lived a tailor named Tyko Lindquist. His house—a lovely building, still standing today—was on the corner of Juárez and Colón, a couple of streets west of the Alameda. Tyko and his wife, Eva, hid Woo Lam Po—front man for Kang Youwei, secretary of the Asociación Reformista, and member of the board of the Banco China—during the hours of the massacre. In the Wah Yick offices were employees who rented the four rooms on the upper floor as living space (for example, Kah Shi Jock, the company cashier, and Wong Ken Dai, in charge of the supply chain of Do Sing Yuen's market garden). Other rooms in the building were occupied by a group of travelers whose original destination had been Chihuahua but who had been stranded in Torreón due to the war. In addition, there were the staff and guests of the Hotel del Ferrocarril, who came to seek refuge there during the siege. They were approximately twenty-five in number. There is a remote possibility that an armed guard was with them. What is more likely is that one of them had a pistol. When the gang began to break down the doors and shout racist threats, someone fired on the crowd from inside the building: or such is the opinion of Ramos Pedrueza, after hearing dozens of witness statements. A highly detailed piece of local lore has it that one bullet was embedded in a horse's rump. In his declaration to Judge Martínez, Benjamín Argumedo describes those scant shots as "heavy gunfire." He admits that, in response, he ordered his men:

"Kill the Chinese."

The soldiers and mass of civilians broke down the door, raced up the stairs, and shot the Chinese dead in the rooms where they found them, then took the bodies into the street through the door, or threw them out windows. Each time a Cantonese body fell into the middle of Avenida Hidalgo, people milled around it to see who would be the first to get his hands on the money in the shoes. Some of the bodies—mutilated and possibly not yet dead—had lassos strung around their necks or feet and were dragged several blocks behind horses. One Mexican man came to a window of the Wah Yick and threw out a decapitated Chinese head.

After this, the mob launched itself on the adjoining building: the El Puerto de Shanghai department store, one of the most luxurious in the city. The same scene played out there: members of the Asian community were taken out into the street and executed by gunshots, machete blows, or kicks and punches. In the meantime, another group rolled the strong box out of the Wah Yick, and spent some time shooting and hacking at the lock before it gave way. Inside they found Mexican and foreign currency, and a pile of gold coins, amounting to a total—according to official figures—of 100,000 pesos: around four centuries of wages for the average worker in La Laguna.

Juan Puig says:

From one of these establishments—probably on one of the balconies of the Asociación Reformista—flew the brightly colored flag of imperial China: a blue horizontal dragon extending its claws toward a red moon on a yellow background [I think it was in fact golden]. There was no lack of people ready to tear it from the flagpole and trample it in the street.

Everything seems to indicate that Dr. William "Billee" Jamieson was not in the square during the killings. But his account, written just nine days after the events, communicates a clear idea of the horror of the surviving foreign residents. A horror in which death and material loss form a rigorous palimpsest:

Little children were stood up against the wall and shot down, crying "*No me matan*" (Don't kill me). Chinese women were served the same way. Mounted troopers rode to the outskirts of the town and dragged Chinamen in to the plaza by the hair to execution. Some took refuge in the Casino, the fine $250,000 club of the city. The mob entered and after killing them sacked the place, leaving it an utter ruin. I saw one fellow with a fine heavy plush silk curtain which he was using for a saddle blanket.

His consternation is echoed by Juan Puig in a dizzyingly Balzacian paragraph:

And the same went for the writing desks, carpets, ebony-work veneer, the silver inkstands, the notebooks bound in fine leather, the chairs, typewriters, sofas, blinds, a great deal of printed, handwritten and typed paper, and the doors, and almost everything that wasn't partition wall, beams, or rails. The river of people who had flooded the [Wah Yick] building departed shouldering all these objects, and many others they had taken from the upper rooms: underwear, and outdoor clothing, "Chinese writing boxes," bedclothes, mattresses, headboards, pillows, small bottles of "Chinese medicines," paintings, portraits, empty frames, shoes and slippers, handkerchiefs and shirts, and dressing gowns, and silk pajamas, books in Chinese, felt hats, spectacle cases . . .

It was not yet nine in the morning.

J. Wong Lim (or Sam or Walter, as he was also called) came to the door of José María Rodríguez's Red Cross station. He watched curiously as a group of revolutionaries made their way to Don Julián Lack's department store; they were firing into the air and howling. He followed their progress until they arrived at the French shoe store, and saw them disappear down Calle Juárez. He stood at the door for another twenty minutes. During all that time, no one spoke to him of his people's misfortune.

Not far away, the various bands had regrouped. They were crossing the city repeating Benjamín Argumedo's order to kill the Chinese and loot their possessions. One of the groups headed west, toward Calle Zaragoza, where Chon Lee's restaurant was located.

They forced the lock. Inside were seven workers and the two owners (Puig speculates they may have been brothers), plus another five
people. All fourteen perished.

Another contingent made for the open market and attacked the
vegetable vendors, destroying their stalls and killing three Chinese.
A third band headed for the steam laundry, seven or eight streets
east of the Banco Chino.

The laundry belonged to Foon-chuck and was splendid: it employed over twenty men, had an enormous cauldron, and a staff
canteen with its own chef. The back wall gave onto La Vizcaína
lumberyard, owned by a professor of uncertain age with an interest
in business studies: Don José Cadena.

All the employees of the laundry were hidden on the premises.
The manager, Wong Nom Jung, and four assistants had slipped between the many stacks of firewood used to heat the cauldron. The
cook hid in the kitchen. The cashier from the Hotel del Ferrocarril
had also come there to find a hiding place: he dived into the well.
When they discovered what was awaiting them, the rest of the staff
ran to the far end of the patio.

The pack hunting the Chinese broke down the door and ran-
sacked the room with the frenzy of a predator that has already
tasted blood. The first thing they took was the wood.

"Smells of Chink," someone is said to have remarked. Then someone else said, "There's a Chinaman here!"

They dragged the men from their hiding place and riddled them
with bullets. The bodies were thrown into the street; two were las-
soed and dragged behind horses.

The cook was found by someone attempting to steal his serving
dishes. He was shot.

Juan Puig continues:

Practically nothing that could be carried or pulled out was left
in the building. Samuel Graham, an elderly American trader
who had lived in Mexico for almost twenty-five years, three of
them in Torreón, witnessed an attack on two laundrymen: he

then asked those who passed carrying their booty why they had killed them: "We don't like 'em," one man replied. [Graham] also saw the plunder his serving man managed to grab: a hand-cart, a cooking pot, a pane of glass from a lattice window, and a lot of firewood. This man's wife was with him, but her hands were empty and she was crying: she had seen another two Chinese laundrymen being killed.

There exists a photograph taken by Gustavo G. Fernández. In the background a number of horsemen are outlined against a wall and what appears to be a large porch, the ground is muddy and lit-tered with a variety of objects: rods, small tables, bundles of clothes, saucepans . . . A woman is crossing the area in the foreground, wearing a white rebozo. The figure that stands out most clearly is also a woman, wearing long, flowing, dark petticoats, and walking toward the camera carrying an enormous box full of *avances*.

The terrified survivors of the steam laundry attack escaped by climbing the wall at the back of the premises and jumping into La Vizcaína before the Maderistas searched the patio. The cashier from the Hotel del Ferrocarril was not so lucky: a Mexican man discovered him at the bottom of the well and shot him dead. Not to take anything from him besides his life. Just because he could.

On the other side of the wall, in the carpentry workshop, the laundrymen and ironers came across a servant with a very fit-ting name: Clemente. The man called to his master, Don José, and showed him the fugitives, none of whom spoke Spanish. It seems that one of them managed to make himself partially understood but, as Puig rightly points out, explanations were unnecessary: you only had to go out into the street and see what was happening to understand the dark shadows of their panic. José Cadena became one of the heroes of the first capture of Torreón, one whose valor is shrouded in silence: no museum or street is dedicated to his mem-ory. He was a small-town prof who, risking his life and the lives of his family, saved twenty migrant workers by hiding them from the hatred.

At about nine in the morning in Gómez Palacio, the British vice-consul and gentleman of the Order of St. George and St. Michael, Herbert Ashley Cunard Cummins, received news that Maderista troops had entered Torreón in the early hours. He pulled on a Red Cross armband and drove there in a car. When he had covered half the distance, a man who introduced himself as Emilio Madero's secretary caught up with him and explained that his boss was ordering the vice-consul to do what he was going to do anyway: go in person to Torreón, where—according to Don Emilio's criteria—relief services were needed. I infer from this declaration that Madero was already aware of the massacre. What I can't work out is how Madero failed to arrive in the city until almost an hour after Cunard Cummins.

While Cunard was continuing on his way from Gómez Palacio, Consul George C. Carothers was still locked up in his house for safety.

Also about nine, or perhaps a little later, Walter J. Lim (or Wong, or Sam) saw townspeople pass by his Red Cross station carrying "many goods, including clothing and groceries."

"Where did you get all that?" he asked one of them.

"From a Chinese store—a Maderista gave it to me."

A car pulled up beside the doctor and a fellow Red Cross worker got out.

"There are a great many Chinese dead and injured in the streets," he finally informed Wong, after three hours of executions.

"Why?"

"I don't know."

They put two stretchers into the vehicle and headed for the Plaza de Armas, just a few blocks away. When they arrived, the Chinese doctor—slightly stunned, I would imagine—realized he was in danger, as he would later testify to Ramos Pedrueza:

At that time, many Maderistas who saw me began to shout they would kill me, and for that reason the man who was with me in the car ran off, leaving me alone, and even though I had the Red Cross insignia on my left arm, and was still wearing the white coat I had on to treat the wounded, they did not respect me, and some Maderistas began to order me to get out of the automobile so they could kill me, while others on horseback tried to defend me: in that way, we reached the corner of the Hotel Central, where a number of Maderistas repeated they would kill me, pointing their weapons at me, while others defended me until, finally, several events were my salvation.

(Lim inside his moving car, one band jumping onto the running boards, hood, and windscreen pointing rifles, and mounted troopers surrounding the vehicle, some with the intention of rescuing the driver and others wanting to kill him, was one of the first images of the massacre to be stamped in my memory. I wrote this book like someone attempting to restore a frame from an old film reel to understand what it refers to.)

A horseman then appeared who must have had some authority over the mob, because he managed to make his way through them, get Lim out of his vehicle, and, shielding him with his body, pull him up onto his horse and put him under protection until he could later bring him before Jesús Agustín Castro.

There must have been just a few minutes between Lim's rescue and the arrival of Cummins in the Plaza de Armas. The scene he describes was probably the same as what Lim saw: "the bodies of nine Chinese, two of them mutilated. In the street, trampled by the horses that filled it at that moment, were the corpses of two other Chinamen, covered in mud."

The vice-consul recounts that disciplined, well-armed troops were present by that time, patrolling the city without becoming involved in the killings, but not attempting to stop them either. One of these squadrons passed a very poor house with ideograms painted on the facade that a group of looters was trying to blow up. The troops stopped for a moment before continuing on their way, without offering the least assistance.

It was approaching ten in the morning, and a mixture of violence and consternation was boiling up in the city. Samuel Graham and Delfino Ríos testified that many townswomen were weeping in the streets at the sight of the bodies of the murdered migrants. But other women ran outside, shouting to inform the troops that there were Chinese hiding in their houses. The fugitives were dragged through the streets and riddled with bullets before they could defend themselves, to the satisfaction of those who had denounced them.

There was also—all accounts agree on this point—the blood of children spilled in the streets: the story of the soldier who took a boy of twelve by the feet and crashed his head into a post is confirmed by dozens of oral sources.

It is probable that an order had by then been issued to stop the murder, and it was known that the leaders of the rebellion—Madero, Castro, Pereyra—were due in the city at any moment. Nevertheless, the small genocide continued.

Erico Notholt, the Belgian consul in Torreón, lived on the corner of Morelos and Jiménez, three or four streets to the west of the Alameda. Opposite his house was a Chinese store that employed four assistants. Notholt maintained that those four had not only kept their distance from the Porfirian defense of the city but had been supporting the guerrillas since Saturday the thirteenth, giving them water and food. He said none of these actions were of any benefit to them: at around ten in the morning, the store was looted, and a couple of men on horseback took two of the assistants a few blocks away. Notholt stated that he did not see the executions, but heard the gunshots in the distance. He also testified that a short time afterward he had an interview with Leonides González, chief of the nearest Maderista post, who confirmed the killing of the four Cantonese from the store. Notholt finally stated that Leonides confessed to having tried to save two of the four by hiding one in a bathtub and the other in a stove, but his bid was unsuccessful: his own men mutinied, and searched the post until the Cantonese were found. They were then shot in the street.

One of the instructions of the still-absent Emilio Madero was to transfer the Cantonese from the market gardens to the center of Torreón, undoubtedly with the intention of protecting them. The problem—one that, a century later, seems to have become a tradition in Mexico—was that he put this mission in the hands of the executioners themselves. The Cantonese were tied with ropes and had to trot alongside the Maderista horses. It had been raining and the ground was muddy. If one of the market gardeners slipped and fell, he was executed on the spot. There exists a statement—published by Dr. Sergio Corona Páez—made by a Brígida Cumpián de García, who saw "two boys, the sons of a certain Eusebio Casiano, owner of the maize mill near El Palomar," bringing in fourteen Chinese from the gardens, tied up and herded as if they were cattle. At a given moment, the Cantonese attempted to take refuge in the witness's house, so the two boys went after them. There was a kerfuffle, and Atanasio Sánchez, the woman's neighbor, came out to see what was going on. Doña Brígida explained (and in this we can see the type of love some of the people of Torreón felt for the Chinese at that time) "that those boys brought out the Chinese, that she didn't know what they were going to do with them, and if they were going to do something, they should do it somewhere else, not in front of her house." Atanasio talked to the boys, and helped them to take the prisoners to a nearby open area. Two minutes later, Brígida Cumpián de García heard gunshots but remained indoors. When she finally did show her face, she saw the bodies of the fourteen Cantonese immigrants some thirty steps from her house.

There is no record of how many of the workers in the market gardens were "rescued" in that way; only eleven made it downtown alive.

Something similar happened in the city. Ten Yen Tea later told Lim that the ten survivors in his group were shot in the back while they were being brought to the Hotel Salvador. Seven died. It is not known how or why the Maderistas chose whom to kill and whom to let live.

In the cool morning air, at ten o'clock, Emilio Madero, Jesús Agustín Castro, and Orestes Pereyra finally entered the city. They set up their headquarters in the Hotel Salvador, a pretty building designed by Federico Wulff, that still stands (although practically in ruins) on the corner of Zaragoza and Hidalgo. While Emilio was settling in, Jesús Agustín dispatched the first matter of the day: the eleven Chinese brought from the market gardens (they had been accused of firing sporadically on the Maderistas since Saturday) and Dr. Lim, recently rescued from the mob, were brought before him. Without making any distinction between them, or checking the facts, Castro ordered the twelve men to be sent to Gómez Palacio as prisoners.

Professor José Cadena made an attempt to communicate to some of the commanders that he had approximately twenty survivors of the massacre hidden on his premises, and that he feared for both their lives and his own. No one spoke to him.

In the meantime, the American consul, George C. Carothers, heard of the arrival of the principal Maderista leaders. He decided to remain in his house a little longer before contacting them, just in case.

Several witness statements confirm that the massacre continued until four in the afternoon. I believe—as does Juan Puig—that most of the victims had already been killed by ten in the morning. There were, no doubt, isolated executions, which the newly arrived Maderistas (Castro's and Pereyra's men) tried to halt by persuasion, and occasionally by force (Delfino Ríos says with sabers; I'd say most probably with machetes). The Chinese were either in hiding or dead, and Emilio Madero had just ordered the survivors to be transferred to an improvised place of refuge (in practical terms, a concentration camp): the Arce lumberyard. The ringleader appointed by Madero to guard the Chinese community was Plácido Orduña, a man for whom an arrest warrant would be issued in 1912 for having taken part in the killings.

In addition to protecting Woo Lam Po, the Lindquists (Tyko and Eva) offered refuge that morning to between fourteen and sixteen Chinese who worked in the restaurant opposite their house. This was achieved by trickery: they placed a table at their front door with beer and sweet cakes served by a pretty Mexican girl. The Maderistas came there six times during the hours of the massacre to demand that the Chinese be handed over. "Each time Mrs. Lindquist refused, insisting they wait till the *comandante* arrived." Later, when the hatred had simmered down, Dr. Billee Jamieson was chosen by Mrs. Lindquist to escort these refugees across the city to the Arce lumberyard. He fulfilled his duty, sweating with every step, fearing the people of Torreón would throw themselves on him and tear him apart along with the Cantonese.

In the ruins of the restaurant, now without food or water, some seventy other Cantonese were hidden; among them was a child called Wong. They spent the night there.

Emilio Madero made his first public appearance before midday— I don't know where, but logically it would have been in Plaza 2 de Abril—and read a proclamation declaring martial law, ordering the suspension of attacks on the Chinese on pain of death, and offering a twenty-four-hour amnesty for the return of stolen goods. He also stated that anyone found in possession of such goods after a period of forty-eight hours would be brought before a firing squad. Tulitas Jamieson says "people began bringing back the things they had stolen. A dry irrigation channel was filled with typewriters. . . ."

On the outskirts of the city, a mounted trooper with "orders from high up" (I imagine from Madero) reached the gang holding J. Wong Lim and the other eleven survivors prisoner. He informed his fellow rebels they could take the eleven market gardeners, but should immediately free the Chinese doctor, as he was a Red Cross volunteer; a vehicle was summoned to take him back to Torreón, accompanied by the soldier who carried his order of safe conduct. They had scarcely started out on the return journey when a group of Sam's or Wong's or Walter's friends came out to meet them, recommending that they should go no farther: Torreón was still an extremely dangerous place for a Chinese man. Authorized by the Maderistas, Lim set out again for Gómez Palacio and took refuge in the Red Cross headquarters, where he spent the night.

It seems that news reached Carothers via the Hotel Central,

adjoining his house. By midday he had heard about the massacre, but it was not until three in the afternoon, when his compatriot W. S. Conduit drove to his house, that he mustered the courage to act. He had received reports that Emilio Madero was lunching in the Hotel Sterneau. Still wary of going out into the street, George sent Conduit with a message for the revolutionary leader. Emilio went straight to the consul's home to give him a personal guarantee of safe conduct for the people he had given refuge to (among them the tax official Villanueva), express his "consternation" at the anti-Chinese acts, and assure Carothers that his people were now under control. This said, he left.

Madero was not lying, but his words need qualification.

The Chinese were no longer being killed: between 180 and 200 of them ended up in the Arce lumberyard, where they were treated as prisoners rather than victims. Their transfer there was the responsibility of Sabino Flores, one of the many ringleaders who lied consistently, and to any official body, about the role of the Chinese community in the defense of the city. The first investigation, conducted by Sixto Ugalde, came to an end that same afternoon with the arrest of the herbalist José María Grajeda as being solely responsible for more than two hundred homicides. The malicious slander that the Chinese died as Porfirian combatants was confirmed at all times by the revolutionary forces. There were even attempts made, after May 16, to obtain forced confessions.

And there were, of course, the corpses: Wong Pack Cuiy, Wong Chew Yong, Fang Hong Mow, Leong Ping Toy, and eight more. The bodies of Kang Shai Jack, manager of the Wah Yick bank, and of Ching Mon King, grocer; of Ching Pin Con and Ching Pin Quon, probably brothers, and owners of La Plaza de Armas restaurant. The remains of Tang Cong, Lio Tong Lon, and Lio Tack Toy in El Puerto de Hon Nam. The murder of the cook Low Son, and the traders Pack Tin Chong and Pack Tin Suy, in Chon Lee's restaurant. The extermination of Mar Tu Lean and Mar Young in the Pabellón Mexicano; of the machinist Wong Hong Quong; of Wong Ken Hing, secretary of the Asociación Reformista China.

The shattered skulls of Woo Kim Young and Wong Yong . . . The dead: names that, because they seem exotic, have been denied the right to be remembered in Mexico.

In his *Chronicle of Torreón*, Sergio Corona Páez published a fragment of a declaration made on May 15, 1911, by Srta. Dolores Ramírez, a native of Fresnillo, Zacatecas, and head nurse at the Torreón hospital. She stated she had personally checked 130 of the 206 bodies of the Celestial subjects she knew of:

> The bodies of the Chinese brought in presented a variety of wounds, some from firearms, and others had suffered machete blows, some with their skulls fractured, or even completely split open, but the majority had bullet wounds to either the heart or the forehead.

When I asked him about this, Corona Páez replied: "That declaration is forensic evidence that the Chinese were unarmed when they were slaughtered. No army has sufficiently good marksmen to hit the majority of enemy soldiers in the heart or the head. And you have to strike at a particular angle to split the skull of someone in two, wielding a machete: I'm talking about an unarmed man on foot being attacked from horseback."

In the afternoon, Jesús Agustín Castro (after all, he was twenty-three: still a child with a new toy) organized a triumphal march of his troops, unconcerned that the streets were littered with bodies (and, what's more, civilian bodies belonging to a specific race). There were sixty-nine corpses on Calle Hidalgo, another fourteen on Zaragoza, eleven more on Juárez, the same number on Abasolo, four on Morelos, and thirty-six on Valdez Carrillo. The Republican Liberation Army rode past those bodies in their first display of public spirit. The only person to note the ferocity (or at least the lamentable lack of decorum) of the parade, worthy perhaps of Genghis Khan, but not of an army that has just taken up arms in the name of democracy, was a more experienced xenophobe than any mestizo: Vice-Consul Cummins. Halfway through the march, he approached the boy commander sporting a Moorish beard and—with great discretion and courtesy, I imagine—pointed out that perhaps "it was time to start the burials." Castro again displayed the intemperance of youth: he gave Cummins command of twenty Maderistas and ordered him to deal with the remains of the small genocide in an attitude that seemed to say, "Why should I?" or "Do it yourself."

Herbert Ashley Cummins led the troops placed under his command to the City of the Dead and ordered them to dig a mass grave just outside the walls. It seems clear to me that his choice of location was—in a very English way—pragmatic and puritanical: as close as possible to where the dead should be laid, but not in hallowed ground, since they were not Christians.

Puig says:

> The cemetery manager put three carters at his disposal—one of them was Spanish—to load the bodies into a similar number of pack mule wagons. This funeral cortege was joined by two nurses from the Civil Hospital, named Elena and María; the five of them collected the dead Chinese, transported them in piles to the ditch, and Agustín Castro's men threw them in, one on top of the other. The great majority were naked, and some of the bodies had obviously been mutilated.

Before nightfall, the businessman and—in his own description—amateur photographer Hartford Harold Miller Cook set up his camera by the road to the cemetery and took a shot of the back of a wagon loaded with bodies. One section of the *guayín* is reflected in a large puddle, as if the water wished to stress the enormity or illusory nature of any form of destruction.

Bernabé Miranda, an eyewitness whose testimony was transcribed years later by Terán Lira, recounts the following:

> When the first wagons were full of bodies piled one atop the other, and they set off for La Alianza, a lot of us kids went after

them . . . and when we took a look [into the mass grave] we
saw them walking about down there, trampling on the Chinks,
searching their pockets and slippers, and taking gold coins from
them, some loose, some in small bags they carried at their waists
or under their shirts.

Cunard Cummins set the operation in motion, checked that
everything was going smoothly, and then at six in the afternoon
washed his hands of the whole affair; he left the Mexicans to bury
the Chinese. The cemetery manager (his name doesn't appear in
the archives) stayed to the end, and so was able to later testify that
a number of the cadavers were decomposing. It seems likely that
the carters had made the effort to go to the market gardens to collect the remains there. The digging, collection of the bodies, and
their burial must have continued well into the night. The manager
counted 205 bodies in the largest of the mass graves.

(Later, 70 more bodies were discovered in two smaller graves
under the waterwheels in El Pajonal.)

Professor José Cadena had a tough day in La Vizcaína. He
struggled against the terror of the Chinese survivors, whose language was incomprehensible to him, and whose first instinct was
to run as far from Torreón as their legs would carry them. He was
also concerned that his property might be affected by the wave of
looting. That night, when the city was calmer, he returned to the
Hotel Salvador and asked, for the second time, to talk to someone.
He was received by Orestes Pereyra. Don José explained his pre-
dicament and the fifty-year-old guerrilla agreed to offer him two
armed guards. Then, at around half past ten, Orestes sent an armed
detachment, and twenty of the Chinese were escorted to the concentration camp in the Arce yard.

Juan Puig does not specifically refer to Cadena's Chinese, but he
does describe the condition of the majority of the survivors:

They were forcibly held there for three days, without being given
anything to eat or drink, and forbidden to leave. At midnight

on one of those days, "a number of Maderistas," Lim stated three months later, "cruelly" beat up some of the Chinese, and then "searched" everyone, and took whatever money they had on them, in this way gathering a "fair sum."

At the end of the declaration he made to Bassett and Ramos on August 12, 1911, the Belgian consul, Erico Notholt, mentioned the person who may have been the last victim of the small genocide:

"Do you have anything else to add?" asked Bassett.

"On the night of Monday or Tuesday," replied Erico, "at around eleven, a Chinese man was killed right in front of our window by four Maderistas on horseback. The Chinaman made no use of arms."

"How did they kill him?"

"His head was split in two from nose to crown."

"By a machete?"

"I believe it was a bullet. The body was left there in the street until the following day, at around eleven. That night when they killed the Chinaman, I thought to go out to the street to see what was happening. They told me four Maderistas were killing a Chinaman. The soldiers were talking in loud voices, and I asked them why they were making such a din. They told me they were arguing about which of them had killed the Chinaman."

"Are you aware of any member of the revolutionary forces being killed by the Chinese?"

"No. I only saw them bringing them out."

From Tuesday, May 16, to Friday, May 19, 1911

On Tuesday, the seventy Chinese hiding in the remains of a restaurant in downtown Torreón woke without water. Without water or food, but safe from the gunfire. They decided to stay there one more day, just in case.

A certain Cristino Hernández heard of the pitiful situation of Orduña's almost two hundred Asian prisoners in the Arce lumberyard: they had not been fed or given anything to drink either. Cristino went to visit them, taking what he could: bread, water, coffee, cigarettes. (I know of no more humanitarian gesture than that of providing tobacco to captives: far from attempting to save them, it imbues them with a lighthearted pleasure, reminding them of that fleeting, inadequate saddlebag we call dignity.) While they were smoking beside him, some of the Cantonese described to Cristino in their pidgin Spanish the abuses they had been subjected to throughout the night.

At three in the afternoon, J. Wong Lim left the Red Cross station in Gómez Palacio and made his way to the barracks commanded by Juan Ramírez, where the eleven gardeners the Maderistas had captured along with him were being detained. Lim requested an audience with the ringleader, and interceded on his compatriots' behalf, but Ramírez refused to release them: he said six of the men had fired at the insurgent troops during the siege. Sam asked for the eleven men to be brought in, and interrogated them in Cantonese. They all denied the accusation. Juan Ramírez had them returned to their cell and, in a display of political perspicacity, ordered the Chinese doctor to talk to them again and persuade six of them—it made no difference which—to plead guilty. Lim entered the cells and questioned them one by one. He left with the conviction that the eleven were innocent.

"Who is accusing them?" he asked.

Juan Ramírez called for a soldier, who said another soldier (whom he could not identify, even by his first name) had assured him the Chinese had fired on the Maderistas in the market gardens.

After a great deal of insistence, Walter J., or Sam, or JW managed to have the gardeners freed under his personal signed guarantee.

●●●●●

On Wednesday morning, a Cantonese boy named Wong came to Carothers. He said that he had assisted Dr. Lim in the Red Cross center during the siege and, rather than guarantees, requested drinking water for the seventy survivors he was representing: those taking refuge in the ruins of the restaurant. The consul took up a collection from members of the foreign community to fund provisions for the group. It was this gesture that reactivated humanitarian feeling in La Laguna.

Lim returned from Gómez Palacio to Torreón. There is no record of his meeting Woo Lam Po or Foon-chuck, the other leaders of the local Chinese community, but it is known that he had an interview with Emilio Madero, in which he demanded guarantees for his people. After convincing the doctor he was on his side, the morose Emilio added another pearl to the necklace of inconsistencies in his faction's investigation of the massacre: he appointed Sabino Flores as representative of the Liberation Army, so he and Lim could make a tour of the market gardens.

The prisoners in the Arce lumberyard were freed that Thursday. Collections were soon under way to feed and clothe them.

As Emilio Madero had arranged, Walter J. and Sabino Flores toured El Pajonal and found it deserted. They went to Lim's country house, where the statements given by his sister and her children finally broke the doctor's spirit. "When I had visited all the houses, businesses, country estates, and all the Chinese residences in general, with true pain, which my pen cannot express, I felt absolute desolation."

On Friday, Lim spoke to George C. Carothers. "He seemed to be stupefied, and not know what was to be done," said the United States consul months afterward. And in this way, the Chinese doctor exited the story: shattered by reality. His leadership of the community evaporated in 1911.

That night, or maybe even the day before—Billee Jamieson does not clearly remember—the La Laguna Maderistas organized a ball in the rooms of the steam laundry. It was their version of a deeper symbolism: dancing on the skulls of the dead.

A MONSTER COURSE

In November 2014, the Mexican arts organization Fondo de Cultura Económica (FCE) invited me to lead a workshop in Apatzingán, Michoacán. It was part of a cultural assistance program aimed at child and young adult victims of the violence generated by confrontations in the Tierra Caliente region between drug trafficking cartels and civil authorities. I accepted. The workshop was called "A Monster Course."[11]

We opened the event with a reading of "The Blue Bouquet,"[12] a short story by Octavio Paz in which a tourist is threatened by a man who wants to gather a bouquet of blue eyes to give to his beloved. I then asked the children two questions: What kind of a monster would you be if you wanted to threaten someone? And, why—as is the case in Paz's story—should you be forgiven? It's easier to imagine oneself as the executioner than the victim. Almost all the girls imagined themselves as vampires or ghosts. Almost all the boys were werewolves or zombies. One very shy girl decided to be a dragon. The eldest in the group, a kid of eighteen or nineteen (in addition to having completed his technical baccalaureate, he was a reporter and, as I later discovered, had worked for the cartels for a couple of years), opted for a serial killer; I adduce that realistic monsters are the most powerful. Naturally, I declared myself an ogre. For three days, we lived and experimented with these avatars; we created stories and poems, gave readings, and produced four short movies. The reader can find the resulting material on the website uncursodemonstruos.tumblr.com.

Our mythic condition gave me the chance to hear some of their stories. I discovered that the former director of Conalep, the institution that hosted the event, was an active member of the Knights

11. "Un curso de monstruos"
12. "El ramo azul"

Templar cartel, and had been in charge of recruiting thugs and drug dealers from among his own pupils. I met a fifteen-year-old who had spent weeks in the hospital after a beating he received from national soldiers when he was found in possession of a stash of crystal meth. I had lunch with a girl whose ambition was to be a writer, singer, and comedian, and whose father had first been hounded out of Apatzingán by La Familia Michoacana (the man, his wife, and their children moved to Tijuana), then arrested and sentenced to thirty years' imprisonment, before finally being exonerated by the authorities and organized crime in exchange for his life savings.

I feel slightly bad about sharing these stories: I'd intended to keep them to myself. That's why I haven't given the names of those involved. But without those accounts, I would be unable to testify that in Apatzingán there is a handful of wonderful kids trying to get by, swimming upriver against a current of shit.

Three emotionally exhausting days. After the morning workshops, I spent the afternoons (and part of the evenings) exploring the city. It wasn't so easy: the FCE had assigned two women, whose day job it was to encourage reading habits, to act as my chaperones; they did show me around, but they also made sure I didn't go to dangerous neighborhoods, seedy bars, the corners where cocaine and crystal meth were sold. I managed to escape a couple of times, but the truth is the Apatzingán I saw was never the real one: little more than the extreme tourist version, under the protection of Mexican institutional culture. They took me to the cultural center, which was being renovated, and from there we went to a nearby seafood restaurant that, according to my hosts, had been the great center of power of La Familia Michoacana cartel, and later the Knights Templar, and was now one of the haunts of the Tierra Liberada, with live music, smiling children, the whole kit and caboodle.

There was a kind of uneasy fiesta feel about the city: the self-defense groups and the federal government had won out over the cartels without doing each other too much harm. But it wasn't difficult to predict that this balance couldn't last. Not a few of the people

I talked to (young and old alike) insisted that the infiltration of the criminal gang Los Viagras (I'd never before heard of them) into the self-defense groups, plus the intransigence and impunity of the army and federal police, augured a flare-up of the war.

Despite all this, while I was walking near the main square in the early morning—risking my life, as became clear after the massacre on January 6—I had my illusions: "It could be," I mused, trying to convince myself that the Mexican government might be something more than a factory for the manufacture of unpleasantness. "Maybe coming here to do 'A Monster Course' has meant something. Something very small. Very small, but perhaps worth the effort."

•••••

On Sunday, April 16, 2015, I found a report by Laura Castellanos on the internet: "It Was the Feds." The document, based on thirty-nine taped witness statements, photographs, anonymous declarations, and a couple of videos, reconstructed a massacre that had taken place on January 6, 2015, in Apatzingán, two months after "A Monster Course."

The official version, released on January 12 by Alfredo Castillo—at that time the regional security commissioner—states that an armed group occupied city hall and, while the building was being evacuated in the early hours of the morning, a civilian was run down and killed, and forty-four armed men were arrested. Castillo also declared that, hours later, in daylight, a paramilitary contingent ambushed a squad of federal police and, during the struggle, eight delinquents were killed in the crossfire: they had been riddled with bullets (mainly, but not exclusively) from their own side.

Laura Castellanos's version is quite different. The statements she taped—including (in addition to the voices of people directly involved) a cyclist, a taco vendor, neighbors, and passersby—established that the first attack was on unarmed rural defense volunteers, people doing their shopping for the Feast of the Epiphany, and the employees of businesses in the streets around the Plaza de Armas (the location of the hotel I stayed in during my visit): civilians. There is no way of knowing exactly how many people died that night. According to statements, the local community refused to report the disappearance of loved ones for fear of government reprisals.

Those who spoke up say that in the second phase of the massacre, the federal police used antitank weapons to disperse the youths carrying sticks and stones who were attempting to rescue the people detained in the early hours. It's also said that some of the latter group were bleeding heavily when they were taken away, but even so were not offered medical assistance by the authorities. There is then a photograph of the bodies of a community leader and his family (a woman and two children); they are lying on the asphalt, covered in blood, with various bullet wounds visible. The father has a gunshot wound to the head, execution style. The photographic evidence suggests the man was unarmed, and at least one witness reports seeing him lift his T-shirt to make that clear to the federal agents: a gesture that didn't keep them from killing him. There is also a recording of a radio dispatch in which members of the self-defense groups themselves stated that their colleagues were being shot by federal police. Medical reports are shown describing gunpowder residue on the craniums of other victims, forensic proof of execution. Several witnesses—whose identity Castellanos says she is protecting for fear of reprisals—identify at least sixteen extrajudicial executions in the recordings: they say the self-defense group members were kneeling with their hands raised when the police agents shot them in the head. Finally, there is a video showing a young man dying in the street. He is bleeding from what appear to be bullet wounds. Spasms course through his body. In the background, uniformed individuals can be made out. Despite the fact that they are not under fire, these individuals evade taking responsibility—no longer legal but humane—for helping the wounded youth.

Although I could give more details, I won't: my intention is to condemn not the events but the syntax. That is to say, in a fairer, humbler way, I'm interested in drawing a dual analogy. First, between the information the Mexican authorities issued about Apatzingán and Macrino J. Martínez's *Extracto* on the killing of the Chinese in Torreón. Second, between Antonio Ramos Pedrueza's *Informe* and the report written by Laura Castellanos.

Both the case of Commissioner Castillo in 2015 and that of the military judge Macrino J. Martínez in 1911 show a political stance attempting to justify its existence by laying claim to "historical truth" (the phrase is not mine, but comes from the attorney general Jesús Murillo Karam; he used it to refer to another emblematic case: the disappearance of forty-three student teachers in Ayotzinapa). Neither Castillo nor Macrino offers criminological, testimonial, or forensic groundings; just the perversion of a syllogism: the truth has authority; authority has power; therefore, the person who has power has the truth.

In technical (*technical*, not political) terms, Laura Castellanos's report is closer to the investigative methodology used by Antonio Ramos Pedrueza: he brings in voices from many different spheres; offers forensic data; shows the documents on which his judgments are based; presents a chronological structure: the temporal elements of the account alternate with the relevant evidence.

That the investigative reach of the highest authority in Mexico today can be likened to that of a rural military judge, while a young, independent journalist undertakes the investigation of an event with methodological resources not dissimilar to those of a former special attorney in 1911, gives a patent demonstration of the idiocy of power.

Repressing (and even eliminating) a particular group within the population, under the pretext of serving the public good and law and order, is nothing more (even when it has to do with criminals) than a schizophrenic illusion: the surreptitious legalization of chaos.

LATER

Who by fire?
Who by water?
Who in the sunshine?
Who in the night time?
Who by high ordeal?
Who by common trial?
Who in your merry, merry month of May?
Who by very slow decay?
And who should I say is calling?
Leonard Cohen

On Monday, May 22, 1911, Mexico's minister for foreign affairs, Francisco León de la Barra, received a wire from Shung Ai Süne, chargé d'affaires of the Chinese Empire: "Would your excellency please be so good as to tell me if this news is true." Included was a copy of another wire, sent from Piedras Negras by the businessman Wong Chan Kin: "I have received a message from my representative [in] Torreón, Coahuila, Mexico informing me that 224 of our compatriots were killed in the recent disturbances there." León de la Barra wrote to the governor of Coahuila, Jesús de Valle, inquiring about the events and, at the same time, responded to the Chinese official that the reports were "judged to be exaggerated." Those were the opening words of a novel that would continue to be written over the course of the next hundred years: the national fiction of a small genocide.

If León de la Barra's first reaction was to issue an unsupported opinion, the truth is that he investigated the affair with diplomatic seriousness after he was appointed interim president on May 25 and had received a wire from Coahuila confirming the news. Governor de Valle was unable to take charge of the inquiry: first, because he had no telegraph connection with (or authority in) La Laguna, which was by then in rebel hands. Second, he himself would be relieved of his office by the Maderista Venustiano Carranza. The person who did take charge of the investigation was Emilio Madero: on May 20 he set up an office for the purpose of recording accusations and formal complaints related to loss of material goods; it was open not only to Celestial subjects but to any inhabitant of Torreón. Macrino J. Martínez, the principal author of the second fictional chapter about the massacre, was promptly appointed by Madero as the military judge of the case. Denial gave way to calumny. Macrino stated in his conclusions that the reason for the deaths of the Chinese was that they had attacked the Republican Liberation Army. In order to sustain this verdict, he gave precedence to statements made by soldiers, falsified and deformed those of foreign residents, journalists, and Mexican civilians, cited nonexistent documents (for example, a supposed sworn statement by Lim in which eleven market gardeners had "confessed" their guilt to the rebel leader Juan Ramírez during their detention in Gómez Palacio), and generally managed to establish as historical truth what was in fact a political stance: the Maderista view of the events.

Macrino's *Extracto* (as it is known) was handed to Emilio Madero on July 15, and very soon reached León de la Barra. It included such gems as "As a humble citizen, and with the patriotic aim of saving our Government from being obliged to pay the Chinese Empire the substantial indemnity their government claims . . ."

Under pressure from León de la Barra, and concerned for *the dignity of the nation*, the relevant undersecretary for foreign affairs, Victoriano Salado Álvarez, asked his counterpart in the justice office, Jesús Flores Magón, to undertake another investigation. This one was at once rushed and sluggish: it was carried out from Mexico City, and didn't see the light of day until the end of December. The document names nine individuals against whom arrest warrants had recently been issued: José María Grajeda, Gonzalo Torres, Anastasio Saucedo, Benito Bradley, Anastasio Rosales (accused of having single-handedly killed nineteen Cantonese), Estrada Baca, Benigno Escajea, Aureliano Villa, and Florencio Menchaca. The first three of these had been imprisoned; the remaining six were, in December 1911, fugitives from justice, and were apparently never detained. Another investigation, carried out the following year by the governor of Coahuila, issued arrest warrants for, among others, Benjamín Argumedo, the Casiano brothers, plus Soto and Plácido Orduña. Not a single member of this second group ever saw the inside of a jail either.

International diplomatic efforts and the consequent reaction of the press revealed another scene in what would become a three-act political farce. Chargé d'Affaires Shung sent a wire to Ching Yi Kuang, the Chinese minister of foreign affairs, that read: "In the Mexican revolution, murder and arrest are carried out arbitrarily. Yesterday in Tsai Yüan, more than 200 Chinese were wounded and killed in deplorable circumstances." This telegram was published, and editorials were written in the most important Peking newspapers, plus others in Japan, Europe, and America.

Juan Puig recounts:

> Prince Ching then sent his emissaries to the Mexican Legation in China with a list of demands, formulated unofficially and in very polite but clear terms. In this missive, the Mexican government was requested to offer its condolences, apologize to the Chinese community, indemnify the dead and the survivors, protect the lives and property of Chinese citizens in Mexico, and punish those responsible for the events.

The man who received this communiqué in a diplomatic residence in Peking was a half-intrepid, half-obtuse personage whom I will soon have the opportunity to mention again: the chargé d'affaires, Pablo Herrera de Huerta. On May 26, Herrera offered his sympathy to China on behalf of the Mexican people but was careful not to include apologies or condolences from the state. This nuance is the third chapter of the anti-Chinese novel, and marked out the direction of Mexico's reception of the massacre: to this day, the government has not admitted responsibility.

In June, what later became the central topic of the massacre began to be debated: indemnity. China requested the equivalent of 60 million Mexican pesos in gold as compensation for the material and human losses. A racist tone tinged with humor, rooted in the Porfirian tradition rather than Maderismo, predominated in the national press regarding the following question: How much is a Chinaman worth? Chapter four of the novel: contempt was added to denial, calumny, and obfuscation.

On June 17, 1911—just over a month after the tragedy—an article defending the massacre appeared in *El Ahuizote*:

> In the price it puts on its subjects, China is not following any economic law: if we apply the law of supply and demand, taking into account the millions [of] excess Chinese in the Celestial Empire and other parts, instead of charging us a hundred thousand pesos a Chinaman, they should pay us for their eradication. But making great concessions to the human feelings of the Celestial citizens, we would agree to pay in the ratio of a hundred thousand Chinamen per peso, not a hundred thousand pesos per Chinaman.

Three jocular texts were published on June 29 in the magazine *Multicolor*. One, signed Karkabel and titled "An Interview with Chin-chun-chan," concludes, among other things, that the most a Chinaman can aspire to is ironing other people's shirts, the Chinese don't wash, even if they have just had a bath in shit, the Chinese deserve to die like rats because they cook rats, the Chinese boast of standing up to unbeatable opponents when they fire (apparently) on Maderistas, Chinese women are free whores ("the lan lalas"), Chinese migrants are slaves who have already been sold (or at least "pawned"), so their lives are worth very little, and (NB), the life of a Chinamen is not worth the same as that of a Mexican, since a Mexican doesn't wear a plait or even a pigtail.

A similar attitude is shown in a text signed V., published in the same issue of *Multicolor*:

Like any living creature, twice a week I'm visited by a Chink of the sort who dedicate themselves to healthful laundering. And to think I saw that Chink as a *thing* of little value . . . !

I believed you could get half a dozen for 75 centavos, but it turns out, according to the famous claim for damages, each one of them is worth a trifling 100 thousand pesos, FOB, because the people who are the cause of the claim are already freight.

Where would a Chinaman keep a cool 100 thousand pesos?

In his pigtail? Impossible: for a pigtail to be worth 100 thousand *machacantes*, it would have to be worn by a member of the Gaona or Machaco families of bullfighters.

How can a Chinaman earn 100 thousand *locos* in his laundryman's life?

Only in one way: washing all the dirty laundry of our politicians, which would need several million Celestials and many thousands of years.

The only way a Chinaman could earn such fabulous sums would be by dedicating himself to exterminating rats and, to my best knowledge, no such valuable a rat catcher has been known to this date.

The case is that they are claiming 100 thousand *gongos* for each son of Confucius.

Chole (a displaced Guadalajara woman) was right when, offering me a lock of her hair, she said: treasure this *chino* [in that city a curl is known as a chino], which is worth so much.

The third text is an anonymous song. In its attempts at wit, it states that China has sent a military cruiser called the *Tellor* to the Mexican coast, claims the empire has demanded the return of its subjects' pigtails, and compares the price of the dead Chinese with a "mother-in-law market," where there are no clients and that has been set up by the proprietor only to honor his own relative by marriage.

The cruiser was not a joke. Around that time, the *Hai-Chi* had in fact set out from China for the coronation of George V in England. In this respect, Puig says, it was

one of the most costly items in the imperial Chinese navy: built in England, with a crew of 452, a displacement of 4,300 tons, a maximum speed of 24 knots, and armed with two large, ten medium-sized and fifteen small gun turrets, six machine guns, and five torpedo tubes.

The ship sailed from Europe toward the East Coast of the United States and weighed anchor in Havana on October 2, 1911, but it never set out for Mexican shores.

In Asia, the Mexican reaction to the claims for indemnity and the crisis of the international image of the country was managed by two officials: Ramón Pacheco, the ambassador to China and Japan, stationed in Tokyo, and his subordinate, the above-mentioned chargé d'affaires in Peking.

Pablo Herrera de Huerta was born in Tacubaya, southwest of the capital. I don't believe he was the smartest bureaucrat of the Porfirian regime, or at least never had the requisite connections to make something of his life. But he was an extremely dedicated official: an upmarket salaryman. At the age of thirty, he gained his first junior appointment in an Italian mission. After that, he worked in the Archivo General de la Nación. In 1901 he was admitted to the Ministry of Foreign Affairs in an unsalaried post in the section dealing with Europe, Asia, and Oceania. He arrived in China in 1904 as third secretary (now salaried), and rose to chargé d'affaires, a post he held—with four breaks, during the last of which Alfonso Reyes stood in for him—for seventeen years. He went through terribly hard times when Venustiano Carranza, with his habitual acrimony, dismissed the officials of every embassy for having collaborated with Victoriano Huerta's government. Pablo rejoined the diplomatic service in 1919. In 1923 he left China, was sent to Guatemala, and, until 1934 (when, I guess, he retired after thirty years in service), occupied the post of chargé d'affaires (he was never an ambassador) in a variety of missions in America, including Washington, DC. He died in 1940. His communications on the massacre (he was forty-three when it occurred) offer a glimpse of the anxiety of a middle-rank official who hopes to stay on the right side of his patriotic duty and ascend the food pyramid of his ministry.

When tempers were most raw, and the Asian press was attacking Mexico on a daily basis, Herrera sent Undersecretary Carbajal a letter bordering on an act of villainy:

> There would be no difficulty in refuting the reportage in ques tion by pointing out the enormous difference between the events we are being reproached for, and the truly barbarous crimes that were committed here in 1900 [during the Boxer Rebellion]. The former are inherent in a state of war in every country in the world . . . while the Siege of the International Legations, and the murder of diplomatic agents (among them a German minister), carried out by troops under the orders of the Chinese government, are acts of savagery, unparalleled in the history of all nations.

Then, in the same letter, Pablo qualifies the preceding and contradicts himself: he states that saying such things in public would be offensive to the Celestial Empire, and that in fact the Chinese have been treating him with great courtesy of late. Reading between the lines, he also confesses that he fears for his safety because, since the killings, the imperial police have been watching his house. He concludes that it may not be the ideal moment to accuse the Chinese of savagery, but adds that later,

> when the inquiries have finished, and we have in our power indisputable facts (if you so consider them), I can make rectifications

and refute once and for all the tasteless articles in the press with
the reminder of the events of 1900, and many others, and it will
not be fear that impedes me from carrying out the instructions
I am given to the full, because our prudence has already been
much abused.

The letter reveals a cross-grain similarity between Mexico and
China: an excess of courtesy masking scorn for the other.

Ambassador Ramón Pacheco wasn't to be left lagging. On
June 29, he instructed Herrera to look into the amount of indemnity received by Chinese subjects who had suffered at the hands
of foreigners within the Celestial Empire itself. His objective was
to reduce the cost to the Mexican government. He even offered to
pay, out of his own pocket, for a voyage to the continent to take
charge of the investigation, since he was convinced "the life of a
Chinese has a minimum value of 10 or 20 pesos, and a maximum
of 150 to 200." The journey was approved but didn't end happily:
the train on which Pacheco was traveling to the east coast of Japan
went off the rails and he suffered a fracture. The person who established for Mexico the unitary price for dead Cantonese was, again,
Herrera de Huerta. He undertook the task with diligence and dis-
taste: there were (both in the empire and other countries) a great
many precedents supporting the demands of the Asian nation.

That same June, Shung, the Chinese chargé d'affaires in Mexico,
was relieved of his post. In his place came Chang Yin Tang, envoy
extraordinary and minister plenipotentiary in the United States,
Mexico, Cuba, and Peru of the emperor of China. The high rank of
this person, and the fact that he was based in Mexico City rather
than Washington, DC, as was usual, constitutes diplomatic pressure. In response, León de la Barra also moved his pieces, and
appointed Bartolomé Carbajal y Rosas undersecretary of foreign
relations.

The new Chinese mission set up an international investigative
commission that included Chang himself, Owyang King (his private secretary), the attorney W. Arthur Bassett, and, unofficially,

Judge Lebbeus R. Wilfley, who was familiar with the Asian context, having been attorney general in the Philippines and first judge of the United States Court for China. In early August, Owyang King and Bassett prepared to travel to Torreón to conduct interviews and gather statements. Keeping a careful eye on what was now an international chess game, and aware that, so far, the investigation had been pedestrian, Francisco León de la Barra moved one of his knights: he named the delegate and lawyer José Mónico Antonio Ramos Pedrueza as prosecutor.

Born in Parral in 1864, but resident in the capital from the age of ten, Ramos Pedrueza was the son of a lawyer, and his whole life was spent in the world of law. He graduated at the age of twenty-two, and then accepted a variety of judicial posts: court secretary, agent of the State Prosecution Service, judge, and, naturally, professor of law. At twenty-eight, he married Luz Mariscal y Piña, daughter of another legal family. The couple settled in the town of Tacuba.

Ramos Pedrueza served as a delegate on a number of occasions during Porfirio Díaz's governments, the last of which saw him in the Twenty-Fifth Legislature. Juan Puig considers him to have been sympathetic to Maderismo. This may be true, but, in his daily practice, he was a conservative legal consultant, as is shown by his views on criminology.

In *Criminal and Citizen in Modern Mexico*, Robert M. Buffington writes:

Antonio Ramos Pedrueza began his revolutionary-era course in penal law with a detailed discussion of the relative merits of classic and positivist criminology that attacked the underlying premises of Mexican criminal law. Taking inspiration from Italian criminologist Enrico Ferri, Ramos concluded that the rational criminal, the foundation of classic criminology, had never existed. "Observed reality in prisons and asylums affirms that delinquents are abnormal," he noted, "admitting nevertheless that they are very different and that the passage from hardened criminal type to normal human type is not a brusque transition but a series of gradations, just as in animal species."

Although this argument is pertinent (there is a glimmer of the notion that sociopaths and psychopaths exist), its absolute nature is unsustainable: it denies society's role in the crime. This theoretical perspective must have influenced the final verdict on the massacre.

Ramos Pedrueza was forty-seven when León de la Barra appointed him investigator. He was an upright citizen, lean and elegant, with a heavy graying mustache and a receding hairline. He requested 400 pesos in traveling expenses, and a fee of 3,000, to be paid on completion of his task. On August 10 he set out on a twelve-day visit to Torreón.

The international representatives (de la Barra's government never conceded them this rank: they considered the Americans to be mere private consultants to the Chinese) were in La Laguna during the same period. At first, it seemed as if the three of them— Owyang, Bassett, and Ramos Pedrueza—formed a single investigative commission and even undertook interviews together, as is demonstrated by the transcriptions presented by the Mexican investigator in his final report. Nevertheless, each team (Owyang and Bassett on one side; Ramos Pedrueza on the other) issued its own verdict. This gave rise to a debate, the legal niceties of which would be onerous to set down here, being more suitable for a quasi-biblical reading of international law than a *crónica*. I will, therefore, confine myself to narrating, *grosso modo*, the points of coincidence and divergence in the two conclusions.

The document of the imperial commission and Ramos Pedrueza's report, submitted on September 13, 1911 (the swiftness with which the Mexican investigator worked deserves praise: if only there were more like him), agree in denying any provocation on the part of the Cantonese community. The evidence was overwhelming. Not only is this version backed up by the testimonies of foreign residents in La Laguna—Cunard Cummins, George Carothers, Dr. Lim, Erico Notholt, Federico Wulff, and Charles W. Enders—

but there are also the facts that the city was lost due to a shortage of ammunition and that the Chinese community in Torreón was peaceful. Added to this were the flyers distributed by Woo Lam Po, and Ramos Pedrueza's claim to have gathered over a hundred oral testimonies from waiters, employees, officials, and middle-class townsfolk contradicting the Maderista version of events. One of the imperial commission's documents states Professor Delfino Ríos, editor of the newspaper *Diógenes*, was authorized by General Emiliano Lojero to refute the report that the Chinese had taken part in the defense.

(Even so, to this day there are illustrious members of the Torreón community who are convinced the Chinese fired on the revolutionaries.)

Another point of agreement between the two commissions was their absolute rejection of the report made by Macrino J. Martínez, whose ingenuity in playing tricks leaves no margin for doubt. They also coincide in concluding that the killings were carried out with extreme cruelty. But then the nuances begin to appear: graphic details abound in the Chinese report, while Ramos Pedrueza is content to give a more abstract version of the events.

There are also points of differences. In the first place, the foreign commission sets the number of dead at 303; Ramos Pedrueza says it was 205, confining himself exclusively to the bodies buried, on Cummins's order, in the mass grave near the cemetery. And while the Chinese version lays primary responsibility on the Maderistas, and in consequence, the Mexican government, the national story exonerates the federal authorities, justifies the actions of federal soldiers, and attributes the massacre to a "law of psychology." In Ramos Pedrueza's words:

A mass of common people is always dangerous, but when they are armed, and feel they have the support of a mob thirsting for loot, and when circumstances make them masters of their own acts for a period of three or four hours, conscious of their omnipotence and, in the absence of any higher authority, both judge and executioner, the consequences of crime will be fatal: this occurred in Torreón.

That was the fifth (perhaps the most enduring and insidious) chapter of the Mexican fiction of the small genocide in La Laguna. After denial, calumny, obfuscation, and contempt, a half-truth was installed: intellectual manipulation of the events.

The main weakness in Ramos Pedrueza's thesis is the following: the massacre did not last four or five hours, but forty-eight (from the night of May 13, according to a great many witnesses, to the night of the fifteenth, according to Erico Notholt). During the greater part of that time, the Maderista leaders were present at the battlefront. Nor is it logical to exonerate the rebel soldiers: the massacre commenced on the night of the thirteenth, in the El Pajonal market gardens, and at that time there were no "mobs" present there: only combatants. True, the climate of violence was at its worst the morning of May 15, but its origins were earlier: at least a fifth of the killings (around sixty) had been carried out earlier, and it was the negligence of the local authorities (both Porfirian and Maderista) that allowed the violence to escalate.

The second weakness lies in its denial of the context. It is easy to state that a gang of poor people bears sole responsibility for a crime when cultural history is discounted; when one believes delinquency to be an abnormality and, therefore, ignores the criminal effects of the racism, expressed in words and carried out in practice for decades by members of the La Laguna cotton-growing elites.

That thorn in the flesh, Chang Yin Tang, offered the Mexican government a list of the names of the 303 people killed (the figure is to this day disputed, but has come to attain official status). He then sent a memorandum in which Wilfley and Bassett gave a preliminary report. Finally, the external commission had a booklet printed detailing Owyang and Bassett's inquiry in La Laguna.

The negotiations became more complex after the arrival of the cruiser *Hai-Chi* in the port of Havana, the insistence of the Chinese government on the payment of the indemnification—first fixed at 30 and later at 6 million pesos in gold—the indiscretions perpetrated by Sown Nai Sown, Chinese consul in Veracruz and supporter of an armed solution (whom Chang appears to have immediately removed from office), and the de la Barra regime's refusal to accept United States mediation or the direct responsibility of either Maderistas or Porfirians for the tragedy.

Nevertheless, toward the end of October, it seemed an agreement was in sight: Mexico was willing to pay a 3-million-peso indemnification. What put the situation on hold was democracy: on November 6, elections were held, and Francisco I. Madero was elevated to the rank of constitutional president. Bassett and Wilfley sent Manuel Calero, the new minister of foreign affairs, yet another legal broadside by attempting to add default interest to the debt. Calero, for his part, tried to reduce the sum by means of legal hairsplitting, the use of geopolitical antecedents, and a trail of exonerating precedents related to the lynching of Mexicans in the United States.

The president had to appear in person to mediate between voracity and miserliness. In a meeting with the representatives of the international commission, Francisco I. Madero saw the sum, and ordered 100,000 pesos to be added to the previously agreed-upon figure. In this way, the indemnity for the small genocide was set at 3,100,000 pesos in gold. What Manuel Calero obtained in exchange was the Chinese mission's acceptance that it be a "grace" payment; that is to say, one that was dictated by the generosity and sympathy of the Madero government, and not obligatory. In this way, the state was inherently protected from any historic involvement in the massacre, and Antonio Ramos Pedrueza's vision of the event was consolidated.

On December 16, 1911, the Convention for Payment of Indemnity was signed. The document set the date for settlement of the debt as July 1, 1912.

Naturally, this commitment was never fulfilled. First, because the Chinese Republic's victory caused the plaintiffs to attempt to postpone the payment. Second, because in Mexico, in February

1913, General Victoriano Huerta led a military coup. It was the Decena Trágica, the Ten Tragic Days that included the shooting in cold blood, in the Zócalo, of General Bernardo Reyes—"the last romantic," as his son Alfonso called him in one of the most fluent darts in Castilian prose—the arrest of Felipe Ángeles, the assassination of the president and vice president of the republic; days of the torture, mutilation, and murder of Gustavo Madero in La Ciudadela market by the soldiery, while a phonograph played "When the bill is paid, is paid, what pleasure I'm going to give you, girl . . ."

Debts and dead bodies flowing like pus.

•••••

In 1924 Billee Jamieson made a business trip to Chicago. He was crossing the street when someone called his name. On turning, he saw a stranger with Asian features who introduced himself as a survivor of the Chinese massacre in Torreón: an assistant in the restaurant that once stood on the opposite side of the street from the Lindquist house. He was one of the Cantonese men Jamieson had risked his own life to escort to the Arce lumberyard on May 15. He invited Billee to a restaurant he owned. They opened a bottle of wine and talked about those dark bygone days. It had been more than a decade since the doctor and his family had left Mexico.

(Yet Tulitas continued referring to Torreón as her town.)

The prosperous city of Torreón had changed in the interim. Its character remained intact, but not its innocence. That was violated on three occasions by the armies of Pancho Villa—whom the people of Torreón either love or hate: there is no middle ground. The Chinese community was still there, but times had changed: it was not the same. The consuls had left. The Spanish residents were expelled. Many rich men were ruined, others continued to prosper; some of them by changing sides. Such was the case of Lauro de la Garza, who became the banker of the Division of the North and instructed Villa on the best ways to extort money from the cotton-plantation caste.

Foon-chuck, the twenty-four-year-old youth who had arrived in La Laguna on one of the first trains to run through the region, would never again experience the prosperity he enjoyed before the slaughter. The Chinese steam laundry closed its doors. Productivity at the Do Sing Yuen market garden fell sharply. The Wah Yick streetcars became historical curiosities. The Banco Chino building passed into the hands of the Banco de La Laguna, and was later left vacant. In the thirties, a Monterrey official by the name of Castillón—Silvia Castro says there is even a street named after him in that city—attempted to gain ownership of the building by no other right than his pistols. And a certain General Ríos Zertuche took over another edifice belonging to Foon-chuck to set up the Torreón military camp. Foon-chuck, a personal friend of Miguel Cárdenas's and the most successful Celestial subject in Coahuila, the man who founded a school where Cantonese was studied in Monclova, moved his residence to a small estate he owned in Tamaulipas: El Limón. He continued to attempt to work with the revolutionary regime: Bernardo Chuck says he had a project to build a dam with the backing of the federal government when Venustiano Carranza was murdered. It seems he had few illusions after that. But he was strong: he lived to see the rise of the Chinese Republic, the return of Mexico to a state of peace, two world wars, and the ascent to power of Mao Zedong in his native land. He died in 1955 at the age of eighty-seven, having lived on the American continent for seventy-five years.

On September 17, 1911, the newspaper *El Criterio de Durango* published a brief report about a new attack on the Chinese in El Pajonal. When, on January 26, 1912, the Torreón Proprietors' League was formed with the aim of protecting and reclaiming property that had been in any way affected by the revolutionaries, no Chinese person was invited to join.

Almost all the old Cantonese businesses were abandoned. According to the office set up by Emilio Madero, the material losses of the community amounted to over 1,300,000 pesos.

On February 20, 1912, the Torreón Chinese asked the local authorities to guarantee their safety, fearing renewed attacks. In June, the Chamber of Commerce reopened; the Chinese were not invited into that organization either. Some survivors, including Dr. Lim, tried to forget the killings and go on living in La Laguna. Others fled. And a new wave of migrants arrived, among them Manuel Lee Tang, father of the current president of the Unión Fraternal China. I wonder what the small genocide represented for the new Cantonese community. A distant rumor? Retroactive resignation? Something that was no concern of theirs?

In the forties, the Chinese were still recognized as excellent market gardeners, even though their main niche was by then in small urban businesses. They were much poorer than before the massacre.

Billee Jamieson sold the little that remained of his medical practice in La Laguna to his cousin Dr. Harmon Cole in the summer of 1911. The family—Billee, Tulitas, and their daughter, Evelyn— then left for El Paso, where they spent the rest of their lives. Federico Wulff, in contrast, decided to stay in the city he had personally traced out on paper.

Tulitas later recalled:

Evelyn went back to visit in Torreón and Tlahualilo in 1927 or '28 and found the town had grown considerably. . . . At each intersection was a statue. Some of the statuary was heroic, some patriotic, and some frankly amatory, including a statue of two nudes curved into an intense embrace.

Federico Wulff passed through the revolution, survived Villa's violence, survived the death of his wife in 1921, and finally decided to sell his properties in La Laguna in 1930. He settled first in El Paso, and then in San Antonio, bought an automobile he drove at fifteen miles per hour, endangering other road users. He sold the vehicle. In 1945 he began to go deaf, and he died four years later, at the age of ninety-three, still with a full set of teeth.

In 1969, Tulitas said:

The Chalet Wulff still stands on the hill at Torreón. For a time, I understand, it was used as an army barracks, but now it is empty . . . : the last tangible evidence of a life now gone forever.

Tulitas Jamieson died in El Paso, Texas, on September 1, 1971, sixty years after leaving the city she adored. She was eighty-five. Memory is a young woman of uncertain age.

●●●●●

The Chinese Empire knew all about indemnity. During the nineteenth century it paid vast sums to England, France, and Japan for the courtesy of invading its territory, selling drugs, making war at will, and killing thousands of nationals. On January 16, 1901, the empire broke a record: as a result of the Boxer Rebellion, it contracted a debt with Japan that reached 980 million ounces of silver: essentially mortgaging the twentieth century. By that time Sun Yat-sen, a rural doctor whose aim was to overthrow the Manchu dynasty and turn the country into a republic, had appeared on the political scene. He incited armed rebellions in 1895 and 1900, but failed on both occasions.

Following the diplomatic disasters of 1901, Empress Cixi agreed—without freeing her imperial nephew or making peace with Kang Youwei, the philosopher and real estate speculator who helped make the Chinese of La Laguna wealthy—to carry out a number of the reforms she had prohibited in 1898. Bureaucratic exams were abolished, and between 1905 and 1909 over one hundred thousand modern schools were opened. In 1906 a constitution based on the Japanese model was approved. Two years later both Cixi and Kuang Su, the captive emperor, died one day apart; power passed into the hands of self-serving members of the Manchu court.

Suang Tung—better known as Puyi or, nowadays, the Last Emperor—came to the throne in 1908, at the age of two. Four years later, Celestial diplomacy named him as the Principal Offended Party in the massacre in Torreón. That same year, he was removed

from power—but not from the Forbidden City—with the inauguration of the republic. This was the outset of a road (the Via Doloroso)
that, during half a century, would lead him to become an excellent
gardener: a hero of disillusion.

In 1909 the first legislative elections were held in the Chinese
Empire. Even though it was assumed the Congress would be a
mere consultative body, participation in its election was confined to
the learned and notable people of each province: less than 0.5 percent of the population.

While the Cantonese community of Torreón was being massacred in May 1911, Puyi's regents were expropriating the national
railroad system. This was perceived by the provincial—but increasingly powerful—chieftains as an assault on their autonomy.
In August (while Ramos Pedrueza, Owyang King, and Arthur
Bassett were interviewing the witnesses of the small genocide in
La Laguna), the inhabitants of Chengdu, Sichuan Province, were
closing institutions and businesses, and refusing to pay imperial
taxes. On October 10 (when Mexico was fearing an attack from
the battle cruiser *Hai-Chi*, at anchor in Havana), an uprising broke
out in Wuchang, the capital of Hubei Province. Li Yuang Jung
was proclaimed head of the provisional military government of the
Republic of China, and Tang Hualong, a landowner of thirty-seven
years of age (he would figure in later republican governments as
minister of education and then of the interior, only to be assassinated
in 1918 by a barber), was appointed prime minister. Tang called for
the provinces to refuse to recognize the authority of the monarchy:
almost all of them seconded this demand. Meanwhile, the plenipotentiary Chang Yin Tang was negotiating payments with Mexico
in the name of the Qing dynasty. By the time Madero had been
elected president and approved the 3,100,000 pesos in gold of indemnity, a civil war had broken out in China.

The first reaction came from the empire: Yuan Shikai, a veteran general with great influence among the troops, but who had
been retired sometime before, was called upon by the court, which,
with its tail between its legs—Yuan had been treated as a politi-

cal rival by the chief regent—presented him with what he wanted: nothing less than the post of prime minister. The Peiyang army advanced on the rebel provinces, and a bloody battle took place between November 10 and 18 in which the monarchists were victorious. It seemed as if Yuan Shikai was then going to march on the city of Wuchang, capital of the newly created republic. To everyone's surprise, he decided to open negotiations. There is still debate as to whether he did this from lack of military reserves, or as a calculated political move: he was well aware that it could be to his benefit to abandon the Qing dynasty to its fate. The fact is that, on December 1 (when the Mexican indemnity negotiations over the massacre in Torreón seemed to be almost concluded), Yuan formed an alliance with the Republic.

Sun Yat-sen's supporters were not long in proclaiming their own chieftain prime minister in the city of Nanking. At almost the same time, a separate republican government was formed in Shanghai. In an attempt to avoid the country being partitioned, a conclave of the three anti-imperialist projects was held in Nanking, the home of Sun, and former capital of the Taiping rebels. On January 10, 1912, Sun Yat-sen was proclaimed president of the Republic of China.

At around the same time, plenipotentiary Chang Yin Tang finally left his residence in Mexico and traveled to Washington, DC, considering his mission to have been successful. A new Chinese chargé d'affaires, by the name of Woo Chung Yen, was appointed. No sooner had this official taken office than he had to deal with another crisis: on February 19, 1912, Secretary of State Manuel Calero received a communiqué from a man who introduced himself as his counterpart in China: Wang Chung Hui. The missive requested him to *please* defer the payment of indemnity until further notice. That was the first contact between the Mexican government and the new Republic of China.

Things became violent in Peking. In late February, the local military garrison held a demonstration, probably in support of General Yuan and against President Sun. Arson and looting broke out in several districts, including the one in which the Mexican legation was located. Pablo Herrera de Huerta informed the Italian ambassador that he feared for his life, and had no armed backup within his place of business. The European official provided him with a guard of five seamen and a petty officer, who lived in Herrera's residence for a number of days. Pablo tried to pay them for their services, but the Italians refused his money. He then presented them with "some silver objects" as a gesture of gratitude.

In March Sun Yat-sen resigned: his political sway had waned, and there was a clear risk of civil war. General Yuan Shikai took power.

In May a new minister of foreign affairs was appointed in Mexico: Pedro Lascuráin, who would later set the impressive record of being president of the republic for forty-five minutes. Lascuráin reopened the negotiations of the famous indemnity, adding a specific detail: the payment would be made not in gold but in government bonds.

The Republic of China had not been officially recognized by Mexico (or the United States), and this contributed to the Mexican senate's refusal to ratify the indemnity convention. From June onward, the Asian republic's complaints multiplied. It was even suggested (by Chargé d'Affaires Woo and Lascuráin himself) that an advance sum of 500,000 pesos should be offered, but high-ranking Chinese republicans refused this proposal: the indemnity must be paid in full.

In December León de la Barra reappeared on the political scene as president of the Twenty-Sixth Legislature. Congress finally approved the convention, and a new date was fixed for payment: February 15, 1913.

On that date Madero was facing the Ten Tragic Days. A week later he was assassinated.

When he took power, Victoriano Huerta placed the former gray president in the post of minister for foreign affairs: León de la Barra did juggling tricks to speed up the sluggish Mexican bureaucracy, while managing to retain his decorum in front of a now very impatient Chinese diplomatic service. Communication was maintained until July 1913, when conflicting sensibilities put the convention on ice.

Judge Wilfley had suggested in May that a discount of 10 percent might help accelerate the payment; both Woo Chung Yen and León de la Barra agreed to this in principle. But as the Mexican response continued to be slow in coming, Woo made the mistake of writing directly to Victoriano Huerta on July 14, complaining of León de la Barra's ineptitude and accusing him of miserliness in attempting to obtain a reduction in the debt. He never should have done this: the former gray president, one of the few sincerely committed Mexicans during the closing stages of diplomatic negotiations on the massacre, abandoned the issue, never to return to it.

On October 10, 1913, Huerta dissolved Congress. Ten months later, defeated by the Constitutionalist Revolution, he set off into exile. The indemnity convention ran aground on that area of Kafkaesque splendor during which Mexico had, simultaneously, two presidents of the republic and a first chief of the army, all from Coahuila.

⸻

Jesús Agustín Castro's later escapades make for a good story. He was first general alongside Lucio Blanco (they ended up in court), and then with Pablo González Garza, under whose command he served in Tamaulipas and Nuevo León. He fought against the supporters of General Pascual Orozco, against the Convention of Aguascalientes, against Francisco Villa's final armies. As a Constitutionalist, he made the hacienda owners toe the line, and suppressed rural workers in Chiapas and Guerrero. He was governor of Durango State and minister of war. He broke with Álvaro Obregón, not when that political leader had Carranza killed, but—transgressing a major taboo of Maderismo—when he was reelected president. Castro, like Foonchuck, survived into the mid-1950s. Before shining in the political heavens, he played a leading role in a beautiful but unappreciated act: the march of the Twenty-First Rurales Battalion.

Jesús Agustín was one of the few irregular commanders to join the army and go to Mexico City with troops under his command after the revolutionary victory. He was in Tlalnepantla in February 1913, at the head of the Twenty-First Rurales, when the military coup took place. Well aware that he stood no chance against the forces in the capital, he ordered his men to march north to Querétaro. He then guided them across half the country, without backup, supplies, a rear guard, or logistics, at times slipping by through the night, at others confronting Huerta's troops (who outnumbered his by thousands) in skirmishes that were lost before they ever began, crossing the Bajío region, then later the Huasteca, on the Gulf of Mexico, and Tamaulipas, Nuevo León, and Coahuila, until he reached his goal: *the desert, the desert, the desert!* I've always been attracted by the humble resemblance between this story and the one narrated by Xenophon in *Anabasis*, or *The March of the Ten Thousand*. The Twenty-First Rurales—hungry, worn down, unarmed—arrived in Coahuila on March 30, 1913: four days after the Constitutionalist Venustiano Carranza launched the Plan of Guadalupe. What would soon become a regiment, and later a brigade, joined the recently formed Constitutionalist Army with a new sobriquet: the Loyal Soldiers of Tlalnepantla.

After his brief transit through Maderismo, Orestes Pereyra joined Francisco Villa's army, with which he fought, in succession, Pascual Orozco, Victoriano Huerta, and Venustiano Carranza. He remained in the movement until 1915, when he was taken prisoner with his two sons—both fighting with him. All three were killed by firing squad. Urquizo, who by then was an enemy of Orestes's, wrote a generous portrait of him, perhaps inspired by the desire to free him from the shadow of the Torreón massacre:

> : . . a pure unsullied revolutionary; his hands were never stained by murder, or robbery, and neither can his conscience ever have been stained by any crime. The life he led and the habits of a simple worker were those he continued to observe in general. . . . That good man, the first military chief I had, that puritanical revolutionary, had been executed by our men.

Enrique Adame Macías, the young dynamiter, was, with Jesús Agustín, one of the few supporters of Madero in La Laguna to join the national army. He was imprisoned during the Ten Tragic Days, but was almost immediately released. Like Castro, he attempted to march north to join Carranza, but was recaptured in León, Guanajuato State. It was there his luck ran out: he faced a firing squad at the age of twenty-nine.

With the passage of time, the obese overseer, Sixto Ugalde—in my opinion one of those directly responsible for the massacre of the Chinese—would attain the rank of general in Francisco Villa's Division of the North. He is buried in his hometown of Matamoros, Coahuila State. In Torreón there is a narrow alley named for him.

Emilio Madero joined Villa in 1913. While on active duty, he continued to hold the rank of lieutenant colonel. He added his voice to the Convention of Aguascalientes and, when that was defeated, went into exile in the United States. He spent his military career in a bureaucratic limbo, attaining the rank of major general in 1961, the year before his death. His greatest grace was to have been called Madero: apart from his disastrous leadership in the first capture of Torreón, his life is irrelevant to the history of Mexico.

Pablo Lavín very soon abandoned Maderismo. In 1912 he joined Orozco's uprising with the hacienda administrator and regional leader "Cheché" Campos and ended up as an irregular colonel in the army that carried through Victoriano Huerta's coup. But that was as far as he ever got: on July 16, 1913, in Gómez Palacio, he witnessed a bitter argument between Luis Caro—one of Cheché's assistants—and the city's military chief, Captain Marco Hernández. Passions ran high. Caro drew his gun and fired on the captain, killing him. This event was the straw that broke the camel's back for the leaders of the regular army in La Laguna; for months there had been complaints of abuse of power, extreme violence, and indiscipline among Cheché's men. The following day, Cheché's staff lined up before the firing squad. Colonel Lavín was second in line. He was executed at half past ten in the morning on July 17.

This story has an epilogue completely unrelated to the massacre of the Chinese. Cheché decamped from Huerta's army when it was billeted in Torreón and took refuge in the neighboring city of Lerdo, where he requested an interview with Venustiano Carranza, intending to offer his services. With characteristic terseness—he was, perhaps, the best writer of telegrams in the Mexican Revolution—Carranza said, "I don't talk to deserters. We'll hold a court martial."

Cheché was executed in August 1913. Oral tradition has it that his last wish was to march to the wall against which he was to be shot, followed by a band of musicians.

●●●●●

For many years, the Republic of China allowed the Mexican government to feel it had won, and filed away the indemnity convention. It is likely that this policy was due to an urgent need to protect Cantonese migrants. Rather than ceasing after the massacre, persecution of the Chinese worsened during the first revolutionary governments, and while there was never another incident involving so many deaths, the climate of racism became more intense in the media, daily life, and the law. Although Mexican diplomacy in China continued to affirm candidly (or cynically, I don't know) that Cantonese people were welcome throughout Mexico, and could rely on the protection of the authorities, in a number of states (most notably Sonora and Sinaloa) they were confined to ghettos and prohibited from marrying Mexican women; obstacles were put in the way of the growth of their businesses, and they were ridiculed and humiliated. This policy (because it was a policy: not only businessmen and small traders practiced it, but also a great many mayors and governors, plus at least two presidents: Obregón and Calles) continued until 1936.

In February 1921, through its new chargé d'affaires, T. K. Fong, China once again raised the issue of the indemnity. A year later, Fong paid Minister of Foreign Affairs Alberto J. Pani a visit in relation to this matter. There was no response.

It was then the turn of Yo Tsao Yeu, a new official who, in April

1924, presented the request to Minister Aarón Sáenz. This was sent on to Pani, then finance minister. There was no response. Yo Tsao Yeu visited Pani in 1927 and was more insistent. Pani told him at best he could pay a much lower sum than had been originally stipulated: between 300,000 and 500,000 pesos. The Chinese representative accepted: "Half a loaf is better than no bread," as the saying goes.

This was followed by three years of silence on the Mexican side. At Sáenz's behest, a specialist in international law examined the agreement again to see if there were any loopholes. The specialist's conclusion was that Mexico was obliged to pay.

A new Chinese representative, Samuel Sung Young, wrote most respectfully to Foreign Secretary Fernando Torreblanca in 1933, twenty-two years after the massacre, requesting that the agreement be honored. The definitive response arrived in January 1934: Torreblanca stated that he *had the honor* of informing them the country was in no position to pay the debt. It was the final communication concerning the issue. No Chinese representative ever again brought up the matter before the government of Mexico.

That was the sixth, and last, chapter of the national novel about the small genocide: to denial, calumny, obfuscation, contempt, and half-truths was added the betrayal of a pledge. The indemnity was never paid.

•••••

Chinese migration to Coahuila never again reached its pre-massacre heights. While there were 759 Cantonese in the state in 1910, by 1912 this figure had dwindled to 506; there were 564 in 1930, 371 in 1950, and 264 in 1960. In Torreón, they continued to be the second-largest national group from 1926 to 1960, outnumbered only by the Spanish, and closely followed by United States citizens, but well above the Lebanese (145), Germans (131), and Palestinians (94).

It is probable that Sinophobia ebbed between 1913 and 1919, but it was back in full force during the following decade. In mid-1921,

Jesús Garza Cabello, minister in the provincial government, sent a circular to the mayor of Torreón, ordering him to refrain from providing Asian immigrants with any form of official documentation. That same year, the CROM (Regional Confederation of Mexican Workers), a group affiliated with the postrevolutionary governments, joined the boycott by refusing to admit them as members. The Anti-Chinese Committee was formed, and a local branch of the Liga Pro Raza (Pro-Race League), whose first president would be the businessman and future councilor Efraín López, was established. Other members of these two bodies were a gentleman by the name of Méndez and Filemón Garza Cavazos, founder of the emblematic newspaper *El Siglo de Torreón*.

Xenophobia was mainly confined to urban centers, and was exercised by the upper classes, businessmen, and workers. The members of the Anti-Chinese Committee even complained that the rural campesinos did not support their project.

In 1922, the businessman Juan Wong was the first person to make a formal complaint about the gangster-like activities of the Anti-Chinese Committee. A further complaint made by Patricio Chang in 1924 shows that the aggression, insults, and attacks (no actual deaths occurred) didn't stop there. That same year, the members of the Cantonese community "requested permission from the municipal authorities to carry weapons, promising to use them only in defense of their lives," says Dr. Sergio Corona Páez. Two years later, on June 9, 1926, *El Siglo de Torreón* published a note on the opening of an anti-Chinese club. The writer does not hide his sympathy for the project:

> This reporter could see the enthusiasm of the business community and railroad workers for the formation of the Anti-Chinese Committee, and with even greater eagerness they will add their support for the pro-race ideals of the anti-Chinese groups, in order to free our country from the peril of the Chinese who have carried out a peaceful invasion, with the aim of exploitation, to the detriment of Mexican interests.

Months later, on December 20, 1926, *El Siglo de Torreón* returned enthusiastically to the theme on its front page: "Anti-Chinese work praised. The president of the republic informed the nationalists of his support for the campaign. . . . General Calles expressed his great admiration for the work that is being done throughout the republic against Chinese immigration."

The Cantonese in La Laguna learned to defend themselves. Not only did they request permission to carry arms, they also used the term "the Chinese community" to refer to themselves, "an otherness," as Carlos Castañón Cuadros points out, a stratum of society that resists invisibility by means of internal cohesion: *we are not part of you, but we are here.* That otherness became more overt when, during Calles's government, the Unión Fraternal, the organization that replaced the Asociación Reformista, was formed. And although racist offenses continued well into the twentieth century, in the long run, the Chinese managed to adapt, find a niche for themselves, and survive—like all good migrants.

●●●●●

I spent a year trying to interview Manuel Lee Soriano, president of the Unión Fraternal China in Torreón, initially explaining to his secretary with a candor I do not repent: "I'm writing a book on the 1911 massacre, and I'd like to know Sr. Lee's views on it."

Nothing: Don Manuel is ill, he's retired, he doesn't have time, leave a message and I'll pass it on . . .

I'd started the first draft of this chapter of *The House of the Pain of Others*, and was resigned to making do without his involvement when Mónica volunteered to talk to his wife.

It was a short, polite phone call. I listened from the adjoining room as Mónica told Sra. Lee I was writing a book on the history of the Chinese community in Torreón, that I now only needed a statement from Don Manuel, that without his help my story would have a predictable ending, and that predictable endings left her husband—that is to say, me—depressed for months.

(I don't know how she thought that one up.)

To hasten the encounter and sweeten the scene, Mónica added that we had a five-year-old son and planned to take him to see the Ojuela Bridge in Mapimí that weekend, which would provide an excellent opportunity to meet up: Torreón was on our way. She assured Sra. Lee the interview would not take more than an hour.

Ten minutes later, the telephone rang. Manuel Lee Soriano agreed to meet me.

I knew I had to honor what my wife had said: I wouldn't take up more than an hour of his life and, since the massacre hadn't been mentioned, would not question him about it unless he broached the subject. Mónica suggested we take advantage of the trip to go through with the plan she had invented for the Lees: visiting the legendary Ojuela Bridge, that actor with a cameo in dozens of Westerns and a masterpiece of nineteenth-century engineering and Germanophilia.

When we set out from Saltillo at nine in the morning, there was a slight chill in the air. Our son, Leonardo, was on edge, a little impatient; he didn't stop talking the whole way, especially after he'd spotted a coyote trotting along the side of the highway. We had to invent a story: the coyote was climbing a mountain of fire, it was crossing a diamond bridge, fighting Darth Vader, and was rescued from a chasm by Ben Tennyson. That relaxed him.

Manuel Lee Soriano and his wife received us in the dining room of a nondescript house, perhaps more modest than I had expected. When he saw me for the first time, the elderly gentleman clasped my hands. While giving a slight bow, he remarked, "It's so good that you're writing a book about the history of Torreón."

Just that. Not even "the history of the Chinese." Then he added, "There's an old saying: however close to the heavens the top of a tree is, its heart will always be a root. My root is La Laguna."

He offered me a chair. I asked if I could turn on my tape recorder. He nodded. His wife disappeared into another room and came back with a box of vintage games, which she placed in my son's hands.

"The history of the Chinese in Torreón is a very rich one," said

Don Manuel, without my prompting. "And full of suffering, too. Many of them didn't speak the language, and those who did were afraid of making mistakes or uttering offensive vulgarities. As they were respectful, they preferred to say nothing. They only expressed their feelings through others."

It was a subtle warning that he did not intend to speak of the massacre.

Manuel Lee Soriano is eighty. He suffered an embolism in 2013, and his movements are awkward: he shuffles, keeps his arms close to his chest, has difficulty articulating his words, his gestures are tremulous. In contrast, his mind is Kublai Khan's palace: *a miracle of rare device.*

"Can you tell me about your father?" I asked.

"He was called Manuel Lee Tang. He came from Taishan with his brother in 1895, but not to La Laguna: their plan was to cross to the United States. They got to Jiménez, Parral, and Delicias, picking up jobs along the way. Then they went to Ciudad Juárez, where they encountered the revolutionary Francisco Villa. My dad heard him and said, 'This man speaks well, he speaks for Mexicans.' But Villa had a reputation for persecuting foreigners.

"He saw him again in Jiménez. The González family had given Dad a job as a cook; they hid him under a woodpile every time Villa visited. He was afraid, my dad. Until one time a girl in the family, the one who taught him the catechism, said, 'Come here. I'm going to introduce you to the general.' My dad came out from under the woodpile all atremble and stood in front of Villa.

"'What's your name?'

"'Manuel.'

"'Manuel?'

"'That's the name they gave me.'

"'Don't be afraid, Manuel. I'm no murderer. I respect the Chinese. You cooked this meal, right?'

"'They told me to do it for the general.'

"'From now on, every time I come here, you're going to cook for me.'

"Later my dad was hired by Juan Abusaíd as an assistant in his grocery store, but Villa came and said, 'No. You're coming with me.'

"'And what am I going to do, General, sir? I don't carry a weapon.'

"'I'm going to put you in charge of the store-wagon for provisions.'

"So he went to work there, but many of the fighters took things without paying. Thinking Villa would believe he was doing the stealing, my dad decided to tell him what was going on.

"Villa had the soldiers line up.

"'Manuelito here tells me some of you are eating and drinking and not paying . . . Manuel, tell me who they are.'

"'No, General, sir. I can't do that.'

"Villa ordered the soldiers to take a step forward if they had ever stolen from the store-wagon. He threatened the firing squad if they weren't honest. Almost the whole troop stepped forward, and Villa had them all whipped.

"My dad stayed with the Division of the North until a cannonball destroyed the store-wagon when they were in Bachimba. That was when he came to Torreón. He was employed here by some fellow countrymen, who later made him a partner when they set up Kuan & Co. on Avenida Iturbide; it's called Carranza now. He was a partner there for many years, and then in another company, until he retired with heart problems and never worked again."

Although it was difficult for him to speak clearly due to the effects of the embolism, I found Don Manuel to be a natural conversationalist. I decided to intrude as little as possible ("let him run with the line," as reporters used to say) to see if he would drift toward some comment on the 1911 massacre.

Meanwhile, Mónica and Leonardo were working on a jigsaw puzzle in the living room.

"And your uncle?"

"That's a very sad story. My uncle also came to live in Torreón, and he won a big prize in the National Lottery in . . . 1925? . . . No, I think it was 1938. He invited Dad to go to China with him to visit their parents, but fortunately Dad couldn't get away because at that moment he had just too much work. Then my uncle went with all his money, and when he wanted to come back, he couldn't: the Bamboo Curtain had fallen. That's what we called the Mao Zedong regime."

"Did he take his children with him?"

"Who? My uncle?"

"Yeah."

"I've got two nieces who were educated by the government there. One is a biologist, and the other a doctor. They couldn't choose their careers, where they studied, or anything: the state made those decisions. That's how it was with the Bamboo Curtain."

Without pause, he added, "I was born in the thirties. There were four of us children. My dad had married a Mexican woman from a Spanish family over in Soria. That's where my surname Soriano comes from."

We spoke of other matters: ELLA (El Estado de La Laguna), a chauvinist, right-wing association Don Manuel had some sympathy with. The insecurity in Torreón. The small factory he owned that made metal commemorative plaques. The Unión Fraternal China.

"The majority of the members were Cantonese Masons, but they didn't get mixed up in politics. I attended some of their events. Dad never knew."

Finally, we spoke about anti-Chinese sentiment during the twenties. He brought it up. I let him complain about Obregón and Calles.

"You know *Entre el río Perla y el Nazas*," I said.

It wasn't a question: I have it from a good source that Don Manuel is a personal friend of the author's. This was my opportunity to get him to talk about the massacre.

Lee Soriano assumed a contemptuous expression.

"I know it. It's an excellent book written by Juan Puig. But people weren't happy around here when it was reissued."

"Why not?"

"Because the story belongs to us, the Laguneros. It's got nothing to do with anyone else."

"It's just that with all the anti-Chinese campaigns . . ."

Don Manuel interrupted me.

"I lived through those anti-Chinese campaigns. Even in 1938, they forced us, the second generation, to fight among ourselves, brother against brother. They liked watching us fight. My brother and I were at the same school, and they would be there when we came out, round the two of us up, and say, 'Go on, you hit him first.' I was in elementary school then. Those people were my classmates. My brother and I never hurt each other; we just *pretended* we were fighting: we used to scratch and slap each other a little, but it never hurt much. We did it so they wouldn't beat us up worse.

"When we were on our bicycles, they used to try to make us fall off. That sort of thing still happens to us. There was a little song they used to sing all the time: *Chinky, Chinky, China, eat lice and give no ting.* They would imitate the way our parents spoke. We paid no attention, and never said anything. We'd get home, and they'd ask us how our day had been. 'Fine,' we'd say. 'They just forced us to fight and sang that song.' 'Take no notice of them,' our parents would tell us. 'You not fight. Respect old people, and children, and authorities.'"

There was a pause.

"I lived through those anti-Chinese campaigns," repeated Manuel Lee Soriano, "and that's how my parents taught me to respond: without offending anyone. 'If you think you might cause offense, better not speak. Better be quiet.'"

I switched off the tape recorder and thanked him. Don Manuel and his wife accompanied us to the door. Our conversation ended with a double handshake and a mutual bow.

●●●●●

Walter J. Lim's former country house is a chalet-style building with green roof tiles and redbrick walls whose color is intensified by lines of white mortar. The roof is curved and seems to break like an emerald wave onto the garden, in which dwell, alongside younger orange and grapefruit trees, a pair of ancient mulberries.

Mónica stopped the Ecosport in front of the Museo de la Revolución, and asked, "Should I park?"

These trees—perhaps members of the same species growing in the Venustiano Carranza woods to the east, where the Chinese-owned market gardens that supplied the town with fresh fruit and vegetables once flourished—testify to an entrepreneurial dream: converting a locality famous for its cotton fields into a silk-producing region.

"No, no need."

There was no time for this dream to be realized. Six months after the outbreak of the Mexican Revolution, Francisco Madero's rebel troops entered the grounds and raped the woman who cared for the house. Later, a mob attempted to lynch Dr. Lim near Plaza 2 de Abril, despite the fact that he was wearing the Red Cross insignia on his left forearm. Walter J. somehow escaped to relate, some months afterward, his version of the small genocide perpetrated between May 13 and 15, 1911 in the northern Mexican city of Torreón, in the region known as La Laguna. Not all of his compatriots were so lucky: some three hundred Chinese immigrants were murdered.

I repeated from memory the first paragraph of this *crónica* of a small genocide in La Laguna while contemplating the dark-green railing around Lim's house. I imagined the ghosts of 303 Chinese people who walk the streets—their feet bare, burned by the asphalt—of a city that does not even recognize them. Oblivion is closer to nature than we are.

Viewed from the rear, the building has a somber air. . . . That's how, I think, the back of any historical construction should be seen: as a zone of basic obscenity.

Mónica repeated, "Should I park?"

"No, no need. Let's go."

I always find it hard to say good-bye to a story.

We joined the traffic, headed for Gómez Palacio, took the highway to Jiménez, arrived in Bermejillo, and turned left over the railroad tracks, toward the mountains. After a while, Cerro de la India appeared before us. We drove up the long, winding dirt road that leads, high up in the mountains, to the ghost town of Ojuela. As we ascended, a mist surrounded the Ecosport. A mist that was dense, but composed of shreds; it was floating like a piece of fabric, and between its folds, down below, could be seen a scorched sea: the Bolsón de Mapimí.

"This is a Western," I thought.

Around the middle of the twentieth century, Ojuela was an important mining town with, at its height, a population of five thousand. The remains of what were once the brick houses belonging to the engineers can still be seen, plus a casino and a clubhouse with a tennis court and offices. Some walls were built into the hillside, incorporating the natural rock. Now covered in vegetation, they have a weird adolescent archaeological relic feel. Nothing is left of the workers' neighborhood, which had been made of wood.

Santa Rita was once the second-largest multimetal mine in the world. There are over 250 miles of tunnels on dozens of levels. It is located by Cerro de la India, on the other side of Ojuela, facing a gully three hundred feet deep. To exploit the seams and transport the ore to the town, in 1892 (some say it was '98) the Peñoles company hired the German engineer Santiago Minguín to design a suspension bridge. The result was a nine-foot-wide construction of steel cables and wooden guides with a span of a thousand feet. Popular tradition has it that, forty years later, Minguín would be inspired to rework this design for San Francisco's Golden Gate Bridge.

(The truth is that the only reference to "Santiago Minguín" I know of is the Ojuela Bridge, and that comes from the miners of Mapimí. The chief engineer on the construction of the Golden Gate Bridge was in fact Joseph Strauss.)

When Santa Rita flooded in the forties, the company decided it would be cheaper to halt work than to drain it. The mine was abandoned, and Ojuela soon ceased to exist. Later, when it was realized that the seam could still be worked at low cost, the board of directors at Peñoles sold the concession to a dummy corporation—or at least this is what the local miners say—that contracted men on piecework. At present, they are paid less than one peso per pound of the multimetal ore extracted from the mineshaft. A man would have to work fourteen hours a day in Santa Rita, risking his life above a chasm of over three thousand feet, and carry over two hundred pounds of rock on his shoulders to earn even a basic income. With no health insurance. With no social security. There are businessmen who never learn a damn thing from history.

Some of the inhabitants of Mapimí combine their mining work with the regional tourism industry. They manage the access to the suspension bridge and to the Santa Rita mine; they give guided tours, sell beautiful pieces of rock, have set up a couple of craft stores . . .

After parking the car, Mónica, Leonardo, and I walked along the approach to the gorge. The bridge was standing there, majestic in the mist. It reminded us of an episode of *Samurai Jack*, when the protagonist fights for days and nights against a Scottish warrior while crossing a suspension bridge as long as a nation.

We held hands and stepped out into the void: the bridge is a thousand feet long. I felt the wood creaking beneath my shoes. Vertigo—I've suffered from this condition since childhood: it began as a vague sensation and has gradually worsened with the years— almost forced me to drop down onto the boards. Leonardo's head was below the level of the handrail, so with each step, the feeling became more intense: I believed my son was falling into the depths. I had to make an effort not to break the bones in his hand with the force of my grip.

Leo seemed nervous but happy, saying, "I love what we're doing, Daddy. What is it?"

I tried to mask my condition by thinking of the cowboy movies that have used the Ojuela Bridge as a location: *The Mole*, *Old Gringo*, a couple of HBO movies starring Julio Alemán . . .

We reached the other side.

The walk through the tunnels of the Santa Rita mine was enjoyable. We viewed the perfectly preserved body of a mule, a photograph of Pancho Villa in a bathing suit, one or two of Federico Wulff's original drawings that the workers of Mapimí treasured as if they were medieval relics.

Leonardo was in ecstasy about his miner's helmet and carbide lamp. At some point, there in the darkness, Mónica embraced me. The problem with the Ojuela Bridge is that you have to cross it twice: there and back. We set foot on the old planks once more. I clung to the handrail, sure I was going to be sick. I tried to look into the void through the dense mist, tried to ignore my desire to throw myself off. "This is a Western," I repeated to myself, pretending I was Clint Eastwood, and held on to my son with all my might.

"Daddy," mumbled Leonardo, "you're—squeezing—my—hand—hard."

"Let go," said Mónica. "I've got him."

He's mine: I didn't let go of his hand until we were back at the far side of the bridge and my vertigo subsided. I freed Leo, afraid I'd hurt him, but I hadn't: I watched him run to the store as if nothing had happened. He asked his mother's permission to buy a phosphorescent blue Popsicle.

I felt the first knot being tied inside me.

Writing this book, interviewing Manuel Lee Soriano, and traveling to Ojuela were becoming a tangled mass, and my guts were twining together like the statue of two lovers Evelyn Jamieson once saw in Torreón, and fusing into a single entity. Everything is in everything, as Pythagoras would have it, like a scorched sea in the mist, like the meeting between a newly born utopia and a philosopher condemned to death, like a mass grave dug by an Englishman near the outer wall of a cemetery: like the light of a thaw. This is a Western. This is the house of the pain of others. Holding hands, it was not a city Mónica, Leonardo, and I traversed that day, not La Laguna, not a small genocide, not the Ojuela Bridge: it was the bridge of horrors. And its name is Mexico.

Saltillo, Mexico City, Torreón
March 2014 to May 2015

SILENCE

I have known the silence of the stars and of the sea,
And the silence of the city when it pauses,
And the silence of a man and a maid,
And the silence for which music alone finds the word,
And the silence of the woods before the winds of spring begin,
And the silence of the sick
When their eyes roam about the room.
And I ask: For the depths
Of what use is language?
A beast of the field moans a few times
When death takes its young.
And we are voiceless in the presence of realities—
We cannot speak.

A curious boy asks an old soldier
Sitting in front of the grocery store,
"How did you lose your leg?"
And the old soldier is struck with silence,
Or his mind flies away
Because he cannot concentrate it on Gettysburg.
It comes back jocosely
And he says, "A bear bit it off."
And the boy wonders, while the old soldier
Dumbly, feebly lives over
The flashes of guns, the thunder of cannon,
The shrieks of the slain,
And himself lying on the ground,
And the hospital surgeons, the knives,
And the long days in bed.
But if he could describe it all
He would be an artist.

But if he were an artist there would be deeper wounds
Which he could not describe.

There is the silence of a great hatred,
And the silence of a great love,
And the silence of a deep peace of mind,
And the silence of an embittered friendship.
There is the silence of a spiritual crisis,
Through which your soul, exquisitely tortured,
Comes with visions not to be uttered
Into a realm of higher life.
And the silence of the gods who understand each other without speech,
There is the silence of defeat.
There is the silence of those unjustly punished;
And the silence of the dying whose hand
Suddenly grips yours.
There is the silence between father and son,
When the father cannot explain his life,
Even though he be misunderstood for it.

There is the silence that comes between husband and wife.
There is the silence of those who have failed;
And the vast silence that covers
Broken nations and vanquished leaders.
There is the silence of Lincoln,
Thinking of the poverty of his youth.
And the silence of Napoleon
After Waterloo.
And the silence of Jeanne d'Arc
Saying amid the flames, "Blesséd Jesus"—
Revealing in two words all sorrow, all hope.
And there is the silence of age,
Too full of wisdom for the tongue to utter it
In words intelligible to those who have not lived
The great range of life.

And there is the silence of the dead.
If we who are in life cannot speak
Of profound experiences,
Why do you marvel that the dead
Do not tell you of death?
Their silence shall be interpreted
As we approach them.

ACKNOWLEDGMENTS

I would like to thank the Archivo Histórico Genaro Estrada of the Ministry of Foreign Affairs, and its director, Jorge Fuentes, for allowing me to consult its material; the Hemeroteca Nacional; the Archivo de la Universidad Iberoamericana Campus Torreón and its director, Dr. Sergio Corona Páez; the Archivo Municipal de Torreón Eduardo Guerra and its director, Dr. Rodolfo Esparza Cárdenas; the Instituto Estatal de Documentación de Coahuila and all its personnel.

In Torreón I would like to thank Silvia Castro and Ilhuicamina Rico Maciel, Manuel Terán Lira, José León Robles de la Torre, and Jesús G. Sotomayor Garza: historians who agreed to be interviewed by me, gave me pointers to sources of information, and explained a number of essential aspects of La Laguna and its society. Particular thanks go to—again—Dr. Sergio Corona Páez; my intellectual debt to him can never be repaid. Thank you to Gerardo Moscoso, Julio César Félix, Daniel Herrera, Daniel Maldonado, *Piti* Ramos, Salvador Álvarez, Adriana Luévano, and Paco Cázares: exceptional hosts. Thank you also to the ghost of Francisco José Amparán: I will never set foot in Torreón without recalling him. I owe thanks to Jaime Muñoz Vargas for his long friendship and for mailing me the gem of microhistory, *Tulitas of Torreón*. Also to Fernando Fabio Sánchez, Tulitas's Spanish-language translator. And to my homie Nazul Aramayo, who taught me how to listen to Chicos de Barrio as they should be heard. Thank you to Carlos Castañón Cuadros because, although we never met, his intelligence runs (or at least I hope it does) through this book. And to the cab drivers I interviewed.

In Saltillo I would like to thank Armando J. Guerra, Carlos Manuel Valdés, and Martha Rodríguez, who offered advice on my bibliographic research and put me in touch with people who could offer me information. Thank you to Bernardo Chuck for agreeing to talk to me about his grandfather, and to Rubén Moreira Valdez, a lover of history, for his friendship and conversation.

In Mexico City I would like to thank Martí Torrens, Hélene Meunier, Dottor Fetuso, and the cab driver Arturo, *Arquine* magazine, the French embassy, and Nathalie Ferreira, who invited me to take part in the *(De)scribe the City* project. I am also grateful to Fernando García Ramírez, the editorial consultant of *Letras Libres* and the first person I spoke to about this book. Thank you to Leonardo Iván Martínez, who put me up in Tlatelolco. And enormous thanks are due to Juan Puig: his voice echoes in every word of this book.

Outside of Mexico, thank you to Laurent Portejoie (*Je t'aime, bordelaise!*), and to my brother, Timo Berger, who helped me to translate a strange biography of Pablo Herrera de Huerta from the German. Thanks also to Aurelio Asiain, whose conversation about Asia (or anything else) is one of the most gratifying territories I have even known.

Within the book, thank you to the anthropologist Lourdes Herrasti Maciá, who, in addition to giving me bottles of tequila or gin on Sundays so I would do nothing but write, gathered information from the Hemeroteca Nacional. (If only all mothers-in-law were like her.) Thank you to Jorge Rangel, who read the manuscript, compiled the references, helped with my research, and translated various texts; thanks also for the friendship, the mezcal, and the music. Thank you to Andrés Ramírez, my friend and Spanish editor, for his faith in this work and his patience.

I would also like to thank Santos Laguna soccer club for winning the Mexican championship on the very same day I finished writing this story.

Thank you to Mónica and Leonardo: connections: bridges.

FOOT(LESS)NOTES

Lim's House

The information regarding the Chinese community's hopes of creating a silk industry in La Laguna comes from a security guard I spoke to at the Museo de la Revolución.

The newspaper advertisement for Walter J. Lim's medical consultancy was published on June 17, 1911, in the *Torreon Enterprise*.

The telegram sent to Piedras Negras is cited in "La terrible matanza de chinos," *El Imparcial*, May 23, 1911.

The reference to the battles in Ciudad Juárez, Torreón, and Cuautla in May 1911 was taken from Wikipedia.

The report from the *New York Times*, May 23, 1911, mentioning the supposed lynching of Lim is "Killed in Torreon Number Hundreds."

The dossier in the Archivo Histórico Genaro Estrada of the Mexican Ministry of Foreign Affairs dealing with the killing of the Chinese in Torreón is filed as 13-2-34.

Leo M. Dambourges Jacques's text was published in *Arizona and the West*. Other books and journals mentioned here appear in the resources section.

The quotation from Manuel Terán Lira ("This writer remembers that in 1946 . . .") can be found in Manuel Terán Lira, *La matanza de los chinos (Torreón, 1911)*, 28.

The story about the free third-grade textbook on the local history of Coahuila was related to me by the book's author, Carlos Manuel Valdés, professor of history at the Université de Perpignan. As I recall, in the Saltillo Museo del Desierto there is a wall text in which Benito Juárez is accused of being personally responsible for the poisoning of sources of potable water that led to the extermination of nomadic groups in the region, but, while helping me to check a short passage in the galleys of this book, Carlos Valdés advised me by email, "The one who sent the order and two barrels of poison to contaminate the desert waters was not Benito Juárez, but Santiago Vidaurri.

That is, unless you have discovered a document belonging to Juaréz proposing such an action. If true, this would be terrible news, but it should still be published. But I am sure about Vidaurri: it's in the Archivo General del Estado de Nuevo León. The letter was sent to Jesús Carranza in Cuatro Ciénegas."

Marco Antonio Pérez Jiménez's thesis, "Raza nación y revolución: La matanza de chinos en Torreón, Coahuila, mayo de 1911," can be consulted at http://catarina.udlap.mx/u_dl_a/tales/documentos/lhi /perez_j_ma/portada.html.

The letter from Antonio de Pío Araujo to Ricardo Flores Magón, dated May 18, 1907, is available at archivomagon.net/obras-completas /correspondencia-1899-1922/c-1907/cor181.

The reference to the robbing of the Chinese victims' shoes appears on the back cover of Juan Puig's *Entre el río Perla y el Nazas: La china decimonónica y sus braceros emigrantes, la colonia china en Torreón y la matanza de 1911.*

In the Land of La Laguna

The main sources used to recount the history of Torreón are Eduardo Guerra, *Historia de Torreón: Su origen y sus fundadores*; and Ilhuicamina Rico Maciel, *Mi cuna, el ferrocarril: Efemérides de Torreón.*

In relation to the sale of the land belonging to Luisa Ibarra, the widow of Zuloaga, see Puig, *Entre el río Perla y el Nazas*, 155–57, and Rico Maciel, *Mi cuna, el ferrocarril*, 16.

For more on the Porfirian regime's racism toward the Chinese and indigenous peoples, and its Europhilia, the following can be consulted: Puig, *Entre el río Perla y el Nazas*; Robert Chao Romero, *The Chinese in Mexico, 1882–1940*; and Grace Peña Delgado, *Making the Chinese Mexican: Global Migration, Localism, and Exclusion in the U.S.-Mexico Borderlands.*

The biographical material on Andrés Eppen Aschenborn is taken from Rosa María Lack, "Los hombres pasan, pero sus obras perduran: Don Andrés Eppen Ashenborn," in Jaime Muñoz Vargas, *Panorama desde el cerro de las Noas: Siete ensayos de aproximación a la historia torreonense*, 85–110.

In relation to Governor Gómez Palacio and the founding of the Ferrocarril Central Mexicano on the Torreón hacienda, see Puig, *Entre el río Perla y el Nazas*, 157–59.

The note from the *Diario del Hogar* is quoted by Rico Maciel, *Mi cuna, el ferrocarril*, 22.

The story about the Jimulco train and the wagon that functioned as a preventive jail is narrated by Puig, *Entre el río Perla y el Nazas*, 162. Puig identifies Santos Coy as the mayor, but according to Rico Maciel (*Mi cuna, el ferrocarril*, 24), Colonel Carlos González Montes de Oca held the office at that time.

Daniel Sada's short story "La cárcel posma" is included in his collection *Registro de causantes*.

There is widespread speculation about the identity of the woman who inspired Othón's "Idilio salvaje." Among other places, it appears in José Joaquín Blanco, *Crónica de la poesía Mexicana*. The versions offered here are to be found in "Manuel José Othón en La Laguna (tercera parte de una serie aumentada a cuatro)," *El Siglo de Torreón*, July 12, 2012, www.elsiglodetorreon.com.mx/noticia/769537.siglos-de -historia.html.

The translation of the extract from "Idilio salvaje" given here is based on the version in José Emilio Pacheco, *Antología del modernismo (1884–1921)*, 93.

For the arrival of the printing press in Torreón, see Rico Maciel, *Mi cuna, el ferrocarril*, 31.

The information on industries and transportation in Torreón is also from Rico Maciel, *Mi cuna, el ferrocarril*, 31–47.

For more information about wages in La Laguna, see William K. Meyers, "Second Division of the North: Formation and Fragmentation of the Laguna's Popular Movement, 1910–11," in Friedrich Katz, *Riot, Rebellion, and Revolution: Rural Social Conflict in Mexico*; and Jesús G. Sotomayor Garza, *Benjamín Argumedo: El Tigre de La Laguna*, 28.

Regarding the smallpox epidemic among black workers, see Puig, *Entre el río Perla y el Nazas*, 163, and Rico Maciel, *Mi cuna, el ferrocarril*, 24–25.

On regional identity in La Laguna, and aspects of its founding, see

Sergio Corona Páez, *El País de La Laguna: Impacto hispano-tlaxcalteca en la forja de la Comarca Lagunera.* For information about the conflict between the agriculturalists of Durango and Coahuila, see Carlos Castañón Cuadros, "Una perspectiva hidráulica de la historia regional: Economía y revolución en el agua de La Laguna," in Muñoz Vargas, *Panorama desde el cerro de las Noas.* The quotation related to Juaréz's arrival in Viesca is taken from 17 and 18.

Pedro Luis Martín Bringas's declarations can be found in articles published in *El Siglo de Torreón* on July 7, 2014 ("Vigilarán que voto de ELLA cuente"), www.elsiglodetorreon.com.mx/noticia/1013607 .vigilavan-que-voto-de-ella-cuente.html, and July 8, 2014 ("Votan por el PRI con marca de ELLA"), www.elsiglodetorreon.com.mx/noticia /1013968.votan-por-el-pri-con-marca-de-ella.html.

My summary of Tulitas Wulff Jamieson's story is drawn from the early chapters of *Tulitas of Torreón: Reminiscences of Life in Mexico.* The first quotation ("I sometimes wonder . . .") from the book is on xv; the second ("On one occasion when I was about 13 . . ."), 32; the third ("[The] train service . . ."), 38–40; the fourth ("[Papa] was on horseback . . ."), 72; and the fifth ("Even though it was only . . ."), 93.

The anecdote about the enlightened citizens of Torreón is in the voice of the fictitious engineer and detective Paco Reyes Ibáñez, hero of the only novel by the Lagunero Francisco José Amparán, *Otras caras del paraíso.*

The information on the Pathé theater and movie house comes from conversations with Silvia Castro, Corona Páez, and Rico Maciel.

The passage from Francisco Luis Urquizo relating to brothels is taken from his novel *Fui soldado de levita, de esos de caballería*; see Francisco Emilio de los Ríos, *Francisco L. Urquizo: Narrativa selecta*, 70.

The collection of poetry by the photographer Jesús Flores, published under the pseudonym Sebastián Margot, is *Chacal y susceptible.*

The book by the photographer Héctor Moreno Robles is *Clausurado.*

On Foon-chuck's arrival, see Terán Lira, *La matanza de los chinos (Torreón, 1911)*, 5.

Cab (2)

On the gender imbalance in the Chinese diaspora, see Romero, *The Chinese in Mexico, 1882–1940*, 12–29; Puig, *Entre el río Perla y el Nazas*, 93; and Elmer Clarence Sandmeyer, *The Anti-Chinese Movement in California*.

Regarding the ages of the Chinese killed in Torreón on May 15, 1911, see the Archivo Histórico Genaro Estrada, dossier 13-2-34, file I, Informe de la Delegación China.

Oblivion of Love

On the Manila Galleons, see the article on Wikipedia and the corresponding link to the Kuroshio Current. I also consulted various maps, a globe, and a number of articles in *National Geographic*.

Regarding the first Chinese to arrive in Mexico, see Romero, *The Chinese in Mexico, 1882–1940*, 12–29.

The translation of "La nave de China" ("The Chinese Ship") is based on a version to be found in Pacheco, *Antología del modernismo (1884–1921)*, 114.

The passage on the mythic origins of China is taken from Patricia Buckley Ebrey, *The Cambridge Illustrated History of China*, 10.

My summary of the history of China, and of the arrival of the diaspora in California, is based mainly on chapter 1 ("China") and chapter 2 ("California") of Puig, *Entre el río Perla y el Nazas*. While I did consult other sources (Ebrey, *The Cambridge Illustrated History of China*; Antonio Escohotado, *Historia de las drogas*; plus a variety of electronic sources), what I include is basically a synthesis of Puig's text.

For Marx's views on the California mines, see Puig, *Entre el río Perla y el Nazas*, 93.

Pablo Chee's story is from Romero, *The Chinese in Mexico, 1882–1940*, 1.

Lee Kwong Lun's story is also recounted by Romero, *The Chinese in Mexico, 1882–1940*, 13–14.

The concept of transnationalism as a tool in the analysis of the diaspora is developed by Romero, *The Chinese in Mexico, 1882–1940*, 3.

The passage by Severo Sarduy on the traces left by the Chinese diaspora in Cuba appears in his 2011 novel *De dónde son los cantantes*; see Sarduy, *Obras ii: Tres novelas*.

The first quotation from Puig (". . . torturers, polygamists . . .") is from his *Entre el río Perla y el Nazas*, 96; the second (". . . There was not in the language . . ."), 104; the third (". . . an infinite multitude . . ."), 106.

Romero's migrant figures are in *The Chinese in Mexico, 1882–1940*, 15.

The article from the *Marin Journal*, March 30, 1876, appears in Sandmeyer, *The Anti-Chinese Movement in California*, 25.

For the massacre in Rock Springs, see the Wikipedia article.

I was told the story of the mass suicide of the Chinese in Matachín, Panama, during a visit to the country in August 2014. I later found documentary evidence: "La tragedia de Matachín," by Rafael Montes Gómez, at panamaamerica.com.pa: www.panamaamerica.com.pa/content/la -tragedia-de-matach%C3%ADn. And "Matachín y el suicido de los chinos," by Alonso Roy: www.alonso-roy.com/hm/hm-02.html.

No Man's Tsai Yüan

On the Italian communities in Mexico, see Puig, *Entre el río Perla y el Nazas*, 143.

The profile of Matías Romero Avendaño is based on information from Wikipedia; Puig, *Entre el río Perla y el Nazas*, 139–50; and Rico Maciel, *Mi cuna, el ferrocarril*, 30.

The article by Matías Romero is quoted in Puig, *Entre el río Perla y el Nazas*, 140.

On the Sino-Mexican Treaty of Amity, see Puig, *Entre el río Perla y el Nazas*, 139–50.

For the geographical distribution of the Chinese population in Mexico between 1895 and 1910, see Romero, *The Chinese in Mexico, 1882–1940*, 56–61.

On the jobs taken by the Chinese in Mexico, see Romero, "Employment and Community," in *The Chinese in Mexico, 1882–1940*.

The story of the five Cantonese men and the undercover immigration agents is to be found in Romero, *The Chinese in Mexico, 1882–1940*, 30–31.

On interracial marriage and its censure in both the United States and Sonora, see Romero, *The Chinese in Mexico, 1882–1940*.

For the schematic view of Sinophobia by social class, see Romero, *The Chinese in Mexico, 1882–1940*, chapter 6, "Mexican Sinophobia and the Anti-Chinese Campaigns"; and Puig, *Entre el río Perla y el Nazas*, 333–37.

The information about the students given grants to study in Bridgewater, Massachusetts, can be found in Rolando Elizondo Arreola, *Benemérita Escuela Normal de Coahuila: Alma de acero*, 20.

The anti-Chinese article published in the *Diario Oficial de Coahuila* in 1892 is attested to in Corona Páez, *Crónica de Torreón*: http://cronicade torreon.blogspot.mx/2007/07/racismo-de-estado-finales-del-siglo-xix .html.

The text "Las medidas sanitarias en Honolulú" ("Sanitary Measures in Honolulu") appears in *El Cómico*, June 10, 1900.

Regarding the Romero Commission Report, see Romero, *The Chinese in Mexico, 1882–1940*, 180–83.

The Programa del Partido Liberal Mexicano (Mexican Liberal Party Plan) can be found on Wikisource: http://es.wikisource.org/wiki /Programa_del_Partido_Liberal_Mexicano.

The anti-Chinese letter written by José Díaz Zulueta, "La inmigración china para el fomento a la agricultura, perjudicará a México," appears in *El Tiempo*, April 10, 1911.

The Chinese representatives' response to Díaz Zulueta's letter "En defensa de la Colonia China" can be found in *El Tiempo*, April 21, 1911, and is signed by Li Chung Ping, Li Yuck Ling, Moy Hah Sing, Chion Ah Wan, Tam Tip Hong, and Chin See Yin.

The biography of Wong Foon Check (Foon-chuck) is in Lucas Martínez Sánchez, *Monclova en la Revolución: Hechos y personajes, 1910–1920*, 63. Certain aspects of this man's life were narrated to me by Bernardo Chuck, his great-grandson.

The profile of Kang Youwei was written using various Wikipedia articles, and Puig, *Entre el río Perla y el Nazas*, 65–73 and 155–77.

In relation to *leng t'che*, an extraordinary novel has been written in

Mexico that also includes a photograph of a man being executed by this method: Salvador Elizondo, *Farabeuf.*

The interview with Kang Youwei, published by *El Popular* in Mexico City, appeared on June 10, 1907, and is cited by Corona Páez in *Crónica de Torreón*: cronicadetorreon.blogspot.mx/2008/09/eminente-intelectual -chino-visita.html.

On the relationship between Foon-chuck, Hop Lee, and Kang Youwei, plus the uniforms of the Yue Mae School in Monclova, see Evelyn Hu-DeHart, "Indispensable Enemy or Convenient Scapegoat? A Critical Examination of Sinophobia in Latin America and the Caribbean, 1870s to 1930s," in Chee-Beng Tan and Walton Look Lai, *The Chinese in Latin America and the Caribbean.*

The reference to the eight miles of electrified streetcar lines laid by Wah Yick appears in Dambourges Jacques, "The Chinese Massacre in Torreon (Coahuila) in 1911," 236.

On the Banco Chino and the prosperity of the Chinese in Torreón, see Puig, *Entre el río Perla y el Nazas*, 169–73.

The notarized document of the Compañía Bancaria y de Tranvías Wah Yick, S.A. can be found among material currently being cataloged in the historical archive of the Universidad Iberoamericana Campus Laguna.

The manifesto published in *El Nuevo Mundo* is cited by Rico Maciel, *Mi cuna, el ferrocarril.*

Both Woo Lam Po's Súplica (Entreaty) and the editorial reply by the newspaper in question, plus Corona Páez's comment, can be found in *Crónica de Torreón*: http://cronicadetorreon.blogspot.mx/2008/04/1907 -destellos-de-tormenta.html.

On the arrival of Antonio de Pío Araujo in Torreón and the *Mexican Herald*'s article on the housing shortage, see Rico Maciel, *Mi cuna, el ferrocarril*, 41.

Regarding the strikes of boilermakers and engine drivers, the elevation of Torreón to city status, and the founding of the Banco de La Laguna, see Rico Maciel, *Mi cuna, el ferrocarril*, 42.

The violent events of 1908, including the capture of Viesca, are attested to by Rico Maciel, *Mi cuna, el ferrocarril*, 43–44.

The disagreements between Foon-chuck and Huang Jih Chuck were noted by Dambourges Jacques in "The Chinese Massacre in Torreon (Coahuila) in 1911," 236.

Regarding the location of Chinese establishments in Torreón, my main sources have been interviews with local historians, plus Puig, *Entre el río Perla y el Nazas*, 172, and Terán Lira, *La matanza de los chinos (Torreón, 1911)*, 22.

On the number of Chinese in Torreón, see Puig, "Tsai Yüan, Coahuila," *Letras Libres*, October 2002.

For Porfirio Díaz's fleeting visit to Torreón en route to his historic meeting with Taft, see Rico Maciel, *Mi cuna, el ferrocarril*, 45.

The Torreón celebration of the Centenary of Independence is narrated by Puig in a manner substantially different from that given here. Puig based his story on Guerra's *Historia de Torreón*, which in turn must have been based on the original event program. Later research into press coverage at the time shows that the program suffered changes due to rain.

Pedestrian

The quotation about the true location of the Banco Chino is from Castro, "Rumbo al centenario / Sobre la ubicación del Banco Chino," *El Siglo de Torreón*, December 5, 2004: www.elsiglodetorreon.com .mx/noticia/122784.rumbo-al-centenario-sobre-la-ubicacion-del-ba .html.

Numerous Bands

The title of this chapter and the epigraph accompanying it are from Ernesto Lumbreras, *Numerosas bandas*.

Meyers's essay "Second Division of the North" can be found in Katz, *Riot, Rebellion, and Revolution*. The quotation ("From 1884 . . .") is from 454.

The biographical sketch of Calixto Contreras is constructed from information on Wikipedia; some individual scenes are from Paco Ignacio Taibo II, *Pancho Villa: Una biografía narrativa*; and passages from Meyers in Katz, *Riot, Rebellion, and Revolution*.

The portrait of Jesús Agustín Castro is taken from *Recuerdo que . . .*, a compilation of the memories of Urquizo anthologized by de los Ríos, *Francisco L. Urquizo*, 162; "De Villa Guerrero, Coahuila a La Laguna," in *El Siglo de Torreón*, March 8, 2015; and other electronic and oral sources.

Regarding the revolutionary preparations in La Laguna, see Guerra, *Historia de Torreón*, 179–202.

The story of the uprising in Gómez Palacio on November 20, 1910, is taken from two sources: Guerra, *Historia de Torreón*, 202–8; and Rico Maciel, "El 20 de Noviembre de 1910 en Gómez Palacio": http://batallaseneldesiertoilhuicamina.blogspot.mx/2011/11/el-20-de -noviembre-de-1910-en-gomez.html.

The popular tradition that has Jesús Agustín Castro guarding the retreat of the troops on November 21, 1910, was recounted to me by a number of Torreón residents, and also appears in Guerra, *Historia de Torreón*, 207.

A profile of the demonic bandit known as La China Apolinaria is given by Urquizo in *Charlas de sobremesa*, a collection of anecdotes compiled by de los Ríos, *Francisco L. Urquizo*, 204.

On sharecropping in La Laguna, see Meyers in Katz, *Riot, Rebellion, and Revolution*, 470.

The portrait of Orestes Pereyra is taken from *Recuerdo que . . .*, in de los Ríos, *Francisco L. Urquizo*, 162; Wikipedia; and various extracts from Taibo, *Pancho Villa*.

The portrait of Enrique Adame Macías is based on oral histories collected in La Laguna; and from Rico Maciel, "Dinamita: También un arma de la revolución mexicana": http://batallaseneldesiertoil huicamina.blogspot.mx/2012/04/dinamita-tambien-un-arma-de-la .html.

Urquizo's words about Sixto Ugalde appear in de los Ríos, *Francisco L. Urquizo*, 163.

For the portrait of Emilio Madero and the strange way in which San Pedro de las Colonias joined the Revolution, see Meyers in Katz, *Riot, Rebellion, and Revolution*, 451–85.

The description of the Madero clan is taken from José León Robles de la Torre, *Cinco coahuilenses, presidentes de México*, 27–115.

The quotations from Francisco Madero Hernández's letter to his son, the revolutionary Francisco I. Madero González, were taken from Robles de la Torre, *Cinco coahuilenses, presidentes de México*, 50–51. The photograph of the children Gustavo and Francisco I. Madero is in Robles de la Torre, *Cinco coahuilenses, presidentes de México*, 33.

The quote by the British consul in La Laguna is from Meyers in Katz, *Riot, Rebellion, and Revolution*, 466.

The quote by Francisco L. Urquizo can be found in de los Ríos, *Francisco L. Urquizo*, 155–56.

The portrait of Luis Moya Regis is taken from Wikipedia and Meyers in Katz, *Riot, Rebellion, and Revolution*.

The portrait of Pablo Lavín is constructed in part from Meyers in Katz, *Riot, Rebellion, and Revolution*; and Roberto Martínez García, "Siglos de Historia," *El Siglo de Torreón*, April 29, 2012.

Cast List: Thirteen Portraits

The description of Benjamín Argumedo is synthesized from Sotomayor Garza, *Benjamín Argumedo*.

The advertisement for Dr. Lim's "antialcoholic specific" appeared in the *Torreon Enterprise*, June 17, 1911.

The biographical portrait of J. Walter Lim is based on various extracts from Puig, *Entre el río Perla y el Nazas*; conversations with a number of inhabitants of Torreón, particularly Silvia Castro; and two documents from dossier 13-2-34, file II, in the Archivo Histórico Genaro Estrada of the Mexican Ministry of Foreign Affairs: the "Protesta que enérgicamente hace el Dr. J. W. Lim súbdito chino contra varios hechos asentados en el proceso que con motivo de la matanza de chinos habida en Torreón Coahuila, el día quince de mayo del corriente año, instruye el juez señor Macrino J. Martínez y su secretario Julio Avino" and the "Declaración del doctor J. W. Lim ante el abogado Antonio Ramos Pedrueza."

The biographical sketch of Emiliano Lojero is based on information from Wikipedia; Juan Manuel Torrea, *La asonada militar de 1913*; and Salvador Alvarado, *La reconstrucción de México: Un mensaje a los pueblos de América*, 18.

The biographical sketch of Federico Wulff is drawn from passages in Puig, *Entre el río Perla y el Nazas*; Guerra, *Historia de Torreón*; Rico Maciel, *Batallas en el desierto*; Wulff Jamieson, *Tulitas of Torreón*; "Museo de la Casa del Cerro" (July 24, 2008) and "La Casa del Cerro, un viaje al pasado" (March 28, 2005) in *El Siglo de Torreón*; plus "Testimonio de Federico Wulff ante Ramos Pedrueza," Archivo Histórico Genaro Estrada, dossier 13-2-34, file II.

José María Grajeda is mentioned in Puig, *Entre el río Perla y el Nazas*, 196; and in "Testimonio de Federico Wulff ante Ramos Pedrueza."

The biography of H. H. Miller appears in "Comparten archivos de imágenes de H. Miller," in *El Siglo de Torreón*, November 19, 2010. The photograph of the ladies and gentlemen walking in the Torreón alameda is reproduced in María Isabel Saldaña Villarreal and Francisco Durán y Martínez, *Recuerdos y sabores de la comarca lagunera*, 43. The photograph of a cart loaded with bodies was published in Terán Lira, *La matanza de los chinos (Torreón, 1911)*, 27.

The biographical sketch of Francisco León de la Barra is based on information from Wikipedia; dossier 13-2-34, file I, of the Archivo Histórico Genaro Estrada; and several passages from Puig, *Entre el río Perla y el Nazas*.

The portrait of George C. Carothers is based on a number of electronic sources; extracts from Taibo, *Pancho Villa*; passages from Jamieson, *Tulitas of Torreón*; Puig, *Entre el río Perla y el Nazas*; and Carothers's declaration to Ramos Pedrueza, Archivo Histórico Genaro Estrada, dossier 13-2-34, file II.

My portrayal of William Jamieson is based on various passages from Wulff Jamieson, *Tulitas of Torreón*.

My portrayal of Herbert Ashley Cunard Cummins is taken from Puig, *Entre el río Perla y el Nazas*; and Timothy J. Henderson, *The Worm in the Wheat: Rosalie Evans and Agrarian Struggle in the Puebla-Tlaxcala Valley of Mexico, 1906–1927*, 122–24.

The description of Francisco L. Urquizo is taken from de los Ríos, *Francisco L. Urquizo*, 13–92; the photograph mentioned is reproduced in Arreola, *Signos para la memoria: Coahuila; Inventario artístico*.

The portrait of Jesús Flores is based on Puig, *Entre el río Perla y el Nazas*, 183–84; "Torreon's Capture," a chronicle published in the

Torreon Enterprise, June 17, 1911; "La verdad sobre los asesinatos de chinos en Torreón: Relación de un testigo presencial," Archivo Histórico Genaro Estrada, dossier 13-2-34, file I; *Diógenes*, July 16, 1911; and "Testimonio de Herbert Ashley Cunard Cummins ante Ramos Pedrueza," Archivo Histórico Genaro Estrada, dossier 13-2-34, file II.

The description of the dangers faced by the Chinese community in Torreón appears in Puig, *Entre el río Perla y el Nazas*, 183–87.

The photograph of the barricades in Torreón manned by civilians was reproduced in Terán Lira, *La matanza de los chinos (Torreón, 1911)*, 13.

The portrait of the Amarillos is from Terán Lira, *La matanza de los chinos (Torreón, 1911)*; "Torreon's Capture"; "La verdad sobre los asesinatos de chinos en Torreón"; and several passages from Urquizo, *Tropa vieja*.

The English-language translation of Woo Lam Po's flyer can be found in Tan and Look Lai, *The Chinese in Latin America and the Caribbean*, 87.

The House of the Pain of Others

The description of Benjamín Argumedo tying his scarf beneath his chin is fictitious.

Benjamín Argumedo's words are taken from Sotomayor Garza, *Benjamín Argumedo*, 16.

The description of the eastern battlefront is based on Puig, *Entre el río Perla y el Nazas*, and, principally, "Torreon's Capture"; see also Meyers in Katz, *Riot, Rebellion, and Revolution*.

The official documents of the Secretaría de la Defensa Nacional establishing Sixto Ugalde's superior rank to Benjamín Argumedo appear in Sotomayor Garza, *Benjamín Argumedo*, 17–20.

Cummins's actions during the battle can be found in his own declaration to Ramos Pedrueza, "Testimonio de Herbert Ashley Cunard Cummins ante Ramos Pedrueza."

The photographs of the federal defense on Cerro Calabazas and Cerro de la Cruz are reproduced in Terán Lira, *La matanza de los chinos (Torreón, 1911)*, 15.

Dr. William Jamieson's words are taken from Wulff Jamieson, *Tulitas of Torreón*, 118.

The description of Lim is taken from "Declaración del doctor J. W. Lim."

Details of George C. Carothers's observation post and the story about the wounded gringo are taken from the declaration of Carothers to Ramos Pedrueza, Archivo Histórico Genaro Estrada.

The quotation by Terán Lira is from *La matanza de los chinos (Torreón, 1911)*, 19.

Almost the whole description of the action on the western front is taken from Urquizo, *Tropa vieja*, 136–60.

The quotation that begins "There was unease" appears in Urquizo, *Tropa vieja*, 148–49.

The sabotage of the electric plant by Enrique Adame Macías, and the submachine guns positioned on the perimeter of the city, is reported in "Torreon's Capture."

The nighttime assault by revolutionaries on Cerro de la Cruz is described in Urquizo, *Tropa vieja*, 151–52.

The story of the death of Jesús Flores is taken from "Torreon's Capture."

The story about the Chinese residents of Torreón shouting, "Viva Madelo!" is commonly heard as a form of ridicule in the oral tradition of La Laguna: historians, cab drivers, housewives, and pedestrians all remember it. It is also cited in dozens of newspaper articles published in the summer of 1911.

The declarations related to the early stages of the attack are from Puig, *Entre el río Perla y el Nazas*, 187–91; and the "Declaración del doctor J. W. Lim."

The testimony of María Antonia Martínez appears in the *Extracto* that military judge Macrino J. Martínez sent to Emilio Madero on May 18, 1911, Archivo Histórico Genaro Estrada, dossier 13-2-34, file II.

The words of Dr. William Jamieson can be found in Wulff Jamieson, *Tulitas of Torreón*, 118–19.

Sabino Flores's assertion about the origins of the various factions to be found in El Pajonal, and the story of the death of Francisco Almaraz, are in the "Declaración del doctor J. W. Lim."

The calculation of the number of Chinese murdered in the market gardens between May 13 and 14, 1911, is taken from the *Lista de los súbditos chinos que fueron muertos por las fuerzas maderistas en los días 13, 14 y 15 de mayo de 1911 ascendiendo a la suma de trescientos tres personas, como sigue*, Archivo Histórico Genaro Estrada, dossier 13-2-34, file IV.

The fictional account of federal soldiers breaking out of Torreón is in Urquizo, *Tropa vieja*, 156–57.

The meeting between the tax official Villanueva and Consul Carothers is described by the latter in his declaration to Ramos Pedrueza.

The exact location of the Second Civil Court, where the adulterated bottles of cognac were found, is described by Carothers in his declaration to Ramos Pedrueza.

"Just before six, as the sun was coming up": I obtained this information from a web page of astronomical calculations.

The portrait of José María Grajeda is taken from Federico Wulff's declaration to Ramos Pedrueza.

Dr. Lim's vicissitudes are recounted in "Declaración del doctor J. W. Lim."

The story of the adulterated cognac is addressed by Puig, *Entre el río Perla y el Nazas*, 193–95; and in Pérez Jiméncz, "Raza nación y revolución," chapter 3.

The description of the onset of the urban slaughter is taken from Puig, *Entre el río Perla y el Nazas*. The quotation "As they were looting . . ." is on 195.

Apolinar Hernández Sifuentes's testimony is given in Terán Lira, *La matanza de los chinos (Torreón, 1911)*, 22.

The quotation by Francisco L. Urquizo comes from de los Ríos, *Francisco L. Urquizo*, 159.

The quotation "Someone discovered . . ." is from Puig, *Entre el río Perla y el Nazas*, 196.

The attack on the country house and the probable rape of Ten Yen Tea's wife are described in the "Declaración del doctor J. W. Lim."

The names of those implicated in the massacre for whom, the following year, arrest warrants were issued, are given by Corona Páez in "99 años del genocidio": http://cronicadetorreon.blogspot.mx/2010/06/99-anos-del-genocidio.html.

The oral tradition that the Lindquists saved Lam Po is reported by Terán Lira in *La matanza de los chinos (Torreón, 1911)*, 28.

Ramos Pedrueza's opinion of the killings is in his *Informe*, Archivo Histórico Genaro Estrada, dossier 13-2-34, file II.

The quotation "From one of these establishments . . ." is from Puig, *Entre el río Perla y el Nazas*, 197.

William Jamieson's words ("Little children were stood up against . . .") can be found in Jamieson, *Tulitas of Torreón*, 119–20.

The quotation "And the same went for the writing desks . . ." is from Puig, *Entre el río Perla y el Nazas*, 199.

The description of Lim's rest period appears in the "Declaración del doctor J. W. Lim."

The quotation "Practically nothing that could be carried . . ." is from Puig, *Entre el río Perla y el Nazas*, 201–2.

The photograph of Gustavo G. Fernández can be found in the Archivo Histórico de la Universidad Iberoamericana Campus Laguna.

Cummins recounts his departure from Gómez Palacio in his declaration to Ramos Pedrueza, "Testimonio de Herbert Ashley Cunard Cummins ante Ramos Pedrueza."

The story of Lim's attempted lynching and the related quotation are taken from the "Declaración del doctor J. W. Lim."

The quotation by Cummins (". . . the bodies of nine Chinese . . .") can be found in his declaration to Ramos Pedrueza, "Testimonio de Herbert Ashley Cunard Cummins ante Ramos Pedrueza."

The statements of Samuel Graham and Delfino Ríos are cited by Puig, *Entre el río Perla y el Nazas*, 207; the description of women denouncing Chinese men hiding in Torreón is in "Torreon's Capture."

Erico Notholt's account is part of his declaration to Ramos Pedrueza, Archivo Histórico Genaro Estrada, dossier 13-2-34, file II.

The executions of the Chinese "rescued" from El Pajonal are attested to by Dr. Sergio Corona Páez, and come from the sworn statement of an eyewitness: Brígida Cumpián de García in Corona Páez, "99 años del genocidio."

Ten Yen Tea's testimony on the murder of his companions is mentioned in the "Declaración del doctor J. W. Lim."

Orduña's appointment as guardian of the Arce lumberyard is given by Puig, *Entre el río Perla y el Nazas*, 210. Orduña's responsibility for the murders is clearly demonstrated by the order for arrest issued against him in 1912; see Corona Páez, "99 años del genocidio."

The story of the pretty Mexican girl and the Chinese saved by Eva Lindquist is in Wulff Jamieson, *Tulitas of Torreón*, 122.

The scene of the seventy Cantonese men hidden in a restaurant is taken from George C. Carothers's declaration to Ramos Pedrueza.

Emilio Madero's first announcement after the capture of Torreón is recounted by Meyers in Katz, *Riot, Rebellion, and Revolution*, 479.

The image of the typewriters thrown into an irrigation channel appears in Wulff Jamieson, *Tulitas of Torreón*, 123.

Lim's travels after his attempted lynching are recounted in the "Declaración del doctor J. W. Lim."

The meeting between Madero and Carothers is recounted by the latter in his declaration to Ramos Pedrueza.

The declaration of Dolores Ramírez is noted by Corona Páez, "99 años del genocidio."

The Maderista march through Torreón and the digging of the mass grave for the 205 dead Chinese in the city are related by Cummins in his declaration to Ramos Pedrueza; and in Puig, *Entre el río Perla y el Nazas*, 208–9.

The Puig quotation ("The cemetery manager . . .") can be found in *Entre el río Perla y el Nazas*, 208.

The declaration by Bernabé Miranda in relation to the burials in the mass grave is taken from Terán Lira, *La matanza de los chinos (Torreón, 1911)*, 28.

The quotation from Puig ("They were forcibly held there for three days . . .") is from *Entre el río Perla y el Nazas*, 210.

The dialogue between Arthur Bassett and Erico Notholt is a literal transcription of the latter's declaration to Ramos Pedrueza.

The account of the freeing of the eleven market gardeners detained in Gómez Palacio, and Ramírez's attempts to incriminate them, appears in the "Declaración del doctor J. W. Lim."

The release of the prisoners in the Arce lumberyard is taken from Puig, *Entre el río Perla y el Nazas*, 210.

The quotation by Lim ("When I had visited . . .") is taken from the "Declaración del doctor J. W. Lim."

Carothers's description of Lim is in his declaration to Ramos Pedrueza.

The ball in the Oriental steam laundry is described by Dr. William Jamieson in a letter written to his father on May 24, 1911, in Wulff Jamieson, *Tulitas of Torreón*, 122.

A Monster Course

Laura Castellanos's report "Fueron los federales" ("It Was the Feds") appeared in *Aristegui Noticias*. (Laura Castellanos was awarded the 2015 Premio Nacional de Periodismo for her coverage of the events in Apatzingán.—*Trans.*)

Later

The three fragments relating the demand and the Mexico-China indemnity convention are summaries of Puig, *Entre el río Perla y el Nazas*, 245–331. Certain aspects of the account come not from the body of Puig's text but from his notes.

The quotation by Macrino J. Martínez is taken from his *Extracto*.

The quotation from Puig ("Prince Ching then sent . . .") can be found in *Entre el río Perla y el Nazas*, 213.

The quotation from *El Ahuizote* is taken from Castañón Cuadros, *Las dos repúblicas: Una aproximación a la migración china hacia Torreón, 1924–1963*, 54–55.

The following is a full transcription of "Entrevista con un Chin-chun-chan," signed by Karkabel and published in *Revista Multicolor*, June 29, 1911:

An Interview with Chin-chun-chan

To understand the impact the massacre in Torreón has within the Celestial Empire, yesterday I interviewed the Chinaman who is kind enough to iron my shirts. He was present in Torreón that day.

His first name is "Chin-chun-chan," and I will not translate it here out of decency. He is a prominent member of the Celestial community of that city and, in addition, is a first-class ironer. For some, an iron can cost their lives. But for this man, an iron is what keeps him alive and feeds him.

But let us not digress.

Once "Chin-chun-chan" had seated himself on the floor (they do not use chairs), the interview began:

"Well, you son of the great China, what can you tell me about the events in Torreón?"

"Madelistas killed all Chinese like lats . . . Vely bad Madelistas!"

"So, the 'lats' covered in egg you give us in restaurants are killed with rifles! Well, just why did the Maderistas attack them?"

"Jus becos Chinese shot bullets at Madelistas—"

"Imagine! And since bullets are nourishing, they should have been grateful, shouldn't they? And how many Maderistas did they kill?"

"Jus two. But the Chinese shout 'Viva Madelo!' and the Madelistas kill."

"But my dear Chin-chun-chan, that's enough to tempt the Devil . . . Why did they fire on you? There's the rub. And you, how did you escape?"

"Ordinary methyl."

"Don't push your luck! And I guess you'd need a week soaking in soap after getting out of there."

"I change clothes . . . Never bath."

"So, your time in hiding was almost like a day in the countryside! And how were your compatriots killed, my little Chinaman?"

"They tie lope to hoss's saddle. Hoss drag them. Den . . . bang!"

"The barbarity of my fellow countrymen must have strongly reminded you of your own! Because over there, foreigners' lives hang by a thread . . . And what do you think of the little sum of 60 million your government wants in indemnity?"

"Vely good . . . vely good!"

"But listen here you son of . . . Confucius. They killed three hundred and you ask for 60 million. Do you think you're worth 200,000 pesos? You've already sold yourself, or at least been 'pawned.' Well, how much is a Chinawoman worth in your country?"

"They give them lalas!"

"So, over there you give, and over here you charge 200,000 smackers. If you came here by airplane, the price wouldn't be so high!"

"I give you 200 thousan peso: I kill you. How you like that?"

"No, my dear Chinaman. It's not the same. What's more, I don't have a plait, not even a pigtail. And what do you think of the 'boycott'?"

"Boycott? You can eat it?"

"No, my dear son of the sky. I'm saying that if you insist on charging 60 million, and sending your big boat to scare us, no one is going to give you clothes to iron or wash, no one's going to eat fried rat in your restaurant, or spend half a centavo on anything that smells of Chink . . . How does that feel?"

"Oh, no! Vely bad . . . vely bad. I no want boy cot . . . I no want demnity . . . I want ion shirts . . . Viva Madelo!"

The poor Chin-chun-chan didn't frown, for the lack of eyebrows needed to do so; but otherwise, he would have!

It seems the thought of never ironing again made him feel flat as a pancake, and faced with this threat, he had no desire to speak further of the events.

"So the truth is, my dear son of China, you don't hold a grudge against Mexico?"

"Oh, no. I luf Mesico. Viva Madelo!"

"In that case, son of Confucius, I admire you. And apart from the sacrifice of eating in one of your people's restaurants, ask me for whatever you will."

Chin-chun-chan asked me to pay for the shirts he had ironed, and left in silence.

I also transcribe here the song "Chinierías," published in the same source on June 29, 1911:

Chinoiseries

They say the Celestial Empire,
Indignant, and without cause,
About three hundred Celestials
Whom the masses did to death
For playing at being heroes
In the capture of Torreón,
Have sent us a battleship
We have to call "The Telluh"
Demanding to be given the pigtails
To see how many they are,
Or rather how many Chinese were killed
By the masses, or Maderistas,
Or their fate, who knows!
But what makes me laugh,
And at a knock-down price
Is to charge ten thousand pesos
per pigtail, yes sirreee;
For every ten Celestial men
They demand from us a million.
If China could sell its people
At such a price, or ten times less,
There is no doubt it would be
A nation of very great wealth.
But they say the market for Celestials
Is depressed throughout the world
That I would even compare it to the
Mother-in-law market opened one fine day
When the man who ran that singular show

Put his own relation-in-law on sale,
But not a buyer was in sight
Until a poor curious man
Strolled by the exhibition
And dared to ask the lady's price.
"She's yours, sir, just take her,"
Was the answer he received;
And the son-in-law closed the deal
With the one and only bidder.
I believe if we were to ask
The value in any place
Of twelve dozen little Chinamen,
The answer would be the same
As that given by the son-in-law
To his mother-in-law's purchaser,
Why they pack them into barrels
In the city of New York
And only as contraband,
Because if not the answer's no.
And our cousins receive them
And lately it would appear
Five hundred of them were fighting
For want of good fresh air
Or because the customs officers
Of the beautiful city of New York
Played that great prank upon then
To teach them what was what.
And I think when their mission
With us is over and done,
They press their claim with the Yankees
For the great ship "The Telluh."
Because to die of starvation
Is more cruel than the sword
Imprisoned in narrow tunnels
As they say it did occur.
We are waiting here calmly

For New York to pay the bill,
And then at just the same price
We'll perhaps liquidate the stock.

The quote from Puig (". . . one of the most costly items . . .") is from *Entre el río Perla y el Nazas*, 276.

The portrait of Pablo Herrera de Huerta comes from a strange source: a Wikipedia article, originally in German, but then translated into Spanish by someone who did not know the target language well. Timo Berger helped me clarify the meaning.

The first of the quotations by Pablo Herrera de Huerta ("There would be no difficulty in refuting . . .") is taken from the notes to the chapter titled "La Matanza" in Puig, *Entre el río Perla y el Nazas*, 239–40; the second (". . . when the inquiries have finished . . .") is taken from the notes to the same chapter, 240.

The biographical sketch of Antonio Ramos Pedrueza is based on fragmentary electronic sources.

The quotation by Robert M. Buffington about Antonio Ramos Pedrueza appears in the chapter titled "Looking Forward, Looking Back: Judicial Discretion and State Legitimation in Modern Mexico" in Buffington, *Criminal and Citizen in Modern Mexico*.

The quotation from Ramos Pedrueza is taken from his *Informe*.

The story about the phonograph playing "El pagaré" while Gustavo A. Madero was being murdered appears in Taibo, *Temporada de zopilotes*.

The meeting between Dr. William Jamieson and a Cantonese man he had escorted in Torreón can be found in Wulff Jamieson, *Tulitas of Torreón*, 122.

Lauro de la Garza is picturesquely portrayed in Taibo, *Pancho Villa*.

The biography of Foon-chuck can be found in Martínez Sánchez, *Monclova en la Revolución*, 63. Certain additional aspects of his life derive from interviews with Chuck, Castro, and Rico Maciel.

The information on the Proprietors' League comes from Rico Maciel, *Mi cuna, el ferrocarril*.

The sale of Dr. William Jamieson's medical practice is recounted in Wulff Jamieson, *Tulitas of Torreón*, 123.

The quotation by Tulitas Wulff Jamieson ("Evelyn went back to visit . . .") can be found in *Tulitas of Torreón*, 145.

The story of Federico Wulff after the revolution is recounted by Wulff Jamieson, *Tulitas of Torreón*, 144–45.

For Tulitas Wulff Jamieson's statement (". . . the Chalet Wulff still stands . . ."), see *Tulitas of Torreón*, 146.

Almost the entire passage on the Chinese political situation during the early years of the indemnity negotiations comes from the first chapter ("China") of Puig, *Entre el río Perla y el Nazas*.

The brief summary I have made of anti-Chinese feeling in Torreón after the massacre is based on Castañón Cuadros, *Las dos repúblicas*.

The two newspaper articles expressing pro-Sinophobic sentiments published in *El Siglo de Torreón* were cited by Corona Páez in "Racismo de Estado en Torreón: las pruebas," in *Crónica de Torreón*, September 13, 2009: http://cronicadetorreon.blogspot.mx/2009/09/racismo -de-estado-en-torreon-las.html.

Edgar Lee Masters's poem "Silence" was first published in Louis Untermeyer (ed.), *Modern American Poetry*.

SELECTED CHRONOLOGY

Torreón	Mexico	Europe/Mexico/USA/China	China
			Ca. 2070 BCE Xia dynasty established.
			551 BCE Birth of the social philosopher Confucius, whose thinking is still enormously influential.
	1519 *November 8* Hernán Cortés is welcomed into Tenochtitlán by the emperor Moctezuma.		
	1565 The first Manila Galleons arrive in Acapulco.		**1616** 18-year-old Kangxi becomes first ruler of the Qing dynasty to ascend to the throne through the line of primogeniture.
	1713 The period known as the Bourbon Reforms establishes the viceroyalty in Nueva España.	**1775–1783** The American Revolutionary War.	
		1776 *July 4* The United States declares independence.	
	Late 18th century Marriages among Spanish nobility lead to creation of vast estates in La Laguna.	**1789–1799** The French Revolution.	

Torreón	Mexico	Europe/Mexico/ USA/China	China
	1810 *September 16* Mexico announces its nationhood with the "Grito de Dolores."		
	1815 The Mexican War of Independence from Spain begins.		
		1833 Slavery abolished in the British Empire.	**1838** Lin Tse Su orders opium cargoes in English ships in the port of Guangzhou to be impounded, resulting in the First Opium War.
		1842 *August 29* The Treaty of Nanking is signed at the end of the First Opium War, giving enormous trading privileges to Britain.	
1848 Leonardo Zuloaga buys San Lorenzo hacienda (later the Rancho de Torreón) from Sánchez Navarro family.		**1848** News of the discovery of gold in California spurs Chinese immigration to USA.	**1850** Hong Xiuquan leads the Taiping Rebellion, which lasts until 1864, and is reputed to have cost twenty million lives.
			1852 The first Jesuits arrive in China and fail to convert the local population.
		1856–1860 France joins Britain in the Second Opium War.	**1858** Kang Youwei, the reformist intellectual, is born.

Torreón	Mexico	Europe/Mexico/USA/China	China
		1861–1865 The American Civil War.	
1862 The *ranchería* Torreón has 225 inhabitants.	**1862** *May 5* Mexico fights the French Army in the First Battle of Puebla.	**1861–1867** Napoleon III unleashes the Second French Intervention in Mexico. **1863** *October* Archduke Maximilian of Austria accepts Napoleon III's invitation to become emperor of Mexico.	
	1867 *April 2* Porfirio Díaz commands the Mexican troops against the French in the Third Battle of Puebla.	**1865** *December 18* Slavery abolished in the USA.	
1881 Federico Wulff arrives in Torreón to draw up plans for a reservoir. **1885** *September 23* First train pulls into Torreón. **1888** Wong Foon Check (Foon-chuck) alights from the train in Torreón, carrying baskets of merchandise.	*June 19* Execution of Archduke Maximilian of Austria. **1884** *December 1* Porfirio Díaz elected president.	**1882** The Chinese Exclusion Act passed in USA, leading to increased Asian immigration into Mexico and the rise of Sinophobic sentiment.	**1885** War with France.

271

Torreón	Mexico	Europe/Mexico/USA/China	China
1889 Torreón gets its first printing press.	**1889** Porfirio Díaz announces the construction of 380-mile telegraph line linking Torreón to northern frontier.		
1895 Dr. Walter J. Lim arrives in Torreón from California.			**1895** *April 17* After the Sino-Japanese War, China signs the Treaty of Shimonoseki, and incurs enormous indemnity.
		1898 The Spanish-American War breaks out after the USA intervenes in the Cuban War of Independence.	**1898** Emperor Guangxu initiates the Hundred Days' Reform under the influence of Kang Youwei. Dowager Empress Cixi organizes a coup against Guangxu; Kang Youwei sentenced to death by *leng t'che*. Kang escapes to Peking and later travels to Canada and USA.
		1899 *December* Sino-Mexican Treaty of Amity, Commerce and Navigation signed, establishing diplomatic relations between China and Mexico.	**1899–1901** The Boxer Rebellion.

Torreón	Mexico	Europe/Mexico/ USA/China	China
1901 First streetcar runs through the town. **1903** Asociación Reformista China founded in Torreón. **1906** Kang Youwei descends from a railway carriage in Torreón, accompanied by Foon-chuck. Compañia Bancaria de Tranvías Wah Yick (better known as the Banco Chino) created by Kang Youwei. **1907** *September 15* Torreón granted city status. *December* Banco de La Laguna founded. **1909** *October 12* Porfirio Díaz passes through Torreón on a train without disembarking.	**1903** *October 17* Porfirio Díaz orders a commission to investigate the impact of Chinese immigration. **1908** PLM (Mexican Liberal Party) uprising in La Laguna. Francisco Madero publishes *The Presidential Succession in 1910.* **1910** Francisco Madero writes the Plan of San Luis Potosí while in exile in Texas, calling for armed resistance.		**1901** *January 16* China incurs a debt of 980,000,000 ounces of silver to Japan after the Boxer Rebellion. **1905–1909** Dowager Empress Cixi undertakes constitutional reforms. **1908** Suang Tung (Puyi; "the Last Emperor") ascends to the throne. **1909** First legislative elections held, leading to the establishment of Congress and a movement toward a constitutional monarchy.

Torreón	Mexico	Europe/Mexico/ USA/China	China
1911	**1911**		
Early May	*May 5*		
Members of the Torreón business community refuse to support the federal defense of Torreón. Colonel Carlos González organizes Los Rurales and Las Chaquetas Amarillas to defend the city.	Maderista troops march through Gómez Palacio in commemoration of the Battle of Puebla. Jésus Flores makes a speech including anti-Chinese references. *May 8* Pancho Villa and Francisco Madero surround Ciudad Juárez; the city falls on May 10.		
May 12 Woo Lam Po distributes a pamphlet warning of the imminent threat to the Chinese community in Torreón.	*May 12* Jésus Agustín Castro marches on Gómez Palacio.		
May 13–15 Rebel forces led by Jésus Agustín Castro and Emilio Madero surround the city. Fierce fighting ensues, and federal troops are finally forced to abandon the city. Approximately 300 members of the Chinese community are slaughtered and their bodies are thrown into mass graves.			

Torreón	Mexico	Europe/Mexico/ USA/China	China
1911 *May 20* Emilio Madero appoints Macrino J. Martínez to investigate the massacre. This will be the first of four reports on the events.	**1911** *May 25* Porfirio Díaz resigns the presidency; Francisco León de la Barra becomes interim president.	**1911** *May 26* Mexican chargé d'affaires in Peking, Pablo Herrera de Huerta, sends a message of "sympathy" to China.	
	June Mexican press publishes articles defending the massacre in Torreón and ridiculing the Chinese indemnity claim.	*June* China requests 60 million pesos as indemnity for the massacre of its citizens.	**1911** *June* Cruiser *Hai-Chi* sails from China for the coronation of George V in London and docks in Havana.
	September 13 Reports by a Chinese commission and another by Ramos Pedrueza are completed, offering different versions of the massacre.		*October 10* Uprisings occur in Hubei province; Li Yuang Jung proclaimed head of the provisional military government of the Republic of China.
	November 6 Francisco Madero replaces Léon de la Barra as president.		*November* Civil war breaks out.
		December 16 Convention for Payment of Indemnity signed, setting the figure at 3,100,000 pesos in gold.	

Torreón	Mexico	Europe/Mexico/ USA/China	China
			1912 *January 12* Sun Yat-sen proclaimed president of the Republic of China.
		1912 *February 12* Mexico receives request from China to defer the indemnity payments. New date for payment of indemnity set at February 15, 1913.	
	1913 *February 9–19* Former Federalist Victoriano Huerta leads a military coup that initiates the Ten Tragic Days.		*March* Sun Yat-sen resigns and is replaced by General Yuan Shikai. Kang Youwei returns to China
	February 19 Pedro Lascuráin is president for 45 minutes.		
	February 22 Francisco Madero is assassinated on Huerta's orders.		
	March 9 Constitutionalist Venustiano Carranza launches the Plan of Guadalupe, uniting the northern Constitutionalist forces.		
1913 *September 29– October 1* Pancho Villa leads his Division of the North in a successful attack on Torreón.			
	October 10 Huerta dissolves Congress.		

Torreón	Mexico	Europe/Mexico/ USA/China	China
	1914 *March* Northern armies begin their march on Mexico City.		
	July 15 Huerta deposed and goes into exile.	**1921** *February* China once more raises the issue of payment of the indemnity.	**1917** Kang Youwei participates in a failed attempt to reinstate Emperor Puyi.
1926 *June 9* *El Siglo de Torreón* announces the opening of an anti-Chinese club in the city.		**1927** China accepts offer of between 300,000 and 500,000 pesos as indemnity.	
		1934 *January* Mexico informs the Chinese government that it is no position to pay indemnity.	**1935** First full edition of Kang Youwei's *Da Tongshu* printed posthumously.
		1945 *July 17–August 2* The Potsdam Conference appoints Council of Foreign Ministers, including representatives from UK, USA, USSR, China, and France, to prepare a peace settlement after World War II.	**1949** *September 21* Mao Zedong proclaims the People's Republic of China. *October 1* First National Day celebrated in Tiananmen Square.

Torreón	Mexico	Europe/Mexico/ USA/China	China
1999 Federico Wulff's former home, La Casa del Cerro, becomes the city's historical museum. **2007** *September 15* Torreón celebrates its centenary as a city.	**2006** *December 10* President Felipe Calderón announces the war on drug cartels in Mexico that is estimated to have cost 80,000 lives. **2012** Juan Puig's *Entre el río Perla y el Nazas* reissued. *September 26* 43 students from a rural teaching college in Ayotzinapa are forcibly disappeared. *November* Julián Herbert participates in "A Monster Course" in Apatzingán, Michoacán. **2015** *January 6* Unarmed citizens killed by federal police in Apatzingán. **2017** *September 19* Central Mexico shaken by strong earthquakes exactly 32 years after the quake that killed approximately 10,000 people.	**2018** *April 6* US president Trump orders the deployment of the National Guard to patrol the frontier with Mexico.	**1989** *June 5* Unarmed man stands in front of tanks in Tiananmen Square after mass killing of demonstrators. **2018** *March 11* The National People's Congress removes the two-term limit, allowing Xi Jinping the possibility of life presidency.

GLOSSARY OF NAMES AND TERMS

Adame Macías, Enrique (1884–1913). A former miner and expert in explosives involved in the 1908 Magonista uprising. He was present during the attack on Torreón in May 1911 and was finally executed by firing squad.

Amarillos de La Laguna, Las. Also known as the Voluntarios de Nuevo León. An elite, possibly fanatical military squadron allied to the federal government.

Anti-reelection Movement. A campaign to oppose the further reelection of Porfirio Díaz in 1910. It was led by Francisco Madero and other democratic sympathizers and was the precursor of the Mexican Revolution.

Argumedo, Benjamín (1876–1916). Also known as the Switcher because he changed sides so frequently. He confessed to giving the order to fire on the Chinese in Torreón in 1911 and was later executed by firing squad.

Aschenborn, Andrés Eppen (1840–1909). The son of Russian immigrants. Educated in France, he returned to Mexico and fought against the French in the War of Intervention (1862–1867). After settling in La Laguna, he persuaded Luisa Ibarra to sell the Rancho de Torreón for development.

Asociación Reformista China. A political club created by Foon-chuck in Torreón in 1903 as the Mexican branch of the Protect the Emperor Society.

Banco Chino. See Compañía Bancaria y de Tranvías Wah Yick.

Banda, Manuel "El Chino" (n.d.). He was present during the attack on Torreón in 1911 and later became a general in Pancho Villa's army.

Calles, Plutarco Elías (1877–1945). President of Mexico from 1924 to 1928 and founder of the PNR (National Revolutionary Party).

Carothers, George C. (1878–). US consul in Torreón until 1913. He later came to be known as Pancho Villa's "Watcher."

Carranza, Venustiano (1859–1920). President of Mexico from 1917 to 1920. He was an early supporter of Maderismo and, after Madero's assassination, led the Constitutionalist army in opposition to Huerta. He was assassinated on May 21, 1920.

Castro, Jesús Agustín (1887–1960). A former streetcar conductor and guerrilla leader in La Laguna. He headed the attack on Gómez Palacio in 1910 and led the siege of Torreón with Emilio Madero in 1911. He was governor of Durango State from 1920 to 1924.

Castro, Silvia (n.d.). Teacher and director of the Museo de la Revolución, Torreón.

Chang Yin Tang (n.d.). Chinese envoy extraordinary. He was head of the fourth report into the massacre in Torreón in 1911. In June of the same year he took up residence in Mexico City and led the indemnity negotiations there.

Chaquetas Amarillas, Las (Yellow Jackets). A Porfirian social defense group led by Col. Carlos González. Not to be confused with the Amarillos de La Laguna.

Científicos, Los. A group of influential Porfirian officials whose policies were influenced by the ideas of Auguste Comte.

Cixi (1835–1908). Dowager empress of China. As regent, she exercised enormous political influence for a period of almost fifty years.

Compañía Bancaria y de Tranvías Wah Yick. Better known as the Banco Chino; a banking and streetcar company founded in Torreón in 1906 by Kang Youwei.

Contreras, Calixto "El Indio" (1867–1918). A member of the Ocuileños tribe who campaigned against the seizure of tribal lands. He joined the Maderista cause, later fought in the Division of the North, and died in battle.

Cunard Cummins, Herbert Ashley (1871–1943). The British vice-consul in Gómez Palacio. He organized Red Cross stations in Gómez Palacio in May 1911 and arranged for the burial of the Chinese bodies that littered the streets after the massacre in Torreón.

Decena Trágica, La (the Ten Tragic Days). The period from February 9 to 19, 1913, which led to a military coup and the installation of Victoriano Huerta as president of Mexico.

Díaz, Porfirio (1830–1915). President of Mexico from 1876 to 1880 and 1884 to 1911. His authoritarian regime, the Porfiriato, centralized powers and, less successfully, attempted a policy of social engineering by encouraging European immigration.

División del Norte, La (the Division of the North). An armed brigade set up by Francisco Madero in the early days of the Mexican Revolution. After Madero's assassination, it was involved in opposing the Huerta regime under the leadership of Pancho Villa.

Flores, Jesús (n.d.). A stonemason allied to the revolutionary cause. He was reported to have made a speech in Gómez Palacio days before the siege of Torreón, inciting violence against the Chinese.

Flores Magón, Ricardo (1874–1922). A member of the Mexican Liberal Party. He led the Magonista rebellion against Porfirio Díaz in 1911 and was alleged to have incited anti-Chinese feeling within Maderismo.

Grajeda, José María (n.d.). The Torreón herbalist who was seen by Federico Wulff riding through the streets of the city on Monday, May 15, shouting "Kill the Chinese." He was later arrested on the orders of Sixto Ugalde, who claimed he was responsible for the massacre.

Guangxu (1871–1908). Nephew of Dowager Empress Cixi. He ruled as emperor from 1875 to 1908. His reign was notable for the Hundred Days' Reform, which he initiated in 1898.

Herrera de Huerta, Pablo (1868–1940). Mexican chargé d'affaires in Peking in 1911. He was closely involved in the indemnity negotiations for the Chinese victims of the massacre in Torreón.

Hong Xiuquan (1814–1886). The visionary leader of the Taiping Rebellion (1851–1864) in China, which left a death toll estimated to be as high as twenty million.

Huerta, Victoriano (1845–1916). A Porfirian military leader. After Díaz resigned from office, he supported Madero's government, but in 1913 he headed a conspiracy that ended in the Ten Tragic Days and the subsequent assassination of Francisco Madero. Huerta then assumed the presidency and installed a military dictatorship that led to civil war in Mexico.

Jamieson, William "Billee" (n.d.). A Canadian doctor who set up practice in Torreón and married Tulitas Wulff in 1906. After the massacre, he escorted Chinese survivors across the city to the Arce lumberyard.

Kang Youwei (1858–1927). A highly influential Chinese intellectual and political reformer sentenced to *leng t'che* by Cixi. Living in exile, he founded the Protect the Emperor Society (known as the Asociación Reformista China in Mexico) and created the Banco Chino in Torreón.

Kangxi (1654–1722). Emperor of the Qing dynasty from 1661 to 1722, and the first to establish the line of primogeniture in that dynasty.

La Laguna. A northern Mexican region of lakes comprising sections of the states of Coahuila and Durango.

León de la Barra, Francisco (1863–1939). Interim president of Mexico from May 21 to 25, 1911, after the resignation of Porfirio Díaz.

Lim, Walter J. (n.d.). A medical doctor who arrived in La Laguna from California in 1895 and lived in Torreón until 1919. He was seen as the "moral leader" of the Chinese community, and gave medical aid to the casualties during the attack on the city.

Lojero, Emiliano (1845–1923). A second lieutenant in the Battle of Puebla (1862). He was a member of the council that sentenced Archduke Maximilian of Austria to death. In 1911 he was given the task of defending Torreón and later supported Huerta's dictatorship.

Madero, Emilio (1880–1920). The younger brother of Francisco I. Madero; an accidental rebel who led the attack on Torreón in May 1911 with Jesús Agustín Castro. After his brother's assassination, he joined the Division of the North and pleaded for Pancho Villa's life.

Madero, Francisco, I. (1873–1913). President of Mexico from 1911 to 1913. The son of wealthy landowners and leader of the Anti-reelection Movement, he wrote the Plan of San Luis Potosí (published on October 5, 1910), which called for an armed uprising against Porfirio Díaz. He was assassinated on Huerta's orders on February 22, 1913.

Magonismo. See Flores Magón, Ricardo.

Martínez, Macrino J. (n.d.). Appointed by Emilio Madero to undertake the first report into the small genocide in Torreón.

Miller, H. H. (1875–1931). US businessman and amateur photographer who lived in Torreón from 1905 until his death. He was responsible for taking many of the iconic images of the siege of Torreón and the massacre of the Chinese community.

Obregón, Álvaro (1880–1928). President of Mexico from 1920 to 1924 and reelected in 1928. Although not involved in Madero's Anti-reelection Movement, he supported his presidency and later joined the revolt against Huerta. He was assassinated shortly before he could take up his second term in office.

Orozco, Pascual (1882–1915). A former muleteer from Chihuahua. He joined the Madero rebellion and was involved in the siege of Ciudad Juárez on May 8, 1911. He later sided with Huerta and was forced into exile.

Owyang King (n.d.) Private secretary to Chang Yin Tang who formed part of the fourth commission to report on the massacre alongside the American lawyers Lewens Redman and Arthur W. Bassett.

Pereyra, Orestes (1861–1915). A tinsmith who joined the Anti-reelection Movement and was involved in the assaults on Viesca in 1908 and Gómez Palacio in 1910. He later became a general in Pancho Villa's Division of the North and was executed by firing squad.

PLM (Partido Liberal Mexicano). The Mexican Liberal Party.

PNR (Partido Nacional Revolucionario). The National Revolutionary Party.

Ramos Pedrueza, Antonio (1864–1930). Porfirian jurist who headed the third investigation into the massacre in Torreón. His report became the basis for official versions of the subject.

Ríos, Delfino (n.d.). Founder of the newspaper *Diógenes*. He reported on the events in Torreón and claimed that the speech made by Jesús Flores in Gómez Palacio had been an incitement to murder the Chinese.

Rurales, Los. A mounted rural police force.

Soriano, Manuel Lee (n.d.). President of the Torreón branch of the Unión Fraternal at the time of writing. He is the son of Manuel Lee Tang, who migrated from China in 1895 and later served in Pancho Villa's army, where he was in charge of the store-wagon.

Ugalde, Sixto (1853–1917). He served under Jesús Agustín Castro and was in charge of the cavalry unit that captured the market gardens on the outskirts of Torreón, where the first killings occurred. He is thought to have been the only authority figure in the city during the massacre until the arrival of Castro and Madero.

Villa, Franciso "Pancho" (1878–1923). One of the most famous of the revolutionary leaders. His Division of the North battled against the Huerta dictatorship. He was assassinated on July 20, 1923.

Wong Foon-chuck (Wong Foon Check; 1863–). A Chinese business-man and associate of Kang Youwei's who arrived in Torreón in 1888.

Woo Lam Po (n.d.). Founding secretary of the Torreón branch of the Asociación Reformista China and spokesman for the Chinese community in the city. He arranged for the distribution of flyers warning the Chinese community of the imminent threat in May 1911.

Wulff, Federico (1856–1949). An American engineer and town plan-ner of German extraction who lived in Torreón until the 1930s. He built La Casa del Cerro (now the city museum) and from there watched the development of the massacre.

Wulff, Tulitas (a.k.a. Gertrudis; a.k.a. Dalla) (1886–1971). Federico's daughter. She came to Torreón with her family as a child and mar-ried Billee Jamieson in 1906. She was absent from Torreón during the massacre. She and her family later settled in El Paso.

Zapata, Emiliano (1879–1919). Leader of the agrarian movement known as Zapatismo. He joined Francisco Madero's rebellion and his small army, the Liberation Army of the South, won a notable vic-tory in Cuautla on May 19, 1911. Although he and Madero soon disagreed over land reform, after the latter's assassination, Zapata joined forces with Pancho Villa, Venustiano Carranza, and Álvaro Obregón to overthrow Huerta.

SOURCES

Books and Journals

Acosta, Teófilo, and José María Mendívil. *Directorio Profesional de Arte y Mercantil de la Laguna 1908–1909*. Mexico: Universidad Iberoamericana, n.d.

Aguirre, Jacobo M. *Torreón*. Mexico, 1902.

Alvarado, Salvador. *La reconstrucción de México: Un mensaje a los pueblos de América*. Mexico City: J. Ballesca, 1919.

Amparán, Francisco José. *Otras caras del paraíso*. Mexico City: Almadía, 2012.

Arreola, Rolando Elizondo (ed.). *Benemérita Escuela Normal de Coahuila: Alma de acero*. Saltillo: Gobierno del Estado de Coahuila/Instituto Coahuilense de Cultura, 2010.

———. *Signos para la memoria: Coahuila; Inventario artístico*. Saltillo: Centro de Estudios Sociales y Humanísticos, 1997.

Barragán Rodríguez, Juan. *Historia del ejército y de la revolución constitucionalista, primera época*. Mexico City: Instituto Nacional de Estudios Históricos de las Revoluciones de México, 2013.

Beltrán Enríquez, Rosa Esther. *Coahuila: Sociedad, economía, política y cultura*. Mexico City: UNAM, 2013.

Blanco, José Joaquín. *Crónica de la poesía Mexicana*. Mexico City: Posada, 1987.

Buffington, Robert M. *Criminal and Citizen in Modern Mexico*. Lincoln: University of Nebraska Press, 2000.

Castañón Cuadros, Carlos (ed.). *Extrañas latitudes: Tres visiones extranjeras sobre La Laguna, 1879–1945*. Torreón: Dirección Municipal de Cultura de Torreón, 2004.

———. *Las dos repúblicas: Una aproximación a la migración china hacia Torreón, 1924–1963*. Mexico: Instituto Municipal de Documentación y Archivo Histórico "Eduardo Guerra," 2004.

Corona Páez, Sergio Antonio. *El país de La Laguna: Impacto hispano-tlaxcalteca en la forja de la comarca lagunera*. Torreón: Parque España de la Laguna, et al., 2006.

Cortés, Alberto Armando Ponce. "El mercado regional económico y la migración extranjera: El caso chino en la comarca lagunera 1900–1930. *III Congreso Nacional: Estudios Regionales* y *la Multidisciplinariedad en la Historia*. Mexico: 2013.

Dambourges Jacques, Leo M. "The Chinese Massacre in Torreon (Coahuila) in 1911." *Arizona and the West* 16, no. 3 (1974): 233–46.

Darnton, Robert. *La gran matanza de gatos y otros episodios en la historia de la cultura francesa*. Mexico City: Fondo de Cultura Económica, 1987.

de Baca, A. C., Jr., and Agustín Aguirre Hermosillo. *Directorio comercial e industrial de La Laguna 1905–1906: Torreón, Gómez Palacio, Lerdo, San Pedro, Viesca, Matamoros*. Saltillo: Instituto Coahuilense de Cultura, 2006.

de la Pedraja, René. *Wars of Latin America, 1899–1941*. Jefferson, NC: McFarland, 2006.

de los Ríos, Francisco Emilio. *Francisco L. Urquizo: Narrativa selecta*. Saltillo: Instituto Coahuilense de Cultura, 2005.

de Mora, Juan Miguel. *El gatuperio: Omisiones, mitos y mentiras de la historia oficial*. Mexico City: Siglo XXI, 1993.

del Bosque Villarreal, Homero Héctor. *Aquel Torreón: Anecdotario y relaciones de hechos y personas que destacaron en alguna forma desde 1913 a 1936*. Torreón: Instituto Municipal de Documentación y Centro Histórico "Eduardo Guerra," 1983.

Ebrey, Patricia Buckley. *The Cambridge Illustrated History of China*. Cambridge: Cambridge University Press, 1996.

Elizondo, Salvador. *Farabeuf*. Mexico City: Fondo de Cultura Económica, 1965.

Escohotado, Antonio. *Historia de las drogas*. Madrid: Alianza Editorial, 2004.

Fabela, Isidro. *Documentos históricos de la Revolución Mexicana: Revolución y régimen constitucionalista; IV, El Plan de Guadalupe*. Mexico City: Fondo de Cultura Económica, 2013.

Go, Ping-gam. *What Character Is That? An Easy-Access Dictionary of 5,000 Chinese Characters*. San Francisco: Simplex Publications, 1997.

Guerra, Eduardo. *Historia de Torreón: Su origen y sus fundadores*. Saltillo: Secretaría de Cultura de Coahuila, 2012.

Henderson, Timothy J. *The Worm in the Wheat: Rosalie Evans and*

Agrarian Struggle in the Puebla-Tlaxcala Valley of Mexico, 1906–1927. Durham, NC: Duke University Press, 1998.

Iturriaga, José N. *Viajeros extranjeros en Coahuila: Siglos XVI al XX.* Saltillo: Secretaría de Cultura de Coahuila, 2012.

Katz, Friedrich. *The Secret War in Mexico.* Chicago: University of Chicago Press, 1981.

———— (ed.). *Riot, Rebellion, and Revolution: Rural Social Conflict in Mexico.* Princeton, NJ: Princeton University Press, 1988.

Lumbreras, Ernesto. *Numerosas bandas.* Guadalajara: Mantis Editores, 2010.

Madero, Francisco I. *El Plan de San Luis: 5 de octubre de 1910.* Mexico City: Centro de Estudios de Historia de México, 2010.

Margot, Sebastián. *Chacal y susceptible.* Saltillo: La Fragua, 2008.

Martínez Sánchez, Lucas. *Monclova en la Revolución: Hechos y personajes, 1910–1920.* Monclova: Colegio de Investigaciones Históricas del Centro de Coahuila, 2005.

Masters, Edgar Lee. "Silence," in Louis Untermeyer, ed., *Modern American Poetry.* New York: Harcourt, 1919.

Morales, Catalina Velazquez. "Xenofobia y racismo: Los comités antichinos en Sonora y Baja California, 1924–1986." *Meyibó* no. 1 (January–June 2010).

Moreno Mejía, Jesús Máximo. *La calle donde tú vives.* Mexico City: Sin Censura, 2013.

Moreno Robles, Héctor. *Clausurado.* Torreón: Ayuntamiento de Torreón / Dirección Municipal de Cultura de Torreón, 2000.

Muñoz Vargas, Jaime (ed.). *Panorama desde el cerro de las Noas: Siete ensayos de aproximación a la historia torreonense.* Torreón: Comisión de Historia de Torreón, 2007.

Pacheco, José Emilio. *Antología del modernismo (1884–1921).* Mexico City: UNAM/Ediciones Era, 1999.

Peña Delgado, Grace. *Making the Chinese Mexican: Global Migration, Localism, and Exclusion in the U.S.-Mexico Borderlands.* Stanford, CA: Stanford University Press, 2012.

Puig, Juan. *Entre el río Perla y el Nazas: La china decimonónica y sus braceros emigrantes, la colonia china en Torreón y la matanza de 1911,* Saltillo: Secretaría de Cultura de Coahuila, 2012.

Rico Maciel, Ilhuicamina. *Mi cuna, el ferrocarril: Efemérides de Torreón.* Self-published, 2012.

Robles de la Torre, José León. *Cinco coahuilenses, presidentes de México.* Saltillo: Consejo Editorial del Estado de Coahuila, 2000.

Rodríguez, José Baltar. *Los chinos de Cuba: Apuntes etnográficos.* Havana: Fundación Fernando Ortiz, 1997.

Romero, Robert Chao. *The Chinese in Mexico, 1882–1940.* Tucson: University of Arizona Press, 2010.

Sada, Daniel. *Registro de causantes.* Mexico City: Joaquín Mortíz, 1990.

Saldaña Villarreal, María Isabel, and Francisco Durán y Martínez. *Recuerdos y sabores de la Comarca lagunera.* Saltillo: Secretaría de Cultura de Coahuila, 2014.

Sandmeyer, Elmer Clarence. *The Anti-Chinese Movement in California.* Champaign: University of Illinois Press, 1991.

Sarduy, Severo. *De dónde son los cantantes* in *Obras ii: Tres novelas.* Mexico City: Fondo de Cultura Economica, 2011.

Saviano, Roberto. *CeroCeroCero.* Barcelona: Anagrama, 2014.

Schell, William. *Integral Outsiders: The American Colony in Mexico City, 1876–1911.* Lanham, MD: Rowman & Littlefield, 2001.

Serrano Álvarez, Pablo (ed.). *Historias de familia.* Mexico City: Instituto Nacional de Estudios Históricos de las Revoluciones de México/ Secretaría de Educación Pública, 2012.

Sotomayor Garza, Jesús G. *Anales laguneros.* Mexico City: Editorial del Norte Mexicano, 1992.

———. *Benjamín Argumedo: El Tigre de La Laguna.* Self-published, 2010.

Taibo, Paco Ignacio, II. *Pancho Villa: Una biografía narrativa.* Mexico City: Planeta, 2006.

———. *Temporada de zopilotes.* Mexico City: Planeta, 2009.

Tan, Chee-Beng, and Walton Look Lai (eds.). *The Chinese in Latin America and the Caribbean.* Boston: Brill, 2010.

Terán Lira, Manuel. *Francisco Villa en La Laguna.* Torreón: Macondo, 2002.

———. *La matanza de los chinos (Torreón 1911).* Torreón: Macondo, 1999.

Torrea, Juan Manuel. *La asonada militar de 1913*. Mexico City: Joloco, 1939.

Tovar y de Teresa, Rafael. *El último brindis de Don Porfirio*. Mexico City: Penguin Random House, 2012.

Turner, John Kenneth. *Barbarous Mexico*. Chicago: Charles H. Kerr & Company Cooperative, 1914.

Untermeyer, Louis (ed.). *Modern American Poetry*. New York: Harcourt, 1919.

Urquizo, Francisco L. *Tropa Vieja*. Mexico City: Populibros "La Prensa," 1992.

Wulff Jamieson, Tulitas. *Tulitas of Torreón: Reminiscences of Life in Mexico*. El Paso: Texas Western Press, 1969.

Newspapers and Other Periodicals

"1000 muertos y 600 heridos en Torreón." *El Diario Nacional Independiente*, May 22, 1911.

"China demanda a México por 33,600,000.00 como indemnización: Un crucero de guerra viene a nuestras costas para hacer investigaciones; Han muerto 316 de sus connacionales y pide $100,000 por cada uno más 2,000,000 por daños." *El Diario*, June 10, 1911.

"China pedirá a México un millón de pesos en indemnización: El señor Lan Poo, banquero chino en Torreón, dice que sus paisanos fueron atacados por los rebeldes." *El Diario*, June 9, 1911.

"China reclama por la muerte de sus súbditos en Torreón: El encargado de negocios del Celeste Imperio solicita ayuda a la Embajada Americana para las investigaciones." *El Diario*, May 24, 1922.

"Chinerías." *Multicolor*, July 29, 1911.

"Colonización e inmigación: Inmigración china a Yucatán." *El Economista Mexicano*, July 29, 1911.

"Cómo fue la matanza de chinos." *El Tiempo*, June 21, 1911.

"Consideraciones sobre la muerte de chinos en Torreón." *Diario del Hogar*, June 15, 1911.

"Detalles del ataque y toma de Torreón por las fuerzas de los revolucionarios." *El Diario*, May 30, 1911.

"Eclipse y peste." *El Cómico*, June 3, 1900.

"En defensa de la Colonia China." Letter signed by Li Chung Ping, Li Yuck Ling, Moy Hah Sing, Chion Ah Wan, Tam Tip Hong, Chin See Yin in *El Tiempo*, April 21, 1911.

"Entrevista con un Chin-chun-chan." Interview by Karkabel in *Multicolor*, June 29, 1911.

"Habla el coronel Macías." *Diario del Hogar*, June 9, 1911.

"Killed in Torreon Number Hundreds: Over 200 Chinese Slain by Rebels after the Federals Evacuated the Town." *New York Times*, May 23, 1911.

"La colonia china fue aniquilada en Torreón." *El Heraldo Mexicano*, May 23, 1911.

"La colonia china fue aniquilada en Torreón." *La Gaceta de Guadalajara*, May 23, 1911.

"La delegación de China hace investigaciones: Se cree que durante los sucesos de Torreón perecieron cerca de trescientos hijos del Celeste Imperio; El encargado de negocios de China envió una comisión a Torreón." *El Diario*, June 5, 1911.

"La inmigración china para el fomento a la agricultura, perjudicará a México." Letter signed by José Díaz Zulueta in *El Tiempo*, April 10, 1911.

"La matanza de chinos en la ciudad de Torreón." *La Opinión*, June 11, 1911.

"La matanza de chinos en Torreón." *El Tiempo*, May 23, 1911.

"La matanza de chinos en Torreón: Informe de dos comisionados." *El Criterio de Durango*, September 17, 1911.

"La peste en Manchuria." *El Abogado Cristiano*, March 10, 1911.

"La reclamación de China." *El criterio de Durango*, December 24, 1911.

"Las medidas sanitarias en Honolulú." *El Cómico*, June 10, 1900.

"Las reclamaciones de los extranjeros: Opinión del Sr. R. García Granados." *La Iberia*, June 21, 1911.

"La terrible matanza de chinos." *El Imparcial*, May 23, 1911.

"La toma de Torreón." *Diario del Hogar*, May 22, 1911.

"La verdad sobre lo acaecido en Torreón." *Diario del Hogar*, June 16, 1911.

"Lo que vale un chino." *Multicolor*, June 29, 1911.

"Los chinos en Torreón se habían naturalizado ciudadanos mexicanos:

El informe rendido parece comprobarse la culpabilidad de los asiáticos." *El Diario*, June 13, 1911.

"Los chinos toman las armas." *Diario del Hogar*, May 24, 1911.

"Los crímenes contemporáneos: Horrores de la libertad." *El Mañana*, July 2, 1911.

"Los sucesos de Torreón." *Diario del Hogar*, May 24, 1911.

"Matanza de chinos en Torreón." *La Opinión*, June 19, 1911.

"Matanza de chinos." *El Diario*, May 30, 1911.

"Matanza de chinos." *La Iberia*, May 24, 1911.

"¡¡Peste!! ¡¡Peste!!" *La Semana Ilustrada*, March 10, 1911.

"Profundas divisiones en el Partido Maderista." *Siglo XX*, July 23, 1911.

"Reclamación china: Demandas exageradas." *El Diario*, June 11, 1911.

"Reclamación por la muerte de chinos." *El País, Diario católico*, May 25, 1911.

"Sigue la barbarie en Torreón." *El Criterio de Durango*, September 17, 1911.

"Torreon's Capture." *Torreon Enterprise*, June 17, 1911.

Theses

Hatcher, Donald C. "The Impact of the Mexican Revolution on Foreign Investment in Chihuahua and Coahuila, 1910–1920." Missoula: University of Montana, 1975.

Pérez Jiménez, Marco Antonio. "Raza nación y revolución: La matanza de chinos en Torreón, Coahuila, mayo de 1911." Unpublished. http://catarina.udlap.mx/u_dl_a/tales/documentos/lhi/perez_j_ma/portado.html.

Sosa Flores, Francisco. "Los chinos en México (1877–1937)." Universidad Autónoma Metropolitana, Facultad de Filosofía y Letras, 1990.

Valdés, Carlos M. "Les Barbares, la Couronne, l'Eglise: Les Indiens nomades du nord-est mexicain face à la société hispanique." Unpublished.

Walker, Joshua Charles. "Immigrants at Home: Revolution, Nationalism, and Anti-Chinese Sentiment in Mexico, 1910–1935." Columbus: Ohio State University, 2008.

Electronic Publications

"Conmemoran la matanza de chinos ocurrida hace cien años en Torreón." *El Sol de La Laguna*, May 15, 2011: www.oem.com.mx /noticiasdelsoldelalaguna/notas/n2078289.htm.

"Interesante conferencia imparten en el Club del Libro." *El Sol de Tampico*, May 15, 2014: www.oem.com.mx/elsoldetampico/notas /n3391745.htm.

"La matanza de chinos ocurrida en Torreón el 15 de mayo de 1911." www .chihuahuamexico.com/index.php?option=com_content&task =view&id=3438&Itemid=40.

"Presidentes municipales de Torreón (60 al 10)": www.estaciontorreon .galeon.com/productos655587.html.

Programa del Partido Liberal Mexicano: http://es.wikisource.org/wiki /Programma_del_Partido_Liberal_Mexicano.

"Te han engañado como a un chino": http://yayalt.overblog.com/te -hanenganado-como-a-un-chino.

"¿Una disculpa por la vergonzosa campaña antichina?" *Nexos*, June 5, 2013: http://redaccion.nexos.com.mx/?p=4915.

Archivo Magón, Instituto Nacional de Antropología e Historia: http:// archivomagon.net.

Instituto Nacional de Estudios Históricos de las Revoluciones de México: www.inehrm.gob.mx.

El Paso Herald via *The Portal of Texas History*, December 20, 1911: http:// texashistory.unt.edu/ark:/67531/metapth137143/m1/1/zoom.

El Siglo de Torreón: www.elsiglodetorreon.com.mx.

Paper of Record: https://paperofrecord.hypernet.ca/default.asp.

Periódico Zócalo: www.zocalo.com.mx.

Wikipedia in English: http://en.wikipedia.org/wiki/Main_Page.

Wikipedia in German: http://de.wikipedia.org/wiki/Wikipedia :Hauptseite.

Wikipedia in Spanish: http://es.wikipedia.org/wiki/Wikipedia :Portada.

Barba, Guillermo. "Antal Fekete: se aproxima una catástrofe económica (entrevista exclusiva)." *Inteligencia financiera global* (blog), April 13, 2014: http://inteligenciafinancieraglobal.blogspot.mx/2014/04/antal -fekete-se-aproxima-una-catastrofe.html.

Castañón Cuadros, Carlos. *Civitas* (blog): http://civitaslaguna.blogspot
.mx.

Castellanos, Laura. "Fueron los federales." *Aristegui Noticias*: http://
aristeguinoticias.com/1904/mexico/fueron-los-federales.

Cerda, Adrián. "La matanza de chinos en Torreón." *El Universal*: http://
www.eluniversal.com.mx/estados/25929.html.

Corona Páez, Sergio Antonio. *Crónica de Torreón* (blog): http://
cronicadetorreon.blogspot.mx.

Gabriel el Justiciero. "La matanza de chinos en Torreón—Año de la revolución 1911." *Crónicas del pantano* (blog): http://cronicasdelpantano
.blogspot.mx/2011/05/la-matanza-de-chinos-en-torreonano-de
.html.

Herrera, Daniel. "Sangre y Polvo." *Replicante*, October 2010: http://
revistareplicante.com/sangre-y-polvo.

Hu-DeHart, Evelyn. "Immigrants to a Developing Society: The Chinese
in Northern Mexico, 1875–1932." *Journal of Arizona History*, Fall
1980: http://parentseyes.arizona.edu/promise/hu-dehart.html.

Llama Alatorre, Fernando. "Cual fue la verdadera historia de la
matanza de los chinos ocurrida de 13 al 15 de mayo de 1911 . . . hace
exactamente 93 años": www.internetual.com.mx/llama/articulos/La
_matanza_de_los_chinos.html.

Mendoza Aguilar, Gardenia. "El reto de ser chino en México." *Contra el
racismo en México* (blog): http://racismoenmexico.blogspot.mx/2007
/11/el-reto-de-ser-chino-en-mxico.html.

Montes Gómez, Rafael. "La tragedia de Matachín." *Panamá América*:
www.panamaamerica.com.pa/content/la-tragedia-de-match%C3
%ADn.

Puig, Juan. "La matanza de chinos en Torreón." *La Jornada*, June 28,
2004: http://www.jornada.unam.mx/2004/06/28/008n1sec.html.

———. "Tsai Yüan, Coahuila." *Letras Libres*, October, 2002: www
.letraslibres.com/revista/letrillas/tsai-yuean-coahuila.

Rico Maciel, Ilhuicamina. *Batallas en el Desierto* (blog): http://
batallaseneldesierto-ilhuicamina.blogspot.mx.

Roy, Alonso. "Matachin y el suicidio de los chinos": http://www.alonso
-roy.com/hm/hm-02.html.

Salmerón Sanguinés, Pedro. "¿Genocidio en México?" *La Jornada*,

October 8, 2013: www.jornada.unam.mx/2013/10/08/politica /019a2pol.

————. "Benjamín Argumedo y los colorados de La Laguna." *Estudios de historia moderna y contemporánea de México*, Universidad Autónoma de México/Instituto de Investigaciones Históricas, 2004: www .historicas.unam.mx/moderna/ehmc/ehmc28/334.html.

Archives

Archivo Histórico Genaro Estrada de la Secretaría de Relaciones Exteriores.
Archivo Municipal Eduardo Guerra de Torreón.
Archivo Papeles de Familia de la Universidad Iberoamericana de Torreón.
Hemeroteca Digital de El Siglo de Torreón.
Hemeroteca Nacional de México.
Instituto Estatal de Documentación.

Julián Herbert was born in Acapulco in 1971. He is a writer, musician, and teacher, and is the author of *Tomb Song*, as well as several volumes of poetry and two story collections. He lives in Saltillo, Mexico.

Christina MacSweeney was awarded the 2016 Valle Inclán Translation Prize for her translation of Valeria Luiselli's *The Story of My Teeth*. She has published translations of two other books by the same author, and her translation of Daniel Saldaña París's novel *Among Strange Victims* was shortlisted for the 2017 Best Translated Book Award. She has also published translations, articles, and interviews on a wide variety of platforms, and contributed to the anthologies *Bogotá39: New Voices from Latin America*, *México20*, *Lunatics, Lovers & Poets: Twelve Stories after Cervantes and Shakespeare*, and *Crude Words: Contemporary Writing from Venezuela*.

The text of *The House of the Pain of Others* is set in Adobe Caslon Pro. Book design by Rachel Holscher. Composition by Bookmobile Design and Digital Publisher Services, Minneapolis, Minnesota. Manufactured by Friesens on acid-free, 100 percent postconsumer wastepaper.